THE EXPRESSMEN

THE EXPRESSMEN

By the Editors of

TIME-LIFE BOOKS

with text by

David Nevin

TIME-LIFE BOOKS / ALEXANDRIA, VIRGINIA

Time-Life Books Inc.
is a wholly owned subsidiary of

TIME INCORPORATED

Founder: Henry R. Luce 1898-1967

Editor-in-Chief: Henry Anatole Grunwald
President: J. Richard Munro
Chairman of the Board: Ralph P. Davidson
Executive Vice President: Clifford J. Grum
Editorial Director: Ralph Graves
Vice Chairman: Arthur Temple

TIME-LIFE BOOKS INC.

Managing Editor: Jerry Korn
Executive Editor: David Maness
Assistant Managing Editors: Dale M. Brown (planning),
George Constable, Thomas H. Flaherty Jr. (acting),
Martin Mann, John Paul Porter
Art Director: Tom Suzuki
Chief of Research: David L. Harrison
Director of Photography: Robert G. Mason
Assistant Art Director: Arnold C. Holeywell
Assistant Chief of Research: Carolyn L. Sackett
Assistant Director of Photography: Dolores A. Littles

Chairman: Joan D. Manley
President: John D. McSweeney
Executive Vice Presidents: Carl G. Jaeger,
John Steven Maxwell, David J. Walsh
Vice Presidents: George Artandi (comptroller);
Stephen L. Bair (legal counsel); Peter G. Barnes;
Nicholas Benton (public relations); John L. Canova;
Beatrice T. Dobie (personnel); Carol Flaumenhaft
(consumer affairs); James L. Mercer
(Europe/South Pacific); Herbert Sorkin (production);
Paul R. Stewart (marketing)

THE OLD WEST

EDITORIAL STAFF FOR "THE EXPRESSMEN"
Assistant Editors: David Lawton, Joan Mebane
Picture Editor: Myra Mangan
Text Editor: Gerald Simons
Designer: Herbert H. Quarmby
Staff Writers: Sam Halper, Philip Payne, James Randall,
Michele Wood
Researchers: Ann Morrison, Loretta Britten,
Jane Coughran, Lea G. Gordon, Mary Leverty,
Donna Lucey, Nancy Miller, Janet Zich, Jane Jordan,
Denise Lynch, Archer Mayor, Mary Kay Moran
Design Assistant: Faye Eng

EDITORIAL PRODUCTION
Production Editor: Douglas B. Graham
Operations Manager: Gennaro C. Esposito,
Gordon E. Buck (assistant)
Assistant Production Editor: Feliciano Madrid
Quality Control: Robert L. Young (director),
James J. Cox (assistant), Daniel J. McSweeney,
Michael G. Wight (associates)
Art Coordinator: Anne B. Landry
Copy Staff: Susan B. Galloway (chief),
Elise Ritter Gibson, Celia Beattie
Picture Department: Linda Hensel
Traffic: Jeanne Potter

THE AUTHOR: David Nevin spent his youth traveling through the West and began his career as a Texas newspaperman. Later he joined *Life* magazine, where he was a writer for 10 years. Since then, he has devoted himself to writing books, which include *The Soldiers, The Texans* and *The Mexican War* in the TIME-LIFE Old West series and *The Pathfinders* in the TIME-LIFE Epic of Flight series.

THE COVER: A stagecoach rumbles through a starry night in Frederic Remington's painting *The Old Stagecoach of the Plains.* Atop the coach, silhouetted against the sky, rides a sentinel with a shotgun, alert for trouble. In the frontispiece photograph, another kind of guard duty is demonstrated by Wells, Fargo express messenger Madison F. Larkin, standing watch over a shipment of silver bullion in 1877. (Detail from the Remington painting courtesy Amon Carter Museum, Fort Worth, Texas.)

CORRESPONDENTS: Elisabeth Kraemer (Bonn); Margot Hapgood, Dorothy Bacon, Lesley Coleman (London); Susan Jonas, Lucy T. Voulgaris (New York); Maria Vincenza Aloisi, Josephine du Brusle (Paris); Ann Natanson (Rome). Valuable assistance was also provided by: Karin B. Pearce (London); Carolyn T. Chubet, Miriam Hsia, Christina Lieberman (New York); Mimi Murphy (Rome); Martha Green (San Francisco).

TIME
LIFE
BOOKS
®

Other Publications:

THE EPIC OF FLIGHT
THE GOOD COOK
THE SEAFARERS
THE ENCYCLOPEDIA OF COLLECTIBLES
THE GREAT CITIES
WORLD WAR II
HOME REPAIR AND IMPROVEMENT
THE WORLD'S WILD PLACES
THE TIME-LIFE LIBRARY OF BOATING
HUMAN BEHAVIOR
THE ART OF SEWING
THE EMERGENCE OF MAN
THE AMERICAN WILDERNESS
THE TIME-LIFE ENCYCLOPEDIA OF GARDENING
LIFE LIBRARY OF PHOTOGRAPHY
THIS FABULOUS CENTURY
FOODS OF THE WORLD
TIME-LIFE LIBRARY OF AMERICA
TIME-LIFE LIBRARY OF ART
GREAT AGES OF MAN
LIFE SCIENCE LIBRARY
THE LIFE HISTORY OF THE UNITED STATES
TIME READING PROGRAM
LIFE NATURE LIBRARY
LIFE WORLD LIBRARY
FAMILY LIBRARY:
  HOW THINGS WORK IN YOUR HOME
  THE TIME-LIFE BOOK OF THE FAMILY CAR
  THE TIME-LIFE FAMILY LEGAL GUIDE
  THE TIME-LIFE BOOK OF FAMILY FINANCE

For information about any Time-Life book, please write:
Reader Information
Time-Life Books
541 North Fairbanks Court
Chicago, Illinois 60611

CONTENTS

When President James Buchanan predicted in 1858 that the country would someday be bound east and west "by a chain of Americans which can never be broken," the links were already being forged by an army of entrepreneurs known as the expressmen. Their freight and stagecoach services moved Eastern goods westward, Western ores eastward, and shuttled people, money and mail both ways. By 1860, Pony Express riders were relaying mail across more than half the country in the amazingly brief time of 10 days. Such labors, celebrated here and on the following pages in paintings by Western artists, were eventually to be supplanted by the railroads and the telegraph. But until then, the expressmen persisted as though the fate of a fledgling civilization rested in their hands — and it did.

A wagonmaster watches his ox-drawn freight caravan roll out of Fort Benton on the Missouri in this scene by Charles Russell.

Through Hostile Country was the title artist Oscar Berninghaus gave this painting of a stagecoach speeding across a desolate landscape—probably western Wyoming or Montana. An escort of cavalry with an Indian scout in buckskin helped deter attacks by local tribes resentful of intrusion.

8

Mounted on a fresh horse, a Pony Express rider, as painted by Frederic Remington, charges out of a station on the mail route from Missouri to California. Couriers changed horses every dozen miles or so, often tiring out as many as six mounts before passing on the mail to the next relay rider.

TODD'S
EXPRESS AND BANKING
OFFICES.

C. A. TODD, — — — Proprietor.

DAILY EXPRESSES
TO AND FROM
STOCKTON, SONORA, COLUMBIA, MOKELUMNE HILL, QUARTZBURGH, AGUA FRIO, MARIPOSA, AND
All Parts of the Southern Mines.

GOLD DUST,
Specie, Valuable Packages, &c., &c.,
RECEIVED AND FORWARDED.
NOTES, ACCOUNTS, &c., COLLECTED, AND
All Business appertaining to an Express,
PROMPTLY ATTENDED TO.

A STAGE will LEAVE the OFFICE ON THE LEVEE AT STOCKTON, DAILY, for each of the above named places.

Office in San Francisco, with WELLS, FARGO & CO., in Brick Building, No. 114 Montgomery street, between Sacramento and California sts.

C. A. TODD.

Launching a war against distance and time

Native wit, a flair for figures and an abiding faith in free enterprise were about the only assets Alexander Todd had to work with when he found himself out on a very long limb in the summer of 1849. A desk-bound bookkeeper back East, he had succumbed to gold fever, and had arrived in San Francisco after a rugged 170-day sea voyage around South America. But Todd lacked the stamina to be a prospector. Now, after only a few weeks of futile wading about in icy mountain streams that held the flecks of yellow metal, he was stranded in the California gold fields and in imminent danger of ruining his health. Obviously, he had to find an easier way to make a living.

It didn't take Todd long to hit on the perfect solution. All around him, scattered through miles of wilderness, there were countless pick-wielding, pan-shaking gold seekers. Fortunes were tantalizingly within grasp, but in one sense the prospectors felt desperately deprived. Their contact with wives, children, sweethearts, friends and the familiar world they had left behind was attenuated almost to the vanishing point. Although mail from home was pouring into the San Francisco post office, the letters were effectively out of reach. Since there was no system for deliveries to the mining country, the only way a miner could get his mail was to make the laborious trek into town to pick it up himself —a trip that would not only cost weeks of precious working time but would leave his digs unguarded against claim jumpers. In this bleak situation, Todd perceived a dual opportunity to render a humane service and also to turn a profit: he declared himself a mail carrier.

Sizing up the potential, Todd concluded that official U.S. postal rates bore little relation to California realities. At the time, the Post Office Department charged five cents for a half-ounce letter going a distance of less than 300 miles, 10 cents for more than 300 miles. While the government held a monopoly over the flow of mail, Todd rightly suspected that in this instance the postal service would not object to a bit of help. And the laws of supply and demand strongly suggested that his remuneration ought to be generous. He devised a system of three fees. For carrying a letter from the gold fields to the San Francisco post office, he stipulated a charge of $2.50. But incoming mail was naturally more prized. Merely for inquiring after a miner's mail at the post office, Todd set a fee of one dollar, and formalized the arrangement by placing the man's name on a subscription list he drew up. And if he found a letter for the subscriber, the price for bringing it back would be exactly one ounce of gold dust, then worth about $16.

Hundreds of prospectors, hardly blinking at these rates, handed Todd their outgoing letters, affixed their names to his subscription list and paid the requisite sums. Todd invested in two horses —one for himself and the other to carry a sack of outbound mail—and rode out of the Sierra foothills to the town of Stockton, a sprawl of tents beside the San Joaquin River. There he planned to board a boat and travel down to San Francisco. However, his lucrative improvisations were just beginning. In Stockton, some merchants heard of his trip and asked him —a total stranger—to deliver $150,000 in gold dust to a certain company in San Francisco. Todd was willing to run the errand, but at a price: 5 per cent of the value of the dust, or $7,500. The merchants, with no alternative, assented.

Stowing the dust in a discarded butter keg, Todd stabled his horses, located a boat bound downstream and

The California gold rush touched off a clamor for the varied delivery services touted in this 1852 advertisement by the West's first major express agency, established by Alexander Todd and later taken over by another Todd —no relation.

Delivering letters at up to $16 apiece, an expressman rides the mining trails in this drawing from prospector Alonzo Delano's *Pen Knife Sketches.* "There's scarcely a gulch he doesn't visit," Delano wrote.

set off with the keg and his mail sack. He delivered the gold to the San Francisco company without misadventure and then paid his visit to the post office.

The scene was bedlam. People stood in lines up to half a mile long waiting to get to a window in the building. The lines barely moved, since each query about a letter required a postal clerk to make a needle-in-a-haystack search through tons of unsorted envelopes.

Todd finally came face to face with the harried postmaster, unburdened himself of his sack of outgoing mail and explained the nature of his subscription list. At that point the postmaster displayed an entrepreneurial instinct of his own. In return for swearing in Todd as a postal clerk and allowing him to sift through the mountain of mail from the East, he levied a kickback of 25 cents for each letter that Todd turned up for a client.

The ex-bookkeeper quickly repaired this small dent in his profits by developing some sidelines. He bought a load of weeks-old New York newspapers for a dollar or two a copy, knowing he could sell them at a healthy markup in the gold camps. Then, to convey his newspapers and mail, he bought a big rowboat for $300 and looked around for passengers who might be willing to help him bend the oars. Sixteen signed on and plunked down $16 apiece for the privilege of rowing Todd and his cargo to Stockton. Todd sold the rowboat at a $200 profit and made his way back to the Mother Lode in the Sierra. The miners not only fell upon their mail but gobbled up the old newspapers — at eight dollars per copy. Todd soon had 2,000 names on his subscription list, and was also earning $1,000 a day, regularly, for delivering and safeguarding gold dust.

Todd's enterprise was the first regular service of its kind in California or anywhere in the West. But other delivery services followed hard on his heels, for nothing moved easily in California — neither the mail nor provisions for miners nor the miners themselves.

The changeover from Mexican to American rule in 1848, as a result of the U.S. war with Mexico, had wrought little improvement in modes of transportation and communication; they ranged from the somnolent to the hopeless. Under Mexico's regime, California's 20,000 inhabitants had lived chiefly by cattle ranching, and when they traveled at all they went on horseback. The nearest thing to a link between California's towns was El Camino Real — The Royal Route — between San Diego and San Francisco. Despite its grandiose name, it was little more than a meandering bridle path.

From San Francisco north the road situation was even worse. Travelers bound for the Sierra foothills, including the hordes of gold seekers who turned up beginning in 1849, could go part way by boat. Small sailing vessels plied the San Joaquin and Sacramento rivers, which led 100 miles or so inland from San Francisco. But beyond the heads of the rivers lay trackless wilderness of steep ridges and narrow gorges.

The adventurers who plodded over this terrain often wondered if the instant wealth that was their objective

might not be won at the price of starvation. Few of them were able to carry with them all the supplies required for existence in the outback. Yet their needs were many: not just food, but stoves, pots, guns, tents, clothing, medicines and mining equipment, as well as tobacco, books, and whiskey to fortify body and soul.

Whoever filled these needs had a guarantee of windfall profits, and one of the first to recognize and seize the opportunity was a man named Daniel Dancer. There was nothing new about the means of transport Dancer employed; he simply organized it better. For almost a century the Mexicans and their Spanish overlords had been using trains of sure-footed pack mules to freight goods in and around California. Each mule could carry a load of about 300 pounds, and the manpower requirements were low; one expert muleteer could handle 15 animals. Dancer sent out as many as 150 mules on one journey along the 55-mile freighting line he established from Marysville, on the Feather River, to the gold camp of Downieville. The mules made their way through plunging canyons and mountain creeks carrying everything from sacks of flour to iron safes — and never

lost a load. The delivery charges, figured at the modest rate of five cents per pound of cargo, brought in more than $2,000 per trip — a return even Alexander Todd would have considered worthy.

While Dancer hauled freight and Todd hauled mail, another transplanted Easterner detected his golden opportunity in hauling people. It occurred to James Birch, soon after he arrived in Sacramento in August 1849, that people would jump at the chance to go from place to place in a vehicle drawn by mules or horses rather than in relative discomfort astride an animal. At home in Rhode Island, Birch had worked as a stable hand for a Providence-based stagecoach line. He now decided to forget about gold seeking and put his staging know-how to use. At the time he was just 21, bursting with energy and possessed of a powerful incentive. He hoped to amass a fortune that would send him back East in triumph to claim the hand of his ex-employer's pretty stepsister, Julia Chace, with whom he had fallen in love.

In lieu of a coach, Birch purchased a battered ranch wagon and nailed boards across the top to serve as seats for some two dozen passengers; his team consisted

A booming business that began in a carpetbag

A decade before the California gold rush made it essential to find a speedy means of getting the precious dust to secure repositories, the basic idea of an express service was successfully tested back East. That first company—founded by William Harnden, a former railroad conductor—had great advantages over the express organizations later set up in the West: its messengers were not required to traverse hazardous, near-wilderness routes, and they could travel by rail and boat rather than by horse or stagecoach. Still, Harnden's enterprise—which carried not gold dust but business documents, bank drafts, currency and newspapers between Boston and New York—provided a model for other expressmen to adapt to their own circumstances.

At the time Harnden launched his business in 1839, the accepted means of shipping parcels between cities was to ask a traveler to carry them as a

Early expressman William Harnden

favor. Stagecoach drivers and steamboat captains often obligingly stuffed a couple of packages into odd cargo spaces. Sometimes even bank notes were brought to train stations to be entrusted to anybody with an honest face who was heading to the appropriate destination.

The system worked tolerably well and cost nothing. But Harnden reasoned that his scheme was worth a fee —from a few cents to a few dollars, depending on the shipment's value —for improved security and regular deliveries four times each week. He launched his service personally, toting a carpetbag packed with valuables by train from Boston to Providence and thence by steamboat to New York.

By 1841, he had offices in Philadelphia, Albany, London and Paris. But when an employee named Henry Wells suggested extending the service westward to Chicago and perhaps beyond, Harnden sputtered, "Do it on your own account." Death at the age of 33 from tuberculosis and overwork prevented him from seeing Wells and a partner, William G. Fargo, turn that challenge to lucrative account indeed.

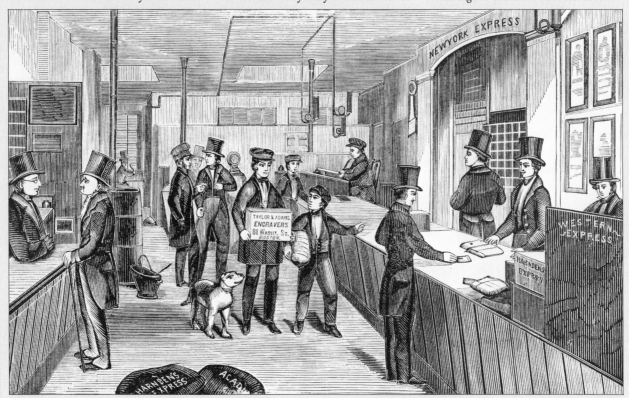

Merchants and delivery boys with New York-bound parcels enlist the services of Harnden's first express depot, opened in Boston in 1840.

of four smallish mustangs that he picked up for probably no more than a few dollars apiece. As a route, he selected a 30-mile run from Sacramento to Mormon Island, not far from Captain John Sutter's mill, where gold had first been discovered the year before. The one-way fare was set at $32, about 20 times the going rate for similar mileage back East.

They were rough miles all, over roads that were not yet roads but tracks made by strings of pack mules, and the horses had to be walked most of the way. Nevertheless, the receipts from the first trip paid for Birch's investment many times over. He promptly extended his run by 10 miles and hired men to build bridges over gullies and to construct relay stations at 10-mile intervals. At these stops, exhausted horses were exchanged for fresh animals, greatly shortening the travel time. By February 1850, Birch was advertising "through-in-daylight service, daily including Sundays" on his 40-mile run. A reporter for the Sacramento *Placer Times* took a trip over the line and wrote: "The horses had never been harnessed but once or twice before, yet they dashed through sloughs and gulches in a remarkably knowing style. These California horses seem to know about as much as most folks. The party returned highly delighted with the ride, and fully satisfied that Birch's line was *the* line to get to the mines in a hurry."

Birch was not content with his "California horses," however. Sparing no expense, he bought blooded stock that had been shipped in from Australia or brought overland by emigrants, sometimes paying $1,000 for a particularly strong animal. He placed orders for the best coaches made in the East and wrote to stage-driving friends, offering them high wages if they came West to work for him. There was no doubt about it: this young man was going places.

Of the varied enterprises of Alexander Todd, Daniel Dancer and James Birch, only Todd's bore the name of "express" service. The word itself had come into usage barely a decade earlier, when a New Englander named William Harnden so described his newly conceived, and instantly successful, service of expeditiously delivering lightweight valuables between Eastern cities *(page 16)*. But in the literal meaning of express as "rapid conveyance"—of any objects whatever, animate or inanimate—the term applied with equal aptness to the endeavors of Dancer, Birch and the many competitors who soon began to emulate them: whole armies of freight entrepreneurs and stagecoach owners who operated not only in California but throughout the frontier. All of them waged a ceaseless battle against distance and time to link the near and the far. All were specialists in conveyance—expressmen.

For two tumultuous decades, from the giddy gold rush year of 1849 to the completion of the first transcontinental railroad in 1869, the expressmen would transport the essentials that nurtured the development of the West: people and food and clothing, household utensils, merchants' wares, farm supplies and mining equipment, bank and government documents, gold and currency, letters and newspapers. Even after the railroads usurped their primacy, the Todds and Dancers and Birches of a new generation would carry on in a long, valiant diminuendo, supplying the needs of the more remote settlements until steam and wheels of steel caught up with them.

Easterners, and the expressmen who served them, were already enjoying and exploiting these technological advances when California's express services came into being at mid-century. By then, contact and commerce among the cities and towns east of the Mississippi took relatively little effort. Nearly 100 railroads, anywhere from five to 150 miles long, connected them. Along the Mississippi, 740 steamboats regularly puffed north and south, and other rivers were just as busy. There was scarcely a spot between the Appalachians and the Mississippi that lay more than 100 miles from navigable streams or the canals—thousands of miles of them—that had been constructed to link natural waterways. And where railroads, rivers or canals failed to reach, stage lines took up the slack, speeding over roads surfaced with stones or wooden planks.

Both the express companies and the U.S. postal service—which maintained 18,000 post offices east of the Mississippi—availed themselves of the railroads, steamboats and stagecoach lines. The individual traveler, too, had a wealth of options. Not for him the mule or horse or bumpy ranch wagon with improvised seats. A man who wished to go from Philadelphia to New Orleans could journey down the Atlantic seaboard and across the South by railway and stagecoach; the total travel time was a week and the cost $94. Or he could go by rail to Pittsburgh, then take boats down the Ohio and

Before express routes spanned the continent, California-bound mail had to be packeted from the East to Panama by steamship, off-loaded into railroad cars—as shown in this 1854 print—and carried across the Isthmus to a ship on the Pacific side. The 6,000-mile trip took about a month.

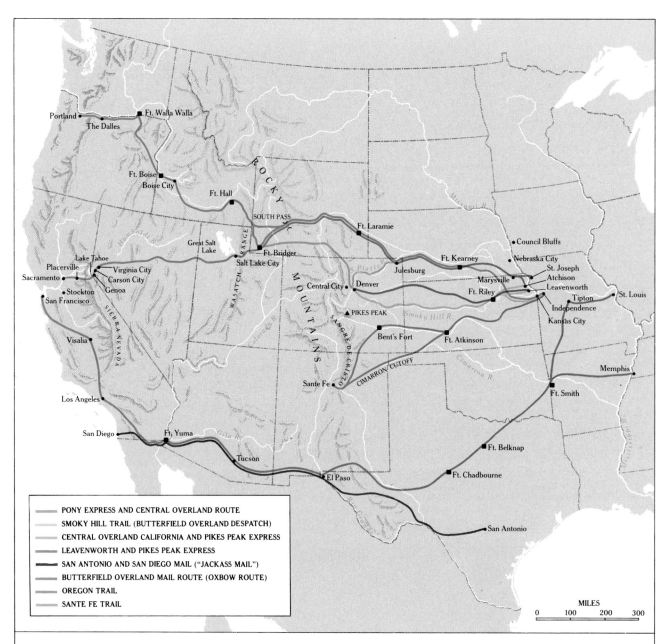

Legend:

- PONY EXPRESS AND CENTRAL OVERLAND ROUTE
- SMOKY HILL TRAIL (BUTTERFIELD OVERLAND DESPATCH)
- CENTRAL OVERLAND CALIFORNIA AND PIKES PEAK EXPRESS
- LEAVENWORTH AND PIKES PEAK EXPRESS
- SAN ANTONIO AND SAN DIEGO MAIL ("JACKASS MAIL")
- BUTTERFIELD OVERLAND MAIL ROUTE (OXBOW ROUTE)
- OREGON TRAIL
- SANTE FE TRAIL

MILES
0   100   200   300

RIVAL ROUTES ACROSS THE WEST

As a rule, the routes that served as major express conduits to the West for mail, freight and passenger traffic grew naturally from paths blazed through the wilderness by the mules and wagons of pioneers and traders. The earliest, the Santa Fe Trail, came into use in 1821. But the great bulk of Western traffic converged on the Oregon Trail, opened by fur traders' wagons in 1830, and on its branches to the Great Salt Lake Valley and California. This central route was used by freight trains from the 1840s on, by the riders of the Pony Express in 1860

and 1861, and by stagecoaches both before and after that time.

The central route's chief rival, and the only one not dictated by the path of population or commerce, was the Oxbow Route, so-called because of the circuitous direction it took to satisfy the regional interests of Southerners in Congress. This route, opened in 1858, was followed part of the way by the "Jackass Mail" (the name suggested what critics thought of it) and by John Butterfield's stagecoach line over its entire length, until the great arc was interdicted on the eve of the Civil War.

Mississippi rivers, arriving at his destination in nine or 10 days; in that case, his outlay was $36.

The East was well knit by 1850, and California was starting to be, thanks to the ingenious efforts of some of its newest citizens. The trouble lay in the lack of adequate linkage between the coasts. Without it, the U.S. remained a nation of separate parts, frustrated in its increasing dreams of continent-wide unity, unable to effect an interchange of news, ideas and important commercial transactions except by means too slow to suit a country that was raring to go—and to grow.

All freight and mail bound for California went by sea, either 13,000 miles around the tip of South America or by ship to Panama, across the Isthmus by canoe and muleback, and then by another ship to San Francisco. The length of the South American trip averaged six months; the Panama shortcut could take as little as a month, but connections with ships on the Pacific side of the Isthmus were rarely predictable.

Most people who wanted to go West could not afford fares of $300 and up for sea passage, and they had only one other option—to travel overland. This was a prospect to give even stout hearts pause. Any thoughts of creature comfort had to be cast aside. Beyond the Mississippi there was not a mile of railroad track. Only one navigable river—the Missouri—crossed an appreciable portion of the Western expanse, and although steamboats plied this waterway, its wandering northwesterly course led nowhere near the Pacific Coast. There were some stagecoaches in operation, but mostly over short distances. One bone-jolting means of conveyance remained for the would-be overland traveler: his own wagon—at his own risk.

Nor was there anything remotely resembling the East's network of surfaced roads. Much of the land between the Mississippi and the Pacific was still as virgin as the entire continent had been a few hundred years earlier. In some parts of the region, passage from place to place was possible only by narrow paths, about 15 inches wide, used by Indians since time immemorial for hunting and for war. There was another legacy from ancient times: trails pounded out, century after century, by herds of deer, elk and buffalo. The buffalo, in particular, had rendered a signal service to transportation. In their habitual roamings, the great beasts had torn out wide swaths of ground many miles long, and hard-packed them by sheer weight of numbers. Such trails could accommodate wagons and in so doing automatically qualified, in the 19th Century, as "roads."

There were two main routes, both starting from western Missouri, from which the wagon traveler could choose. Neither offered him a roadbed of roses. Each had stretches of miring sand and mud, points at which dangerous river fords had to be dealt with, and only a scattering of way stops where supplies or fresh draft animals could be procured.

The more northerly of the two routes was the 2,000-mile-long Oregon Trail, essentially a trunk line of old Indian paths that had been widened by the wagon wheels—and grazing oxen—of pioneers traveling to the Pacific Northwest to settle. Crossing the Rockies was but one crucial test of the trail; beyond the mountains, people wishing to go to California had to branch off, traverse the grim wastelands of Utah and maneuver through one of several passes of the towering Sierra Nevada. The second major route was the 800-mile-long Santa Fe Trail, which went southwest from Missouri to the 17th Century Spanish city for which it was named. Two extensions, the Gila River Trail and the Old Spanish Trail, led to California from the south.

The Santa Fe Trail was a classic example of the part played by pure chance in forging a vital link between widely separated points in the West. William Becknell, a Missouri trader, had no thought of making history when he set out in 1821 to sell some goods to the Cheyenne Indians. He did not even have a wagon; a string of pack horses carried the calico, knives, needles and other wares he hoped to peddle. Starting from the town of Franklin in western Missouri, he went across the prairies of what is now Kansas and on into Colorado, where he expected to find the Cheyennes—only to learn that they had gone south on a horse-stealing foray. Reluctant to write off the trip as a total loss, Becknell crossed the Arkansas River and ventured deep into what he thought was hostile Spanish territory. But in the Sangre de Cristo Mountains, he met some friendly Mexican soldiers who informed him that Mexico had just overthrown Spanish rule. On he went to Santa Fe, where he exchanged his wares for astonishing sums of Mexican silver.

Then and there Becknell decided to return the next year and reap even larger profits by bringing his goods

in wagons, each of which could hold six times the load a pack horse could carry. But he foresaw one major obstacle: he did not think wagons could get through the Sangre de Cristo Mountains. And so in 1822, as he headed back to Santa Fe, Becknell providently explored a route that skirted the mountains, going across 60 miles of parched desert between the Arkansas and Cimarron rivers. In succeeding years, with other traders, he took his wagons through the Cimarron Cutoff, as it came to be known. Soon afterward the Sangre de Cristo Mountains were proved hospitable to wagon travel after all, by way of the Raton Pass; though this route took longer, it did not have the water-supply problems of the Cimarron Cutoff, nor the same dangers from the notably belligerent Comanches and Kiowas in the region.

Either route between western Missouri and Santa Fe was feasible, and before long both were bustling with traffic. Following in the wheel ruts of the traders' wagons rumbled the heavier vehicles of freight operators. Freighting became so routine that after the U.S. took the Southwest from Mexico in 1848 and set up a garrison at Santa Fe, the staggering task of supplying thousands of soldiers with food, firearms, tools and other needs was achieved with comparative ease.

Hundreds of miles to the north, nonmilitary wagon traffic was starting to surge over a route parallel to the Oregon Trail, and leading from South Pass in the Rockies, through the Wasatch mountains and into the Great Salt Lake Valley. This trail, with its final descent from dizzying heights into scorching desert, had been pioneered in 1847 by the Mormons at an immense expenditure of toil and sweat. They had removed obstructing boulders and timber, established ferries across streams and even erected guideposts. No other emigrants had bothered with such matters, but the Mormon vanguard knew that bands of their brethren would be following in their footsteps. Though this alone was reason enough to inspire their labors, other benefits were soon to emerge.

By 1849, some 4,000 members of the sect—safe at last from the harassment and persecution that had driven them westward—lived in the Mormon stronghold of

Salt Lake City, but they were woefully short of supplies. The clothes they had brought on their hegira were now in tatters; women went about in burlap. Moreover, the ever-industrious Mormons had big plans: they proposed to build tanneries, ironworks and a clothing factory, and they urgently needed machinery, tools, textiles and a host of other items.

In the spring of 1849, when two St. Louis merchants named James Livingstone and Charlie Kincaid took a calculated risk and on their own initiative freighted $20,000 worth of merchandise to Salt Lake City, they received a stunning welcome. Within two weeks they had sold their entire cargo, and even some of their wagons—at $500 for a wagon that had cost them only $120 in St. Louis.

"The cry of the people is goods, Goods GOODS!" Livingstone and Kincaid jubilantly informed their fellow Missourians. For anyone with an eye to freighting, the message was loud and clear. Awaiting the inevitable influx, the Mormons lavished more care than ever on the road that led to their domain.

In an age that believed in self-reliance, no official approval was needed for a solitary William Becknell to establish a route or for dedicated teams of Mormons to maintain one. Any number of lesser local roads, crude but serviceable, were constructed by ordinary, unsung citizens of the new communities that were popping up here and there on the plains and prairies of the West. The federal government itself did comparatively little road building beyond the Mississippi until the Civil War's end brought new waves of settlers from the East. In the late 1840s and early 1850s Washington's chief contribution was to send out survey expeditions, under the aegis of the Army Corps of Topographical Engineers, to locate possible new routes and suggest means of shortening those that existed. Captain Howard Stansbury probed the way to Salt Lake City from Fort Laramie, at the eastern edge of what is now Wyoming, and shaved 61 miles off the main overland route. The new passage, his report proudly noted, "varies but a trifle from a straight line." At the same time Lieutenant James Simpson, who was later to be promoted to captain and to come up with a still more valuable shortcut (page 39), surveyed the possibilities of a wagon road from Fort Smith, Arkansas, to Santa Fe, noting prominent landmarks that would serve to guide travelers and locating campsites that were conveniently near water, timber and grass.

But the findings of Stansbury and Simpson essentially looked to the future, to a time when the government would send out engineers to judge the necessity or feasibility of grading and drainage, and construction crews to do the actual road work. When the surveyors' reports came in, Congress had a problem on its hands that more insistently demanded solution if the continent was to be linked. The problem concerned the mail, and the means by which it should go overland if—as contended by Californians and residents of the interior of the West—its customary dispatch to and from the Pacific Coast by sea was intolerably slow.

Mail did not mean only letters from home for forty-niners marooned in the gold country or lonely emigrants in the Oregon backwoods. Mail also encompassed newspapers and government printed matter. In the early 1850s telegraph lines were still a novelty, limited to a few areas in the East; print was the sole medium of communication that could inform Westerners of happenings in the world at large, of debates in Congress, of Presidential signatures on laws that could affect their lives. There was yet another crucial, long-distance function that mail performed: it conveyed currency and bank drafts and business documents.

The delivery of mail had been the government's obligation since the infancy of the republic, but in practice much of it was contracted to private carriers, using whatever mode of transport seemed suitable. There was no major problem, by the mid-19th Century, delivering mail in the East, where roads and rails and riverways and canals were excellent.

The usual procedure in establishing a new postal route was for Congress to decide on the route, set a delivery schedule and stipulate the maximum allowable compensation for mail service; the Postmaster General then advertised for bids on the contract and chose the contractor. If he failed to perform properly, his contract could be annulled; and in the event that his costs exceeded expectations—due to increased mail flow, natural disasters or whatever—his only recourse was to appeal to Congress to raise the level of compensation, a favor that legislators were not always disposed to grant.

This arrangement held obvious risks for a contractor, but also a promise of tidy returns. For the sea route between the Atlantic and Pacific by way of Panama, $290,000 a year went to the steamship line that brought mail every month to the Caribbean side of the Isthmus, and $199,000 went to the line that brought mail from San Francisco to the Pacific side. A third transportation firm, which exchanged westbound and eastbound mail across the Isthmus by mule and canoe, received 12 cents for every pound of mail carried.

But senders as well as receivers of mail were chafing at the delays and uncertainties of the route, and so Congress addressed itself to proposals for an overland delivery system. One of those it examined was a singularly audacious plan by William Bayard, a businessman who clearly liked to think big. Bayard proposed to carry the mail between Fort Smith, Arkansas, and the southern California town of San Diego in coaches that would also transport passengers. He would not only set up the stage line but also build the road it would travel, with relays every 10 or 15 miles and—in Apache country —50 armed men at each relay to protect travelers. After 15 years, the road and improvements on it, such as bridges, would revert to the government.

Bayard asked for the right to use government timber and stone for the road, and to charge tolls to cover the cost of repairs. But that was not all: he also wanted the right to preempt four square miles of land, at 10 cents an acre, along every 30 miles of the road. Finally, he wanted a stipend from the government for his services —no more, no less than $750,000 a year.

To many members of Congress, Bayard's flamboyant scheme smacked of a raid on the Treasury. He was turned down. Instead, the early mail contracts that were let for hauling mail overland went to men of more modest vision, willing to accept terms that less than matched the risks.

The sum of $19,500 was agreeable to the first contract winner, one Samuel H. Woodson of Missouri, and indeed it was not a sum to be taken lightly—except for the nature of the undertaking that was involved. Woodson's route, in accord with the mood of caution inspired in Congress by Bayard, did not go all the way to the Pacific Coast; still, it was long enough. The distance between Independence, Missouri, and Salt Lake City—the specified terminal points of the run—was some 1,200 miles of the Oregon Trail, 400 of them over tricky mountain terrain. Moreover, the agreement

called for Woodson to complete each one-way trip in 30 days, using either pack animals or wagons.

Woodson gamely launched his venture on July 1, 1850, and almost immediately realized that the schedule was impossible; among other reasons, he could exchange exhausted animals for fresh ones at only three stops en route—Fort Kearney, Fort Laramie and Fort Bridger. As a result, deliveries were slow that summer and practically nonexistent during the following winter.

In 1851, knowing the contract was in jeopardy, Woodson struck a deal with Feramorz Little of Salt Lake City to take over the western end of the run, between Fort Laramie and the Mormon capital; the two men would meet at Fort Laramie on the 15th of each month, exchange consignments and fulfill delivery schedules. The plan worked more neatly in theory than in practice. On one November run, after a blizzard struck Little and his helpers near South Pass, they had to labor through drifts for a month to reach the Wasatch mountains. There they had to abandon their animals and the printed matter and haul the letters 40 miles across the mountains to Salt Lake City on foot.

Woodson and Little continued to have trouble, and their deliveries proved so undependable that the Mormon leader Brigham Young wrote in a letter to a Utah Territory delegate in Washington: "So little confidence have we in the present mail arrangement that we feel considerable dubiety of your receiving this or any other communication from us." After four years of discouraging travail, when the mail contract came up for renewal, Woodson chose to step aside and let fresher hands compete for the job.

When Congress authorized mail service between Salt Lake City and Sacramento—a run of about 900 miles, the final link in the first full transcontinental service between East and West —the winning bidders on the contract were two men as obscure as Woodson and Little, and destined for even greater grief. Absalom Woodward and George Chorpenning committed themselves to once-a-month deliveries each way by pack mule, in return for an annual compensation of $14,000. The partners decided on an eminently sensible scheme adapted from that of Woodson and Little. They would split the task evenly, simultaneously working from opposite directions, each

man with a string of mules and a number of helpers.

In November 1851—just six months after the enterprise got underway—Absalom Woodward met a curiously poignant end. He set out from Sacramento for Salt Lake City with four experienced mountain men, all of them on horseback and armed with long-range government rifles. One morning about 70 Indians attacked them at Clover Patch, near the Humboldt River in central Nevada. Woodward and his friends killed several of the attackers and thought they had driven off the rest. That day and nearly all night they traveled on a forced march, and the next morning crossed paths with Chorpenning and his party bringing the mail from Salt Lake City. That was the last that was seen of Woodward and his companions until their bodies were found—four grouped together in death and one, Woodward's, strangely far away. According to information later gathered from other Indians, the attackers, bent on revenging their losses, had followed in pursuit, ignored the Chorpenning party and launched a second assault on their original target along the Humboldt River. Wood-

ward's men were killed and he was mortally wounded. But he escaped on his horse and covered some 150 miles of terrain before slipping from the saddle.

Chorpenning did his best to maintain the delivery schedule on his own, only to run afoul of a winter of especially heavy weather. On one trip in February all of the firm's stock—13 mules and a horse—froze to death in a single night in the Goose Creek Mountains in northern Nevada. Chorpenning and his helpers loaded the mail on their backs and slogged some 200 miles through deep snow to deliver it to Salt Lake City.

Small-scale operators like Chorpenning struggled on heroically with the transcontinental mails until the late 1850s, but their days were numbered. The seeds of William Bayard's idea had begun to sprout. Combining the transport of passengers and mail via transcontinental stage coach now seemed entirely practical; if strings of pack mules made links in a transcontinental chain, stage lines could do even better.

Californians were particularly eager for the change. In May 1856, California's Senator John B. Weller

Building roads in gold-rich Montana and Idaho from 1858 to 1862, Army engineers cut this trail out of a mountain to bypass a river. A map maker with the party drew this sketch and the one opposite.

Field Sketch showing the Side-cut by which
the 1st and 2nd Crossings of the Hell Gate River are avoided
Fort Walla Walla & Fort Benton
Military Road Expedition
Lieut John Mullan in Charge
April 6th 1862

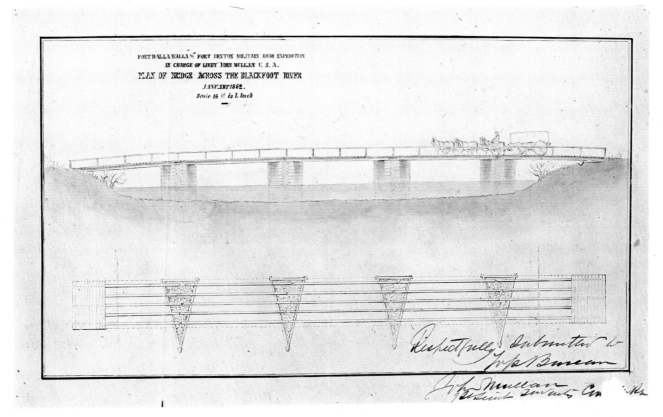

FORT WALLA WALLA TO FORT BENTON MILITARY ROAD EXPEDITION
IN CHARGE OF LIEUT JOHN MULLAN U.S.A.
PLAN OF BRIDGE ACROSS THE BLACKFOOT RIVER
JANUARY 1862.
Scale 16 ft to 1 Inch

placed on the desk of the Senate's presiding officer two heavy volumes, bound in hand-tooled leather. The volumes contained a petition and the signatures of 75,000 of Weller's constituents. Having effectively seized his colleagues' attention, Weller boomed: "California, when she speaks, desires to be heard." He then read what his constituents had to say: "We are a population of five hundred thousand in number, occupying the Western limits of American possessions upon the Pacific. Our State is the growth of little more than five years. Our mines, not yet fairly opened for successful working, have realized a moderate estimate of $300 million, which we have sent forth to the world." The people of California then went on to demand that the government commit funds for the improvement of the main overland trail so that stages could run to what the Californians' petition described as their "distant colony."

Seventy-five thousand signatures could not be ignored, but the plea raised an exceedingly sticky issue. The nation was already feeling the tremors that would explode in civil war. Southern Congressmen were loath to establish a communications link to California along a route through Northern territory, which would be the case if the main emigrant trail were chosen for a transcontinental stage line. Antislavery legislators were equally determined to keep this vital link safely distant from Southern control. Moreover, both factions believed that the first transcontinental railroad—a project already in the wind—would follow the route of the first overland stage line; hence the stakes were high indeed.

In August 1856, Congress sidestepped the issue by authorizing a mail contract for a stage line that, as one wag later said, went "from no place through nothing to nowhere." This assessment was not far off the mark; the route was to run between Texas and California, with the terminal points at San Antonio, which was reachable from the East via New Orleans, and San Diego. To travel between the two cities the stages would be compelled to cross 1,475 miles of desert-and-mountain wilderness.

But the man who got the contract boasted a record second to none in pushing stagecoaches through raw wilderness. The winning bid—$149,800 for semi-monthly service, to begin the following year, on July 1,

Old Glory flutters over Fort Collins, garrisoned in 1864 to guard the main wagon route in northern Colorado territory. Utah-bound freight caravans on the route, which ran through hunting grounds of the Utes, Cheyennes and Arapahoes, sometimes faced attacks by as many as 1,000 warriors.

Swift couriers who defied the wintry Sierra

In grappling with the assorted adversities of Western weather and terrain, expressmen who specialized in the transport of mail and small parcels tried almost every imaginable mode of transport — even their own slogging feet. But the daunting combination of winter and mountains called for a special kind of resourcefulness.

In the Sierra Nevada, where drifting snow closed passes to horse and foot travel much of the winter, some expressmen got through by wearing Indian snowshoes. This method was too slow to satisfy an enterprising Californian named Fenton Whiting. In the winter of 1858 he hitched some large mongrels to a $75 sled and launched the West's first dog-team express. Whiting's sledges, which transported up to 600 pounds of packages and mail to miners on each trip over wintry mountain trails, lasted until 1865, when a snowshoe for horses was introduced. Thus shod, horses were hitched to stage-sleighs — stagecoaches that had runners instead of wheels — that replaced the dog express for mid-winter service.

Another unusual express service had been inaugurated earlier in the mining town of Placerville, California. In 1856, after a severe blizzard had closed the road to the Nevada hamlet of Genoa, a hulking Norwegian named John Thompson informed the Placerville postmaster that he knew a way to get the mail through. When this declaration met with frank disbelief, Thompson produced a pair of long skis, whose use he had mastered in his native land. The postmaster decided to give the Norwegian and

Fenton Whiting's dog team darts through a Sierra blizzard in this 1861 engraving.

his then-strange contraptions a whirl. Within hours, Thompson was on his way to Genoa, 90 miles across the Sierra. Navigating by the sun during the day and by the stars at night, with a 75-pound mail sack strapped to his back, he skimmed through an obstacle course of snowslides, tangled trees and deep crevasses. Three days later he dropped the mail sack at the feet of an astonished Genoa postmaster.

Thompson made the return run to Placerville, most of it downhill, in only two days — again carrying a bulging sack of mail. On his arrival, he

was mobbed by grateful miners, who, never having seen skis before, dubbed him "Snowshoe" Thompson.

The skiing mailman continued to make regular wintertime runs, in the course of which, it was said, he could outpace and even outhowl wolves. Unfortunately he didn't howl loudly enough about his spotty pay. In 1874, after risking his neck for nearly 20 years, he petitioned Congress for about $6,000 in back salary due him. The money was promised, but unlike the mail that Thompson always saw through, it never did reach him.

1857—was submitted by James Birch, California's pioneer stage operator.

Now 29, Birch could look back on a career of virtually unbroken triumphs, both professional and personal. Within four years, he had built up the largest staging network in California, amassed a fortune and won Julia Chace, the girl he loved back East. Shortly before winning the Texas-California contract he had retired from active management of his company, left California and moved into a splendid mansion in the seaside spa of Swansea, Massachusetts. On his estate of rolling lawns, lakes and wooded vistas, he built elaborate stables and filled them with the finest horses and coaches and carriages. In October 1856, Julia gave birth to a son whom Birch showered with exquisite miniature coaches and toy horses. But despite domestic bliss, Birch had not lost his itch for staging, and when he learned of the San Antonio-San Diego route, he could not resist the challenge.

In the summer of 1857, Birch was on business in California. Service on his new San Antonio-San Diego stage line was fairly well underway, and he decided to return home by sea to Julia and his son. In August he sailed for New York by way of Panama. Three weeks later the man whose whole life had been bound up with overland transport went down with the steamer *Central America* in a savage storm off Florida.

Birch's death had sad consequences for his new stage line—the first to span the continent. In his own brief time with it he had had to use mules instead of horses to draw the stages—earning for the venture the tag of the "Jackass Line." After his death the nickname turned from a mild jest to an epithet. The contract went to one George Giddings, who had held a mail contract for the shorter run between San Antonio and Santa Fe, and Giddings presided over a veritable disaster. At times, coaches were dispensed with, and mail and passengers alike had to cross the mountains on muleback.

Travelers' tales helped warn off new customers, and so did a San Diego newspaper's listing of the clothing and gear that a prudent passenger of the Jackass Line ought to take along. The journal specified: "One Sharp's rifle and a hundred cartridges; a Colt's navy revolver and two pounds of balls; a knife and sheath; a pair of thick boots and woolen pants; a half dozen pairs of thick woolen socks, six undershirts; three woolen overshirts; a wide-awake hat; a cheap sack coat; a soldier's overcoat; one pair of blankets in summer and two in winter; a piece of India rubber cloth for blankets; a pair of gauntlets; a small bag of needles, pins, a sponge, hair brush, comb, soap, etc. in an oil silk bag; two pairs of thick drawers, and three or four towels."

During its four-year history, the number of passengers who availed themselves of this pioneering stage link with California probably totaled only a few score. Postage revenues from the trickle of letters that moved over the line fell far short of the amount of the subsidy. According to one estimate, every letter delivered between San Antonio and San Diego cost the government approximately $65.

Congress agreed that both the government and California deserved better than the Jackass Line, and it was in business only a year when, in September of 1858, an alternative line went into operation. As enacted by Congress, the alternative had seemed to satisfy both Northern and Southern factions on Capitol Hill. It called for a maximum compensation of $600,000 per year for semiweekly mail deliveries by stagecoach between "such point on the Mississippi River as the contractors may select, to San Francisco." The Eastern terminus was likely to be St. Louis, a thriving railway center on the Mississippi. But as Northern legislators saw it, to get from St. Louis to San Francisco the stage line would logically have to follow the great emigrant trail, thus traveling in a generally northerly direction. Southern legislators, however, had paid more heed to a clause in the enabling act that left the exact choice of route up to the Postmaster General—who at the time was Aaron Brown, a proslavery Tennessean.

The only route Brown would accept was marvelously attuned to his regional concerns. It had not one but two starting points, St. Louis and Memphis, Brown's hometown. These roads joined at Fort Smith, Arkansas; then the route described an enormous southward arc, to El Paso and Fort Yuma on the Mexican border, and thence to Los Angeles and San Francisco —a total distance of 2,795 miles. The Northern press howled. New York newspapers dubbed it "the oxbow route," "the horseshoe," "the side line." The *Chicago Tribune* called it "one of the greatest swindles ever perpetrated upon the country by the slaveholders." The reaction in California was no less outraged. "A foul

A triumphant timetable for the southern route

Stage line operator John Butterfield

A lesser man than John Butterfield might well have faced instant bankruptcy in undertaking to run a stage line over the roundabout Oxbow Route. Starting from Memphis and St. Louis in the east and ending in California, the route was nearly 1,000 miles longer than it needed to be, as a result of the maneuverings of Southern politicians. Furthermore, it lay across unsettled country and would produce little profitable way-station traffic.

Butterfield nonetheless set to his task, buoyed in part by a $600,000-a-year mail subsidy. Though his government contract called for a one-way schedule of 25 days, he saw to it that his vehicles usually made the trip in 24 days or less, at an average speed of four and a half miles an hour. The extra day afforded a little leeway for breakdowns.

For his passengers' comfort, Butterfield did the best he could. Near the line's terminal points—where the roads were better—he provided handsome Concord coaches. But for most of the route, over what one rider described as "the worst road God ever built," travelers had to take their lumps in "celerity wagons"—comfortless vehicles designed for rough going.

Go they did. Butterfield preached, "Remember, boys, nothing on God's earth must stop the U.S. Mail," and indeed, for more than two years, nothing was permitted to. By the time the Oxbow was finally suspended on the eve of the Civil War, Butterfield's stages were delivering more mail to the Far West than all of the ships at sea.

Butterfield station hands transfer mail and passengers' baggage from a stagecoach to a mule-drawn "celerity wagon" built for rough terrain.

The Oxbow Route's westbound schedule called for two stage departures a week, and completion of a run of some 2,800 miles in 25 days, with exactly 576½ hours allotted for actual travel time between way stops.

No. 2.	GOING WEST.			Jan. 1859.	
LEAVE.	**DAYS.**			**Hour.**	Distance, Place to Place.	**TIME ALLOWED**
					Miles.	No. Hours.
St. Louis, Mo., and Memphis, Tenn.,	Monday	and	Thursday,	8.00 A.M		
Tipton, Mo.	Monday	and	Thursday,	6.00 P.M	160	10
Springfield, "	Wednesday	and	Saturday,	7.45 A.M	143	37¾
Fayetteville, Ark.	Thursday	and	Sunday,	10 15 A.M	100	26½
Fort Smith, "	Friday	and	Monday,	3.30 A.M	65	17¼
Sherman, Texas.	Sunday	and	Wednesday,	12.30 A.M	205	45
Fort Belknap, "	Monday	and	Thursday,	9.00 A.M	146½	32½
Fort Chadbourne, "	Tuesday	and	Friday,	3.15 P.M	136	30¼
Pecos River Croessing,	Thursday	and	Sunday,	3.45 A.M	165	36½
El Paso,	Saturday	and	Tuesday,	11.00 A.M	248½	55¼
Soldier's Farewell,	Sunday	and	Wednesday,	8.30 P.M	150	33½
Tucson, Arizona	Tuesday	and	Friday,	1.30 P.M	184½	41
Gila River,* "	Wednesday	and	Saturday,	9.00 P.M	141	31½
Fort Yuma, Cal.	Friday	and	Monday,	3.00 A.M	135	30
Los Angelos, "	Sunday	and	Wednesday,	8.30 A.M	254	53½
Fort Tejon, "	Monday	and	Thursday,	7.30 A.M	96	23
Visalia, "	Tuesday	and	Friday,	11.30 A.M	127	28
Firebaugh's Ferry, "	Wednesday	and	Saturday,	5.30 A.M	82	18
(Arrive) San Francisco,	Thursday	and	Sunday,	8.30 A.M	163	27

* The Station referred to on the Gila River is 40 miles west of the Maricopa Wells.

This Schedule may not be exact—all employes are directed to use every possible exertion to get the Stage through in quick time, even though ahead of this time.

No allowance is made in the time for ferries, changing teams, &c. It is necessary that each driver increase his speed over the average per hour enough to gain time for meals, changing teams, crossing ferries, &c.

Every person in the Company's employ will remember that each minute is of importance. If each driver on the route loses 15 minutes, it would make a total loss of time, on the entire route, of 25 hours, or, more than one day. If each one loses 10 minutes, it would make a loss of 16½ hours, or the best part of a day.

If each driver gains that time, it leaves a margin against accidents and extra delays.

All will see the necessity of promptness; every minute of time is valuable, as the Company are under heavy forfeit if the mail is behind time.

JOHN BUTTERFIELD, President.

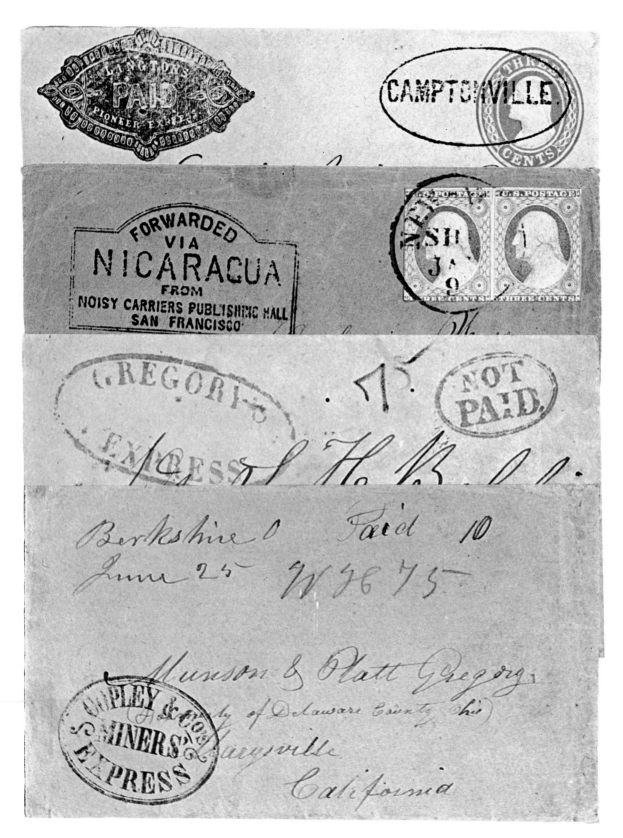

James Birch, a former New England coachman, emigrated to Sacramento in 1849, bought a ranch wagon to carry passengers to mining camps, and in five years built a stage company worth one million dollars.

wrong: a Panama route by land," cried the *Sacramento Union.*

Yet the man to whom Brown awarded the contract, a New Yorker named John Butterfield, made the route work — and work beautifully. A thoroughgoing pragmatist, Butterfield was a most logical choice. He had been a stage driver in his youth, went on to win control of all the principal stage lines in central New York State, and in 1850 helped form the American Express Company, which quickly became one of the giants in its field. For his new enterprise, Butterfield dipped deep into his corporate coffers, came up with one million dollars, built 139 relay stations and way stops, cut new roads, bridged streams and graded hilly stretches. Then he bought 1,800 head of stock and 250 of the best coaches, and hired some 800 men to keep the stages rocking along.

On September 15, 1858, the Butterfield Overland Mail Company was ready for its maiden run. For the first time in history, a traveler could buy — for $200 — a ticket to ride overland by coach all the way from the banks of the Mississippi to the far edge of the American domain. The first stage completed its trip in exactly 24 days, 18 hours and 26 minutes. Thereafter, the stages continued to traverse the great arc twice a week in as little as 21 days each way.

One passenger's view of the nature of Butterfield's accomplishment was published in the *New York Post.* Referring to the bugle used by stage drivers to announce their approach, he wrote: "The blast of the

stage horn as it rolls through the valleys and over the prairies of the West, cheers and gladdens the heart of the pioneer. As it sounds through the valleys of Santa Clara and San Jose, it sends a thrill of delight to the Californian. He knows that it brings tidings from the hearts and homes he left behind him; it binds him stronger and firmer to his beloved country."

Within California, the Butterfield Overland Mail Company connected with a system of transportation and communication that bore only a faint resemblance to the rude network of the first Western expressmen. Alexander Todd had fallen by the wayside. Though he had moved from the gold fields to Stockton and established branches there and in other towns, he was overtaken by a series of costly mishaps, notably the theft of $160,000 by embezzling employees. He had sold out, and the company he had so shrewdly nurtured wound up in the hands of an unrelated namesake, C. A. Todd. In turn, C. A. Todd, like hundreds of other small- and medium-sized operators, had sold out to a firm that would come to dominate the express business in California and all across the West — Wells, Fargo & Company. Daniel Dancer's pack-mule operation, too, was a part of the past. Where mule tracks had once led from his old base of Marysville to gold country, there were now roads jammed with massive freight wagons, hundreds in a single week. As for James Birch, though he was dead, his mark was visible everywhere. In 1854, he had initiated a move to consolidate his own stage lines with those of his smaller rivals. The result, hammered out at the conference table, was the California Stage Company.

By the time John Butterfield's coaches began rolling into the state, the California Stage Company was a colossus. It had been able to survive a vast financial panic in 1855 that toppled a number of large businesses of every sort. Fron Sacramento and Mother Lode country its routes ran almost the entire length of the state, reaching north into Oregon. The company had become California's foremost road builder, sending

Each of California's many express companies put its own mark, or frank, on the mail it carried; four examples appear on the letters at left. The delivery charge was often scrawled above the address, as in the "75" (cents) on the two lower envelopes. This fee was due from the recipient, a point some firms stressed by an ink-stamped "not paid." Beyond express fees, all mail after 1855 also required prepaid U.S. postage. If a postmaster was short of government stamps, he wrote "paid" and the amount, as on the bottom letter. The "WH" on the line below, jotted down by the expressman, stood for the recipient's whereabouts — Whiskey Hill.

out crews to construct ferries and bridges, carve zig-zagging switchbacks down the face of mountain barriers and widen narrow canyons by blasting. It had routes of its own totaling some 1,970 miles, and its stage drivers traveled more than a million miles a year.

Everywhere along this immense, humming network, towns were growing into cities with civilized niceties. San Francisco's population had vaulted from some 2,000 in 1848 to perhaps 100,000 by 1858. Signs of stability were appearing in lesser towns that had been brawling mining camps a few years earlier.

But it was Sacramento, more than San Francisco or the mining towns, that epitomized California in the late 1850s — still raw beneath its veneer of amenities, and bursting with a sense of its own vigor. Sacramento was not only the hub of California's road system, but an important river port, linked to San Francisco by more than two dozen steamboats popularly referred to as "floating palaces." One of them, the *Wilson G. Hunt,* was a 186-foot vision of white enamel, gold-leaf decoration, brass fixtures and plush interior. It had been built in New York as a Coney Island excursion boat, and had made the long journey around the Horn with a load of forty-niners under its own steam.

Twice a day, Sacramento's populace, interest and energy came to focus on the docks. Everyone turned out at 4 p.m. to see the night boat off for San Francisco. Scores of stagecoaches would draw up through the milling crowds to deliver outbound passengers, mail, and as much as one million dollars' worth of gold dust.

Next morning the process was reversed; the people turned out to meet the steamer inbound from San Francisco. Now the stages were ready and waiting with fresh horses. The drivers roared out the destination of their lines to passengers coming down the gangplank. When the seats were filled, the drivers cracked whips over their teams and clattered off in all directions, bellowing the familiar warning of stage coachmen everywhere: "Clear the road!"

And behind all the din was an odd chuffing noise that, in time, would grow louder and louder until it drowned out the expressmen. The single locomotive of the Sacramento Valley Railroad—the only one in California—was setting off on its 22-mile run to the mining town of Folsom, offering an insolent blast of its whistle as a harbinger to the West of the road of iron to come.

ORNIA STAGE COMPANY.

Incorporated December 1853.

A spectacular cascade spills into the Timpanagos River canyon, traversed by a Mormon road that joined Simpson's eastward route.

Uncle Sam's own shortcut to California

The first wagon trails westward were pioneered by traders and emigrants, but the U.S. government, eager to speed settlement, followed close behind. The Army's Corps of Topographical Engineers was assigned to grade and bridge treacherous spots along the early trails, and to survey and build new roads.

Nowhere were these services more needed than in the Great Basin, a vast, arid depression east of the Sierra Nevada. To get through this region to California, most travelers took a roundabout trail along the brackish Humboldt River and across desert wastes—a route that was dotted with the graves of people who failed to make it. In 1859, Captain James Simpson of the Corps of Engineers began surveying a shortcut across the harrowing expanse.

Simpson's prospective route would start out from Camp Floyd, a military post south of Salt Lake City, and thrust almost due west to the town of Genoa. There it would connect with a road that had been recently built across the

James H. Simpson in 1865

Sierra by Californians as a mail route to Nevada mining camps.

After preliminary forays to look over existing Mormon roads in Utah Territory *(left)*, Simpson set out for Genoa with 12 supply wagons and a party that included 23 soldiers, two guides and the artist Henry von Beckh, whose

sketches formed the basis of the watercolors shown opposite and on the following pages. Striking across the Great Salt Lake desert, the party entered a series of little-known mountain ranges. As the guides roved ahead to find passes, Simpson compiled notes on the availability of water, grass and timber, and used an odometer to record mileage. He encountered only two arduous stretches—in the Lookout Mountains, where the guides themselves got lost and had to be found, and in the alkali flats beyond, where the party almost ran out of water.

Six weeks after leaving Camp Floyd, Simpson and his helpers reached their destination—and exultantly calculated that they had cut 288 miles off the Humboldt River route. They turned east again to map a second way across the Great Basin. But the outbound passage proved shorter by 28 miles, and within a year emigrants, freight haulers and Pony Express riders had adopted it as the fastest way to the Far West.

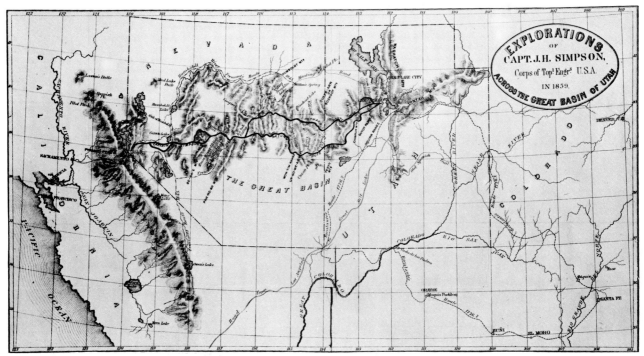

Simpson's map traces his surveys from Camp Floyd to Genoa and back, through the mountains south of the trail along the Humboldt.

On the first easy leg of the trip, Simpson's caravan rolls across the Salt Lake Desert toward the mountain chains of the Great Basin.

"Beautifully embosomed in the Sierra" was Simpson's description of Lake Bigler, named for a California governor and later given the Indian name

Hauling on a rope secured to trees, the surveyors raft a supply wagon over the Carson River in Nevada, while the animals swim across.

of Tahoe. An existing wagon road around its southern shore linked the western terminus of Simpson's exploration to Placerville, California.

Exactly 531 miles from the starting point of their reconnaissance, Captain Simpson's party rides into the Mormon settlement of Genoa, nestled

in the foothills of the Sierra Nevada. The town's 150 citizens marked the occasion by raising the American flag and firing a 13-gun salute.

2 | Caravans on a crucial mission

Pre-Civil War geography textbooks often denominated the immense region west of the Missouri River as the Great American Desert. Even though thriving pockets of settlement gave the lie to this description, there were difficulties enough to make travelers believe it: stretches of alkali dust and sucking mud, bitter extremes of cold and heat, unfriendly Indians and, above all, exhausting distances. No one faced these challenges more intimately than the men on the freight-wagon caravans that supplied frontier towns and military posts with goods from the 1840s until well after the Civil War.

Every spring, thousands of mule- or ox-drawn wagons creaked forth from supply depots along the Missouri. A column of wagons, driven by rugged mule skinners and bullwhackers who urged the animals on with vicious snaps of their rawhide whips, covered only 125 miles or so each week. But at journey's end, such a column might disgorge as many as 75 tons of food, animal feed, cloth, implements and machinery—the wherewithal to sustain budding frontier communities and to keep them growing for another year.

A wagon train pulls out of Nebraska City in the 1860s, loaded with goods brought up the Missouri by steamboat.

A wagon column rumbles past a massive Sierra escarpment along the Lake Bigler Toll Road in the 1860s. The road was one of a network of eight routes built and maintained by private capital to link the booming mining towns on either side of the border between California and Nevada.

With much of their cargo already off-loaded at previous settlements along the trail, wagons inch along a path cleared between steep snowbanks near the summit of the Sierra Nevada. Mountain passes were snowbound half of the year, restricting wagon freighting to spring and summer.

49

Ox-drawn wagons bearing cargo to replenish the stock of merchants roll down the main street of Crook City — a gold-mining town in the Black Hills of Dakota Territory named for General George Crook, the renowned Indian-fighter.

51

A massive push to deliver the goods

Horace Greeley had seen all sorts of novel sights in his years as New York's leading newspaper editor, but never one like the spectacle that spread before him on a plain near Leavenworth, Kansas, one spring day in 1859. "Such acres of wagons!" Greeley rhapsodized. "Such pyramids of extra axletrees! such herds of oxen! such regiments of drivers and other employees! No one who has not seen can realize how vast a business this is, nor how immense are its outlays as well as its income."

Greeley was given to excesses of enthusiasm, but in this case his exclamation marks were justified. The great concourse of wagons and animals and men he beheld was a freight caravan forming up for the mammoth task of hauling supplies to U.S. Army outposts scattered across the Western frontier. What quantities of supplies were involved Greeley did not specify; however, the total certainly came to millions of pounds.

Leavenworth was not the only jumping-off point for these astonishing freight odysseys. Other Missouri River towns, all along the 325 miles from Independence to Council Bluffs, were duplicating the scene on a smaller scale with civilian goods. Hundreds of wagons drawn by thousands of oxen or mules were being loaded with food, clothing, boots, shoes, tools and other necessities

---

A brawny bullwhacker, braided rawhide whip at the ready to urge his oxen on, strides alongside his freight wagon in this 1867 engraving from *Harper's Monthly*.

NEW ADVERTISEMENTS.

ARMY OF THE WEST!

16,000 YOKE

OF

GOOD WORKING CATTLE,

From Four to 7 years of age, wanted at

NEBRASKA CITY,

for hauling freight from this point to Utah, for which SEVENTY-FIVE DOLLARS per Yoke will be paid. Notice will be given through the newspapers of the time they are to be delivered, but suppose they will be wanted about the first of May.

FIFTEEN HUNDRED MEN

Wanted for teamsters who will be found and paid Twenty-five dollars per month out and back.

None but men of good habits need apply; as drinking intoxicating liquors, card playing; and profane language will not be permitted while in employment. Each man will be presented with a Bible and hymn book. Forty Wagon Masters wanted who must come well recommended and who will be paid the usual wages.

A number of houses will be rented in Nebraska City, and one large store room. Apply to

RUSSELL, MAJORS & WADDEL.

by KINNEY & HOLLY, Agents.   Mr 20-t

---

to sustain isolated frontier settlers for another year.

One did not have to be a stranger like Greeley to marvel at the hustle and bustle. Young Frank Root, who traveled the frontier as a stagecoach messenger, was fairly brimming with excitement as he stood on the levee at the town of Atchison and watched a Missouri River steamboat put in, bearing a cargo from the East for a westering wagon train. The deep blast of the steamer's horn brought townspeople flocking; the boat's crew thrust planks out to the dock and the stevedores swarmed aboard. Within a few minutes, Root recalled, the first of them were coming back down the gangplanks, "carrying ham, bacon, sacks of coffee, sugar, potatoes, dried apples and peaches, flour, meal, beans, etc., and piling them up in front of the warehouse on the levee."

At Westport Landing—later part of Kansas City—another sort of consignment fascinated a reporter for the *Missouri Republican*. Prowling the business district back of the port, he came upon "a patent reaper and mower, a steam engine and boiler, together with all the machinery necessary for a new flouring mill at Albuquerque." He was barely able to contain his local pride. "Sometimes," he said, "it is difficult to tread one's way across the streets on account of the blockade of wagons, mules, cattle, bales, boxes, etc."

The freighting season began between mid-March and mid-April, when the ice broke at the port of St. Louis, permitting the passage of the cargo-laden river boats. By the time the first of them poked upstream, freight

53

At a Colorado mine pack mules, some unloaded and some still bearing cargo, stand sure-footed on terrain that would balk a wagon. Even where roads did exist, heavy snows often compelled muleback deliveries.

wagons had been repaired and taken out of their winter storage in wagon yards, hordes of draft animals had been mustered, and teamsters had poured in from all over the East. Some were youths looking for adventure, whose dude suits had to be replaced quickly by more serviceable garb; some were newly arrived emigrants; some were disheartened farmers eager to work their way west to settle; many were veterans of past caravans, their clothes dirtied and well worn, their hats battered, their language imaginatively sulfurous.

The loading of the wagons started as soon as the river boats deposited their cargoes. Time was of the essence, yet utmost care was required, for misplaced loads could shift, toppling a wagon en route. The wagonmaster of each train supervised the proper stowage of the freight; at the same time he drew up a bill of lading that recorded the goods consigned to each wagon. At last the draft animals were hitched and the wagons pulled into line. "The streets resound with barbarous vociferations and loud cracks of heavy whips," a Topeka newspaperman reported. "The rumbling noise made by the clumsy, lumbersome 'prairie schooners,' while propelled along by patient oxen, is heard incessantly." As each wagon train moved out, the sheer numbers of vehicles involved—sometimes as many as 780 wagons in all—made an unforgettable impression on spectators. At one caravan marshaling point—the little town of Lone Elm, Kansas—burdened wagons waiting to depart jammed an entire quarter-section of land: 160 acres. A local resident named Ainsworth watched them set out and timed them. The first wagon of the first train left at midnight; the last wagon in the last train did not pass him until 4 o'clock the next afternoon.

The journey ahead, whether it led southwest, northwest or directly west, held perils both known and unknown. Since a wagon train could cover an average of only 15 to 20 miles a day, distance itself posed problems. Wagons and animals and men alike had to be made of sturdy stuff to endure the 800 miles from Westport Landing southward to Santa Fe or the 1,200 miles of the northern route from Atchison to Helena, Montana. Way stations were few and far between, Indians watched for chances to attack, and there were natural hazards as well. To get to the Santa Fe Trail's Cimarron Cutoff, the Arkansas River had to be crossed, and quicksand made the passage a treacherous under-

Pending the mounted wagonmaster's command to roll out of a way stop en route to the Black Hills gold camps, an ox train forms into two wings—the standard arrangement for travel in open country. This train's heavy cargo required outsized teams—10 pairs of oxen to pull three linked wagons.

taking; at Raton Pass, on the trail's Mountain Branch, the going was so precipitous that wagons had to be eased down by ropes, chains and windlasses improvised from tree trunks. On Oregon Trail caravans, fording a river like the unruly South Platte terrified the calmest oxen and taxed the toughest teamsters; adding to such ordeals, the travelers had to contend with the alkali dust that lay as deep as six inches on much of the overland trails, waiting to be churned into gritty, blinding clouds by wagon wheels and animal hoofs.

Even in the best of circumstances, the long hauls of the freight caravans were grueling ventures, yet they were of vital moment to people on the frontier, serving quite literally as life lines. Until 1869, when rails spanned the continent, both the survival and the economic growth of the West depended on the durability of wagon axles, the hardihood of oxen and mules, the tenacity of wagon drivers and—perhaps most important —the vision and daring of the freight entrepreneurs.

Wagon-freighting was a business that could enrich a man, or bankrupt him. A company that undertook to carry Army supplies on one 1858 journey from Nebraska City to Utah might, for example, receive $1.80 per 100 pounds hauled per 100 miles. The distance covered was about 1,200 miles. If 25 wagon trains

were sent out—each train consisting of 25 cargo wagons, each wagon holding 7,000 pounds—the gross receipts would have totaled more than $945,000. Even with the company's outlay of roughly $500,000 for wagons, oxen, and wages and provisions for the teamsters, the net profit from this journey would have been a handsome one indeed.

Not all Army contracts involved such great quantities of cargo or such long distances to travel, and civilian freight caravans tended to be much smaller. Still, the profit was always potentially good—unless events intervened. Any one of a number of unpredictable mishaps—freakish weather, spoilage of cargoes, trail accidents—could bring financial ruin. The vagaries of the business required men of special strengths.

The massive operation that dazzled Horace Greeley at Leavenworth lay in the hands of three such men. William Hepburn Russell, William Bradford Waddell and Alexander Majors were as incongruous a trio as ever formed a business partnership, yet their very differences proved the key to their joint success. Russell, the senior partner, was a comfort-loving aristocrat more at ease in the banks and board rooms of the East than on the sweaty caravan trails; an irrepressible promoter, he excelled at wooing the financial backers the firm

needed. Waddell, dour and stolid, had worked his steady way up the ladder from lead miner to prosperous wholesaler and retailer of produce, grain and hemp; it was he who oversaw day-to-day office matters. Majors, a former farmer, much preferred the outdoor life; a man of iron discipline and austere ways, he took naturally to the heavy responsibility of supervising the wagon trains en route. Perfectly complementing one another, the three partners made a team that was soon to dominate the Western freighting business.

The name of Russell, Majors & Waddell became so synonymous with freighting that it sometimes seemed as if the firm had invented the idea. Actually, by the time the partners got together in 1854 their opportunity lay in adapting and improving techniques already well tested by earlier entrepreneurs. Among these were William Becknell, the Missourian who in 1821 had pioneered trading on the Santa Fe Trail, and the men who followed in his wake over the next three decades. Though Becknell and his successors were primarily interested in trading, a development crucial to the future of freighting came out of a chance experiment on the journey of a wagon train bound for Santa Fe in 1829. Up to then, the wagons' motive power had been supplied occasionally by horses but primarily by mules. In

1829 oxen were introduced, and their use had a stunning impact on the entire economics of freighting.

The man responsible for this revolution was interested neither in trading nor in freighting but only in doing his duty as an officer of the U.S. Army. He was Major Bennet Riley, commander of a battalion of 180 infantrymen who had been assigned to escort the wagon train from Round Grove, Kansas, to the Arkansas River — then regarded as the border with Mexico — to prevent harassment by Indians. No sizable American military unit had ever traveled that far, almost 500 miles, without sources of supplies, but in this uninhabited area such sources did not exist. So Riley assembled his own supply wagons, 19 in all, and he chose oxen to draw them. The traders he was to accompany were dismayed; they did not think oxen were strong or fast enough for the trip. Still, Riley had his reasons, one of them decidedly pragmatic: a lack of sufficient funds to buy mules. But he also saw advantages in oxen that others did not. As his men ate into the supplies, he could slaughter some oxen for beef; moreover, he would not have to carry feed for the animals because, he figured, they could live on grass.

From the start, the military's oxen consistently kept up with the wagon-train mules. Riley and a member of

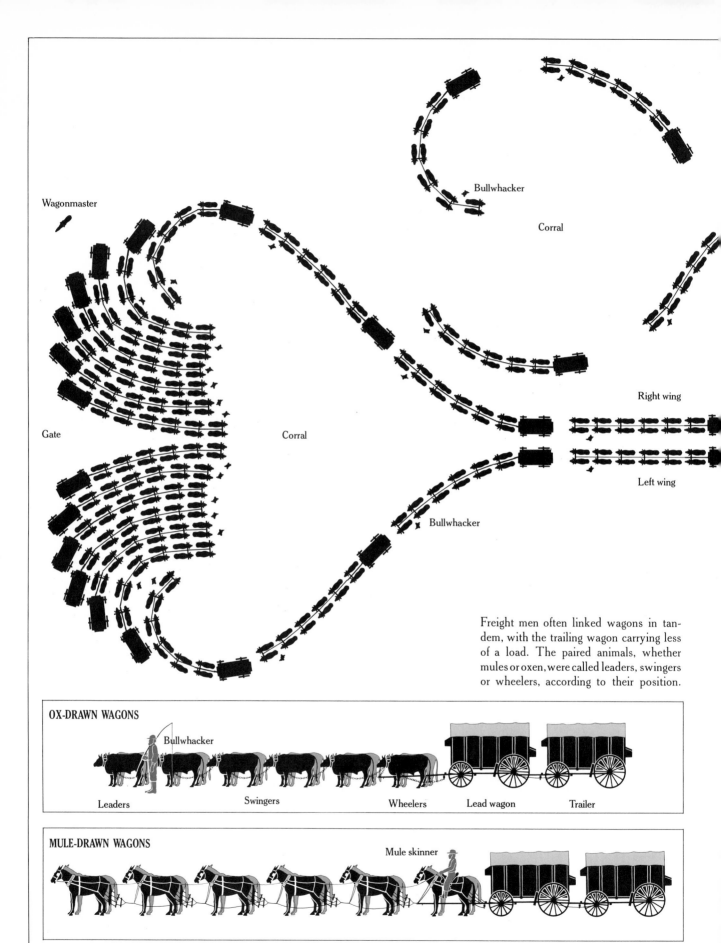

Wagonmaster

Bullwhacker

Corral

Right wing

Gate

Corral

Bullwhacker

Left wing

Freight men often linked wagons in tandem, with the trailing wagon carrying less of a load. The paired animals, whether mules or oxen, were called leaders, swingers or wheelers, according to their position.

OX-DRAWN WAGONS

Bullwhacker

Leaders   Swingers   Wheelers   Lead wagon   Trailer

MULE-DRAWN WAGONS

Mule skinner

SINGLE-FILE OX TRAIN

In a single-file wagon train, wagons swung out alternately in opposite semicircles to form a corral. Wagon wheels were jammed against each other, making a solid wall, impenetrable except for one or two openings.

DOUBLE-WING OX TRAIN

A double-wing train could corral twice as fast because the two wings swung out simultaneously. As the arcs formed, the wagon tongues were turned inward; the animals were then unhitched inside the corral.

Assistant wagonmaster

Herder

Mess wagon

Calf yard

Herder

Military precision in a civilian wagon train

Wagon freighting, which was first used on a large scale to haul supplies for the U.S. Army, resembled a military operation in many ways. Each wagon train, called an outfit, was led by a wagonmaster, whose authority over his men equaled that of a commanding officer. He patrolled the train and also rode ahead of it, setting the pace and scouting stream fords and campsites.

The assistant wagonmaster rode near the rear of the train, where newer drivers were generally assigned, and also kept an eye on the mess wagon. If the train was ox-drawn, he also watched over the "calf yard"—a herd of extra cattle that supplied replacements for lame or injured animals.

The teamsters who actually kept the wagons on the move either walked or rode, depending on whether the train was being pulled by mules or oxen. Mule skinners rode one of their charges and guided the team with a single rein called a jerk line; bullwhackers walked at the left of the oxen, directing them by cracking a whip over the head of one or another animal.

Freight men hotly disputed the relative merits of the two species. What it came down to was that mules were faster, oxen cheaper. Mules pulled wagons at two and a half miles an hour, versus two for oxen—a difference that could knock a week off the run from the banks of the Missouri to Denver. But a pair of oxen could be purchased for only $40 to $160, while a pair of mules cost $200 to $400.

After 1860, many freight companies replaced large wagons with smaller versions that could be coupled together

(left). Although this arrangement improved maneuverability, guiding an entire train still required a precision similar to that of a close-order drill. The column lurched into motion when the wagonmaster bellowed his command of "stretch out!" or "roll on!" On narrow trails the formation was single file. Parallel files, called wings, often were used on the open plains and permitted quicker defense in Indian country.

The basic defensive maneuver, employed under attack and also as a matter of course every night, was to corral, or circle, the wagons, one abutting the other in a solid phalanx. With the animals grazing outside the corral—tended by night herders and teamsters whose turn it was for guard duty—the rest of the company had reasonable assurance of safe, though exhausted, sleep.

the wagon train, the famous fur trader Charles Bent, then started keeping a systematic check on the oxen. The animals were still in fine fettle when they reached the Arkansas River, having traveled 485 miles. As a further test of the oxen, Bent took a yoke, or pair, all the way to Santa Fe, and they returned in better shape than the mules he matched them against.

What had begun as an expedient opened a broad new opportunity for freight entrepreneurs. The ox thereafter supplied the basic motive power of freighting and continued to do so until the railroad steam engine supplanted him. Mules continued to have their fierce partisans, however, and the choice usually depended on the work to be done. Mules were faster than oxen, taking one or two weeks less than oxen to cover the same distance; and so merchants sometimes specified mule freight for speeding delivery of food, light hardware and luxuries. But they paid premium rates, because mules had to be grain-fed, and the grain that had to be taken along reduced the amount of pay cargo they could haul.

Ox teams, on the other hand, "ate their way to market," as one observer put it, feeding on the grasses en route. Moreover, they cost as little as $40 a pair, one fifth the price for a pair of mules. Furthermore, mules posed a temptation to thieving Indians, because they could be ridden; oxen could not, so they traversed Indian lands at less risk. And, in a pinch, oxen made good eating, whereas teamsters loathed mule meat.

All in all, oxen had advantages that a cost-conscious freight entrepreneur could not overlook. Though they were steers—often range cattle from Texas or Cherokee country—they were invariably called bulls; hence the terms "bullwhacker" for the man who goaded them on and "bullwhip" for the means of persuasion he used. The bulls varied in size; many beasts weighed 1,000 pounds or more in maturity.

A young, unbroken steer was trained by being yoked to an experienced beast of similar size and weight; the two, their tails tied together, were walked back and forth in a pasture until the newcomer got the idea. If they got along well, they became a pair. They were then hitched, with four or five other pairs, to an unloaded wagon; the entire team was driven around the pasture until it was accustomed to working together.

Six pairs of oxen to a wagon were the usual rule. When a wagon was ready to get underway, the wheel position, directly in front of the vehicle, was taken by a pair known as wheelers; the strongest and heaviest of the team, they bore the major brunt of pulling the wagon. Progressively lighter cattle were used in front of the wheelers. Just ahead of them, not as heavy but also well trained, came the pointers, who helped pull. Immediately in front of them were three pairs of so-called swing cattle, whose function was to help turn the direction of the wagon; they were relatively young and fractious and most in need of the bullwhip. Finally, ahead of the swing cattle came the pair of leaders, who set the pace and started the wagon turning when necessary. Properly broken longhorns made the best leaders, for they were light, long-legged, and deft on their feet on a rough road. They were also the most intelligent of the beasts, but unfortunately they could run as fast as horses when frightened, which often set off a chain reaction of panic in the animals behind them.

Larger ox teams were sometimes employed for unusually heavy hauling, and they made a striking sight. Their owners often planned it that way, matching the animals for visual effect. Colonel J. F. Meline, a cavalry officer who was riding west one year, passed a wagon train in which each wagon was drawn by ten pairs of oxen, each set of twenty "either all black, all white, all spotted or otherwise marked uniformly."

The boom in freighting began in 1848, at the end of the war with Mexico. The two-year conflict, and the added territory the U.S. acquired as a result, stretched Army supply lines beyond the military's capacity to deliver. The traditional Army practice of hauling its own food, feed, guns and ammunition to frontier outposts had never worked too well. Soldiers made poor teamsters. Many had never laid eyes on an Indian; far more than civilians, they were terrified of Indian attacks on their wagons. Their West Point officers knew little or nothing about handling draft animals.

The solution, Army commanders now decided, was to turn over the job of delivering the Army's supplies to a civilian with greater knowledge of what the problems were about. In May 1848 the quartermaster of the Army's Kansas outpost at Fort Leavenworth signed a contract with James Brown of Independence, Missouri, an experienced handler of civilian freight who had also been wagonmaster of an Army supply train to Santa Fe in 1846. Brown was to haul a maximum of 200,000

The rugged construction of a cargo carrier

Most wagons built in the United States during the early 19th Century were produced slowly and in varying quality by small concerns that were often one-man operations. The nation's westward surge from the 1840s onward changed all that. Scores of companies sprang up to supply vehicles for the transport of people and goods beyond the Missouri. Some firms even boasted of specialties; Peter Schuttler of Chicago, for example, made wagons that could be coupled together *(below)*. However, Schuttler's output never matched that of the wagon industry's two giants: the J. Murphy Company of St. Louis and the Studebaker Brothers Manufacturing Company of South Bend, Indiana.

Studebaker featured an extensive line of vehicles ranging from ambulances for the military to carriages for the gentry. For both companies, however, freight wagons were the staple product, as meticulously crafted as the most glittering surrey. Irish-born Joseph Murphy would not allow his workmen to use augers to bore holes when they had to bolt planks together; instead they burned the holes through with red-hot irons to keep the surrounding wood from cracking or rotting. John, Clem and Peter Studebaker enforced equally high standards. They aged the hardwoods in their wagons for a period of three to five years to prevent shrinkage in the dry Western climate, and they had their black hickory axles boiled in oil to drive out moisture. For all such perfectionism, the cost of most freight wagons was held to less than $200 by quantity production. By 1874 the 550 workers at the Studebaker brothers' plant, with the help of a steam-powered production line, were turning out more than 30 wagons a day.

Like Joseph Murphy, the Studebakers were able to retire as millionaires. The brothers had the added pleasure of seeing their enterprise chalk up a record as the largest of its kind in the world — producer of a total of three quarters of a million wagons.

An advertisement for the Peter Schuttler Company features tandem wagons winding their way down a mountain road toward an idyllic campsite.

High-living William Russell *(left)* and tightfisted William Waddell *(right)*, though poles apart in personality, joined in successful ventures ranging from real estate to a freighting empire that covered the West.

pounds of military supplies to the garrison at Santa Fe. He had enough capital to invest in the necessary stock and provisions, but not enough to buy wagons. Since the Army officers knew and respected him, they arranged for the Army to sell him wagons on credit. Brown executed the contract, made $23,000 on it and paid for the wagons. He managed the entire project with such efficiency that the Army decided to advertise for more civilian contractors—and the boom era of Western freighting had begun.

Brown's success did not escape the notice of William Hepburn Russell, the future promotion genius of Russell, Majors & Waddell. Russell came from Vermont, but he was now living in Lexington, in western Missouri—a roughhewn setting for the blue-blooded descendant of Lord William Russell, who had been beheaded in England in 1683 for plotting against King Charles II. On the frontier, Russell remained an uncompromising grandee. He was always well tailored and well barbered, and he prized fine food—a trait that gradually rounded his figure. He avoided physical exertion; the body below his animated face was soft. But he was a shrewd, tough high-stakes speculator, full of self-confidence. He conceived a new business venture every few weeks, and by early middle age was a full-

fledged capitalist—president of an insurance company and a road-building company, a director of two local railroads and of a branch of the Bank of Missouri, and a partner in a land speculation venture.

Such a man could hardly have stayed out of the lucrative freighting business. Russell, indeed, had taken a flyer in it before the boom, in 1847. With a partner, E. C. McCarty, he had dispatched the first wagon train ever to carry civilian cargo from Westport Landing to Santa Fe. Russell didn't take to the trail himself, of course; he helped assemble the goods, wagons and stock, sent them on their way and then went about with an ear cocked for news. Much could happen out there in the Southwest, and he eagerly queried returning travelers about conditions on the trail and the rumors that flew along it. In a way, Russell was like an 18th Century Yankee shipowner who dispatched his sailing vessels from Boston harbor to China and waited months to learn if he was rich or ruined—the answer depending on the weather and the economy and honesty of his ship captains.

The 1847 civilian cargo venture paid off, and Russell and McCarty repeated it in 1848. But with James Brown's success that year in hauling supplies for the Army, Russell predictably decided that he wanted a

62

chunk of the military business. The following spring he and Brown formed a partnership and won an Army contract for the Santa Fe route. Their performance bond of $150,000 was signed by, among others, William Bradford Waddell, one of Russell's neighbors in Lexington and a member of the same Baptist church.

Waddell and Russell were antithetical, but drawn to each other nonetheless. To Russell's effervescent optimism, Waddell counterposed a stern sobriety. His sharp, flinty face bespoke his Scottish origins. Virginia-born, he had worked in Illinois lead mines, clerked in St. Louis and farmed for a while before setting up at Lexington as a dealer in farm commodities. Waddell was bothered by Russell's taste for high living and his zest for risky enterprise. But that did not stop Waddell from signing the performance bond for Brown & Russell's Army contract in 1849, and he rallied to his friend again after disaster overtook the partnership one year later. An unexpected snowstorm descended on a Brown & Russell wagon train that was carrying emergency supplies to the Army garrison at Santa Fe. Most of the oxen, including the extras, perished. The economic calamity was bad enough, but it was compounded by personal tragedy when Brown, who had been on the expedition, died of typhoid.

Two years later Waddell and Russell became partners in freighting, and by 1853 they had picked off a prize plum: an Army contract to carry military supplies to Fort Riley, Kansas, and Fort Union, New Mexico. But they were not yet dominant in the field. By now a lot of other people were in the freighting business too. In one recent year, the Army had made deals with 16 different companies, partnerships or individuals. Among the lone entrepreneurs was Alexander Majors, who was eventually to round out the triumvirate of Russell, Majors & Waddell, and who was unquestionably the most remarkable man of the three.

In 1853 Majors was 39, two years younger than Russell and seven years younger than Waddell. But his beard was already streaked with gray and his face, with its piercing eyes and high forehead, was that of a practicing ascetic. Majors had been at freighting since 1848. A Kentuckian transplanted to Missouri, he had married early, farmed a little and begun to worry when his three children turned out to be girls. Without boys a small farm wasn't likely to support a family, and in 1846 Majors loaded a farm wagon with a variety of goods and set out to trade them to Indians. When the venture netted him a little capital, his thoughts turned to more ambitious undertakings.

In 1848 he managed to buy six wagons and the oxen to draw them, and loaded each wagon with about 4,000 pounds of goods to be delivered to merchants in Santa Fe. He hired six men to drive the wagons and

To help finance their vast operations, Russell, Waddell and associates launched their own bank in Atchison in 1857 and issued notes like this $50 bill. The design included Waddell's portrait—a bank president's privilege—and partner Russell's name as cashier.

Alexander Majors, the trail-wise partner of Russell and Waddell, gave every employee of the freighting firm a pair of Colt revolvers for defense against Indians and a Bible for defense against "moral contaminations."

then did something characteristic: he made each man sign a pledge. "While I am in the employ of A. Majors," it said, "I agree not to use profane language, not to get drunk, not to gamble, not to treat animals cruelly, and not to do anything else that is incompatible with the conduct of a gentleman. And I agree, if I violate any of the above conditions, to accept my discharge without any pay for my services."

The pledge reflected Majors' faith in the Bible he carried, the sermons he preached, and the practice he instituted on that first trip of pausing Sundays to rest the stock and give the teamsters time to meditate on their duties to their Maker. People joked about Majors' devoutness, but the jests were tempered by respect for the man's fairness, decency and good judgment. If his dedication to Scripture surpassed that of most of his men, he was still always one of them on the trail, even after

he grew rich. Sometimes he rode along as wagonmaster; sometimes he walked beside his teams. When he had several trains on the road, he would shuttle from one to another with a blanket and a mess kit tied to his saddle. At nightfall he would stop with the men, share their food, sit around the fire swapping tales and, after prayer, sleep on the ground beneath a wagon.

Those Sundays off, which Majors insisted upon in obedience to the command of God, provided practical rewards from the start. Majors' six wagons, with their rested oxen, made that first round trip to Santa Fe and back to Missouri in 1848 in the record time of 92 days, and their owner cleared $650 on each wagon. He repeated the trip in 1849; that year, with 20 wagons and 100 oxen—an unusually large operation for the time—he netted the substantial sum of $13,000.

Like Russell, his partner-to-be, Majors quickly sensed the attractions of a military contract. In the summer of 1850 he heard that the Fort Leavenworth quartermaster had 20 wagonloads destined for Fort Mann near the present Dodge City, some 300 miles from Leavenworth. It was well past the normal starting time for a freight odyssey, but Majors contracted to transport 103,644 pounds. He reached Fort Mann on schedule and found the place still under construction, so he hired out his wagons and men to haul logs from a creek 25 miles away. His first military contract had worked out even better than he expected.

By 1854, only six years after Majors had gone into freighting, his stock and equipment were worth more than $100,000, and he was the leading freight operator in Missouri. He was running any kind of freight, military or civilian, and he still took regularly to the trail, moving from train to train and sleeping where night caught him. His military contract in 1854 alone required the use of 100 wagons and some 1,200 oxen, and the employment of 120 men.

At the peak of Majors' career as an independent, change overtook the young freighting business, or at least the military part that was then its mainstay. The Army decided that dealing with a variety of contractors was unsatisfactory. Negotiating separate agreements took too much time; moreover, dividing responsibility for deliveries was not altogether a reliable method. The system had a disadvantage for a contractor as well. A contract ran for only a year, and the holder had no way

Majors set forth these commandments for all of his wagon crews. Hard-bitten teamsters may have observed some of his pious strictures in the breach, but his highly practical advice became gospel for freighters.

of knowing whether his bid for the next year would prevail over a competitor's. And so he was faced with a choice of disposing of his stock and wagons at the end of a freighting season, or keeping at least some of them over the winter — an expensive gamble.

Late in 1854 the Army announced that the next year it would award a single contract, for two years, for all of its hauling west of the Missouri River. It would be the biggest and most remunerative freighting contract ever awarded in that area. But there was a problem. Whoever got the contract would have to buy the necessary wagons and stock, pay the teamsters' wages and provision them adequately. No single freighting firm with experience west of the Missouri had the capital or credit to make the immense outlay of funds that was required — or to sustain losses that might be incurred en route, since the Army would not be responsible for them. But two or more freight operators could swing the deal, so Majors and Russell and Waddell began discussing a merger, and in December of 1854 formally joined forces. On March 27, 1855, the Fort Leavenworth quartermaster, on behalf of the War Department, signed a two-year contract giving the new partners a monopoly on military freighting originating from the Missouri westward. Under the terms of the agreement, they would be paid at varying rates depending on the month in which a wagon train traveled. For example, in May, when the weather was no longer chancy, the rate for moving 100 pounds of freight every 100 miles from Leavenworth to Fort Union in New Mexico was $1.14; in the fall, when the elements were more threatening, the rate increased to $2.

The firm of Russell, Majors & Waddell was to net a profit of $300,000 on this first contract. No doubt the partners glimpsed the glittering potential, for they set about meeting the initial challenge with a remarkable show of efficiency and harmony. Each man contributed $20,000 to the $60,000 capital and each assumed the role for which his talents fitted him. Russell, with his connections and flair, was to obtain the added bank credit that was vitally needed. Waddell was to run the headquarters and keep a canny Scottish eye on all expenditures. Majors was to take charge of manning, organizing and operating the wagon trains.

As their headquarters, the partners chose the town of Leavenworth, conveniently close to the big quar-

A wagon train preempts a Denver thoroughfare in 1868 to display the defensive maneuver of corralling — probably for the benefit of a local photographer. In an embarrassing aftermath a few days later, Indian raiders made off with this caravan's mules while the teamsters were out cutting hay.

termaster depot at Fort Leavenworth. They built offices, warehouses, a blacksmith shop and a sawmill. From western Missouri they moved in the oxen and wagons they already owned. They brought more wagons from St. Louis, each disassembled into 14 components and shipped up the Missouri by steamboat. For additional oxen, Waddell sent expert stockmen scouring western Missouri. Some of the beasts were driven to Leavenworth; others rode the steamers. Eventually the partners had 7,500 head pastured around Leavenworth.

Trusted hands who had served Majors as wagonmasters helped him interview the applicants who poured into Leavenworth seeking teamster jobs. The story goes that Majors doubtfully asked one man if he really believed he could drive an ox team across the plains without swearing, as Majors' pledge required. "Why," the man shouted, "I can drive to hell and back without swearing!" He did not get the job. But Majors did take on 1,700 men that spring of 1855, made each one sign his pledge, gave him a Bible and admonished him to heed its lessons. One of the 1,700 was a 10-year-old wagon-train messenger, William F. Cody, later more celebrated as Buffalo Bill.

A total of 500 wagons, 7,500 oxen and 1,700 men to carry 2.5 million pounds of freight —there never had been anything like it. Yet this was just the beginning. By 1858, the Russell, Majors & Waddell military contract, again a two-year agreement, would call for hauling a maximum of 25 million pounds, and the partners would be operating 3,500 wagons drawn by 40,000 head of oxen.

But that was in the future. Now, in the spring of 1855, the 20 wagon trains of 26 wagons each that set out for Army posts in Nebraska, New Mexico and Wyoming represented an investment of almost $500,000, most of it borrowed. With their contract as security, the three partners were easily able to obtain credit, paying for their purchases with drafts due in 90 to 120 days. Such was their reputation that these written obligations were readily accepted as cash, and even circulated in western Missouri as a medium of exchange among banks, merchants and individuals.

Majors organized the caravan in a system that was eventually copied all over the West. Each train of 26 wagons—25 for freight and one a kitchen wagon—car-

ried at least 150,000 pounds of cargo (6,000 pounds to the wagon); enough men to discourage Indian attacks, and as many oxen as were necessary for hauling and replacements but not so many as to exhaust the supply of forage en route. Besides the six pairs of oxen that pulled each wagon, about 25 to 30 extra head—to serve as replacements if necessary—were driven in a herd behind the train. Each wagon had a driver—the bullwhacker—and each train had a wagonmaster, an assistant wagonmaster, two day herders and a night herder to handle cattle going to or from pasture. In addition there were three or four extra hands to guard the cattle and also to replace men who fell sick, were killed by Indians or simply deserted because the job was too much for them. There were saddle mules for the wagonmaster and his assistant as well as for the herders and messengers like young Bill Cody, who rode between the wagon trains carrying messages of all sorts.

The wagonmaster was almost invariably a powerful figure who had risen from the ranks of bullwhacker on the basis of his leadership qualities. His word was law on the trail, comparable to that of a ship's captain, and his pay of $125 a month ranked near that of an Ohio River steamboat skipper. He earned it. His responsibilities began long before his train set out. He chose his bullwhackers. He oversaw the training of unbroken animals and the loading of wagons. On the trail, he had to be forceful enough to impose his authority on men who were themselves tough and often restless about being miles from the nearest town. He regularly patrolled his train and reconnoitered ahead on the lookout for Indians and difficult stretches of road. He chose routes, timed the march and decided where to camp. When rivers ran high at crossings, when wagons mired down, it was he who made decisions and gave orders.

The bullwhackers who drove the wagons were anonymous men, and few of them cared that they were helping to open up the West. Anyone experienced with farm stock, or ready to learn, could sign on as a bullwhacker, and many newcomers used bullwhacking as a way to earn a stake and survey the frontier country. The bullwhacker's life was hard, monotonous and punctuated by terror, and it tended to make the veteran bullwhacker "taciturn and peculiar," wrote R. D. Holt, a Texas historian. Holt told of one bullwhacker who "was passing through a big pasture and came up to a

windmill and a water tank. It was so fixed that a person could not secure any water without climbing to the top of the storage tank and there was no ladder. The old freighter was hot and thirsty and his team needed water. He drew his six-shooter and shot the bottom of the tank full of holes. He secured the water."

Mark Twain, who happened to eat dinner at a stagecoach stop in company with some 20 teamsters, described them as "a very, very rough set." Little wonder. A bullwhacker walked most of the time, for freight wagons had no seats and the only place to ride, sitting or standing, was on the wagon tongue. When there was mud the bullwhacker waded. When it rained, he got drenched and then slept on wet ground beneath his wagon. His pay was usually $20 or $25 a month, plus dubious victuals. His clothing was stained with mud, dust, sweat, food grease and flying tobacco juice.

Frontier communities welcomed the teamster because he displayed a mighty capacity in the saloons and little

discrimination about what he consumed. Frank A. Root, the stagecoach express messenger, described the potable purveyed as "old Bourbon whisky" in a saloon that sprang up on one freight trail: "To a few gallons of sod corn juice [a distillate of corn fodder] the proprietors would add a quantity of tobacco and some poisonous drugs. The vile liquid was sold to thirsty customers at enormous prices." The customers rarely objected, Root added; they were satisfied if a drink had "even a faint smell of liquor about it."

Fights among teamsters were frequent, for a job that required controlling and inspiring oxen made a man strong and stubborn. Unlike other frontier folk, however, bullwhackers usually battled not with knives or pistols but with their own powerful fists.

And just as fists were a bullwhacker's weapon, his bullwhip was his badge. Men fashioned their whips to their tastes, with stocks of hickory or ash or pecan, one and a half to three feet long. The lash might be as short

Under a bullwhacker's sharp eye, an extra-long team of 30
oxen fords Nebraska's muddy-bottomed Niobrara River
with a wagonload of timber. Added brute strength recruited
from teams of wagons still on dry land *(rear)* increased pulling power, reducing the chance of a mired-down crossing.

Wagons loaded with pipes and mining gear pause at a High Sierra way station for mule-feeding. Though fodder took up valuable cargo space, the fact that mules were faster than oxen helped to offset the cost.

as 10 feet or as long as 20; it was of heavy braided rawhide with a "popper" of thonged rawhide or buckskin on the end to make it crack. A whip weighed a good five and a half pounds, light enough for a healthy male to carry; but it had to be wielded virtually without letup, and that, one teamster recalled, "required all the strength of a man's groins." It always required the use of both hands. Several skilled men cracking their whips together could produce sounds like infantry picket fire, and there were legends in the trade of drivers who could flick a fly from the ear of a lead ox without touching the animal. The whip was rarely intended to strike an animal, for when it did, "you could see a mist of blood and hair start where the cruel thing had cut like a bullet," as a contemporary put it. Merely cracked overhead, a whip could inspire the dumbest ox to greater effort. The same held true for the most obstinate mule when being urged on by a mule skinner, the bullwhacker's counterpart on a mule train.

The great wagons used in freighting were descended from the famed Conestogas of the trans-Appalachian traffic. They varied from wagons of one-ton capacity for fast freight to 10-tonners that hauled mining machinery, though most wagons carried from five to seven thousand pounds. The usual freight wagon box was 16 to 18 feet long and four and a half feet wide. Its bottom was curved slightly, its sides sloped outward, its front thrust forward like a boat's prow. Hickory bows, fitted into sockets on either side of the wagon and covered with canvas, arched high overhead.

The most popular wagon in the West when Russell, Majors & Waddell acquired its first military contract was the creation of Joseph Murphy, a wheelwright born in Ireland who learned and perfected his trade in St. Louis. Murphy produced wagons of one to three tons in size. But because he made wagon boxes to order, his wagons had no recognizable pattern; to identify them he painted "J. Murphy" on the side of each box, making his name one of the best known on the frontier. Like other wagonmakers, he added a touch pleasing to patriotic hearts: the wagons had blue boxes topped with white canvas, and bright red running gear.

Most manufacturers used hickory for axles and Osage orange, a particularly hard and wiry wood, for the 18-inch-deep wheel hubs. The spokes in each wheel were made to flare outward from the hub, resulting in a shape like that of a giant saucer; the tapered ends of the axle that connected parallel wheels fitted into the hubs, enabling them to exert maximum counterpressure against the axle's sideways thrust, thus keeping the wagon from swaying. Spokes and wheel rims were of white oak or other hardwood, and the tires — six to eight inches wide and an inch thick — were of iron, worked tightly into place. Even so, the wagons usually encountered such dry weather on the high plains that the wooden wheel rims would shrink. Teamsters would either throw the wheels into the nearest stream to let them soak overnight and expand back into shape, or they would drive wedges between the rim and the tire to compensate for the shrinkage. As a last resort, a trailside wheelwright would try to heat and reset the tires.

With their curved bodies, sharp prows and clouds of canvas, freight wagons looked like boats — thus the term "prairie schooner," which was often tagged to emigrant wagons but more properly referred only to freight wagons. One veteran of the trail, perhaps the only poet ever to drive an ox team, summed up the sight of a wagon train this way: "From the shining white of the covers and the hull-like appearance of the bodies of the wagons, truly [they] look like a fleet sailing with canvas all spread over a seeming sea."

The rules of procedure promulgated by Alexander Majors for his trains — and adopted by many smaller outfits as well — primarily reflected Majors' concern for the comfort and safety of his animals and his men. After yoking up and setting out at about six each morning, his instructions cautioned, "Do not travel more than one half to one mile before stopping eight or ten minutes for the cattle to urinate, particularly if the weather is warm and the cattle very full." About ten in the morning, having covered some eight miles, the wagons were to stop and the cattle were to be turned out to graze while the men had their first meal, a super-breakfast, and greased their wagon wheels. In three hours they were to start again and go another eight miles before stopping at about 5 p.m. for their second and last meal of the day. Two meals a day, Majors believed, were "sufficient for men on the plains, as they eat hearty." After the cattle had grazed, and if there was still light, the wagons might roll on again for another hour or so.

Majors based his rules on a personal knowledge of the miseries of the trail. Most of the time the weather

One of the few female freighters, a South Dakotan known as Madame Canutson rose from herder and bullwhacker to ox-team owner in the 1880s. In skirts here, on the trail she dressed — and swore — like a man.

was too dry or too wet, too cold or too hot. When the sun burned down, the teamsters walked for miles in clouds of their own dust; even with kerchiefs wrapped around their faces, many suffered lasting damage to their eyes and noses and throats. Alkali dust burned even more than regular dust. Buffalo gnats almost too small to see worked their way into men's ears. Rattlesnakes, abundant on the prairie, lurked to bite both man and beast. Ticks infected oxen with Texas fever; disease and exhaustion made the life expectancy of an ox on the job a single freighting season.

When rain relieved the dryness, the heavy wagons sometimes sank so deep in mud that three teams — 18 pairs of oxen — had to be used to pull each wagon free. After one such episode the men driving the teams were near exhaustion, and somebody discovered that one wagon was carrying a load of beer. With that, a man who was along reported, the trip went easier; his companions emptied several kegs before arriving at their des-

tination, and the saloonkeeper to whom the beer was consigned let them pay for it at cost — $13.

In storms, which broke with awesome speed, lightning could kill men and animals, and huge hailstones often pelted those who escaped with their lives. Josiah Gregg, one of the rare teamsters who kept a diary, recalled one frightening day: "We were encamped at noon, when a murky cloud issued from behind the mountains, and, after hovering over us for a few minutes, gave vent to one of those tremendous peals of thunder. A sulphurous stench filled the atmosphere; but the thunderbolt had skipped over the wagons and lighted upon the *caballada* (the herd), which was grazing hard by. It was not a little singular to find an ox lying lifeless from the stroke, while his mate stood uninjured by his side, and under the same yoke."

Haphazard sanitation on the trail posed its own dangers. Majors' autobiography recorded that cholera struck several of the first wagon trains the partners sent out from Leavenworth in 1855. "Not more than two or three died, but quite a delay and additional expense were caused on account of this dire disease among our teamsters," Majors wrote. "This was in June, and the train was almost deserted. Another train was entirely deserted, the sick men being taken to some of the farmers in the neighborhood, the well ones leaving for their homes, our oxen scattering and going toward almost every point of the compass."

Every journey, eventful or not, presented the nightly problem of finding a good spot to camp. The ideal place was on high ground, for safety against Indian attack, and with water and grass nearby. Oxen could eat the plains grass even when it was brown and dry, but as freight-wagon traffic increased, trains sometimes had to detour for miles to find sufficient pasture.

Their wagons corralled and their beasts unhitched, the weary men formed mess units to haul water, gather fuel, dig a fire trench and start cooking supper. A Russell, Majors & Waddell kitchen wagon carried flour, corn meal, dried fruits and vegetables, bacon, pickled pork, beans and coffee. There might be fresh meat as well, if the men were lucky enough to kill a buffalo, though hunting was discouraged by Majors lest it disrupt his carefully planned routine.

The wagon men were coffee addicts, and they liked it hot. The pot was "always on the fire, always full, red hot and boiling," reported a Texan, T. U. Taylor. "I never saw a wagoner yet who would not use the half-pint tin cup, pour his coffee out of the pot into the cup and drink it without waiting for it to cool off. On one occasion, at a dare, one of the wagoners took the coffee pot off the fire and drank the coffee right out of the spout. He never flinched or batted an eye lash."

Supper done, the men smoked their pipes and, though bullwhackers were taciturn most of the rest of the time, they joked a bit, sang a bit and fell to spinning yarns or bragging. Occasionally a bullwhacker would slip away from the fireside to give a little personal attention to the cargo in his wagon, especially if the cargo included whiskey. "I saw one ingenious wagoner who understood the laws of physics secure a bottle of whiskey," Taylor wrote. "He took advantage of the fact that the whiskey had a specific gravity of about .75 or three-fourths that of water. He bored a hole in the top of the whiskey barrel through which he could fit the neck of the old Bourbon bottle of whiskey, filled the bottle full of water, suddenly inverted it, pushed it through the hole in top of the barrel, and gravity did the rest. The water went down, the whiskey came up. He then whittled a plug of soft pine, drove it through the hole, smeared it over with grease and the deed was done."

This inventive fellow, it should be added, was not on a Russell, Majors & Waddell train. No teamster working for the partners would have tried such a stunt. Alexander Majors not only exacted an antidrinking pledge from his men, but took the added precaution of having the canvas on his wagons nailed down tight.

Around the campfire, most bullwhackers told their last tale early, spread their blankets under their wagons and slept while they might. Before dawn the wagonmaster and the night herder would be walking around the corral of wagons rapping their iron tires and crying, "Roll out! Roll out!" Sometimes the men were already awake because of trouble with the animals during the night. In dangerous country the beasts were returned to the corral after dark; otherwise the herder left them out to graze. Usually they did so placidly, but they took fright on occasion, particularly in storms; and when their leaders dashed off, the herd would follow. At such times the herder would gallop in front of the oxen, yelling, firing his pistol, slashing at their faces with a whip, hoping to turn them into a circle until their fright dissipated. It was not always easy. After a night stampede, sleepless bullwhackers might find a few stray oxen as far as 40 miles from camp.

Sometimes the cattle stampeded while still hitched to their wagons. One morning on the trail, a Russell, Majors & Waddell train set out with the usual extra herd behind. A young herder, Robert Wright, was driving the cattle, and by afternoon the sun was so hot that he took off his coat. It was a heavy woolen garment, with the sleeves lined in red flannel. Wright carelessly turned the coat inside out as he removed it and casually tossed it over the horns of Old Dan, a gentle ox that was lagging. Then he urged Old Dan back into the herd. "No sooner did Old Dan make his appearance among the cattle," Wright said later, "than a young steer bawled out in steer language, as plain as English, 'Great Scott, what monstrosity is this coming to destroy us?'" Then, Wright continued, "with one long, loud beseeching bawl, [he] put all possible distance be-

Some luckless challengers of the mule and ox

Asian camels pick their way across the Nevada desert, with silver miners in the role of camel drivers. Most Westerners loathed the animals.

Despite the proven merits of wagons drawn by mules or oxen, imaginative freight men were ever on the lookout for faster, cheaper or more reliable means of transport. Attempts to achieve this goal sometimes adorned the Western landscape with sights as strange as any a frontiersman could hope—or care—to see.

Caravans of camels were one such novelty. Though not native to the United States, the camel—as any Bible-reading American knew—was a certified beast of burden. In 1855 Secretary of War Jefferson Davis, whose responsibilities included all military freighting, cajoled an appropri-

ation out of Congress and directed that camels be acquired for tests as pack animals. Navy ships duly put in at Alexandria, Constantinople and ports farther east, picked up the bizarre creatures and eventually disembarked 34 of them in Texas.

Their first field trials, on a caravan across the southwestern desert to California, were judged extremely promising. The camels ignored rattlesnake bites, traveled for days without drinking water, subsisted on sagebrush, thistles and creosote bushes, which mules would not touch, and overcame the Army's biggest worry when they willingly swam across rivers. Further-

more, their cargo capacity was stunning: one camel managed a load of 1,256 pounds. The officer in charge of the experiment, Lieutenant Edward Beale, concluded that a camel did the work of four good mules.

Hearing of the results, a California newspaperman optimistically predicted that a "lightning dromedary express" would deliver mail from Missouri River towns in as little as 15 days. Private enterprise soon latched onto what appeared to be a good thing. In 1860 the American Camel Company, Incorporated, began running caravans of Asian camels—better inured to cold weather than the

Arabian variety—around the silver mines of Virginia City, Nevada.

But within a few years the camel boomlet burst. The Civil War suspended official Washington's interest in the subject, especially since the camel project was linked in Northern minds to Jefferson Davis, who had become President of the Confederacy. Nor had the camels' personal habits endeared them to people—least of all the teamsters who were asked to drive or ride them. Camels were prodigious spitters; they also sneezed and vomited in remarkable volume; and they tended to attack strangers with snapping teeth. Dogs barked hysterically whenever they appeared, and oxen and mules sometimes stampeded at the sight of them.

Dismayed by such traits, camel-freight operators finally turned the animals loose to fend for themselves. They survived on U.S. soil for more than half a century, the last of them doing duty as circus attractions and mounts at resort hotels for Southwesterners with exotic tastes.

Ill fortune also befell a freighting scheme thought up in 1853 by a Nebraska entrepreneur whose name is recorded in history as "Windwagon" Thomas. Deciding that the freighting business could dispense with draft animals of any kind, Thomas rigged a 20-foot mast over a wagon, then raised a billowing sail and tried to prove that prairie breezes provided power enough to tow an entire wagon train. Before any wagons could be hitched to the lead vehicle, a wind blew it, like a child's kite, to splintery wreckage at the bottom of a ditch.

Other inventors believed that technology, not nature, held the answer to more efficient freighting. In 1861 the propitiously named Thomas L. Fortune of Mount Pleasant, Kansas, constructed a cross-country steam engine designed to pull 25 loaded freight wagons. His 60-horsepower trackless locomotive rode on wheels eight feet high and weighed 10 tons. The great engine was rolled out of its shed on the Fourth of July. Since it was not sufficiently maneuverable to negotiate a street corner, it had to be backed out of town for its trial run. The engine bogged down in a mudhole, embarrassingly failed to develop a head of steam strong enough to extricate itself and never pulled a wagon.

Meanwhile, other steam engines were being designed and tested by such would-be industrial giants as the Overland Traction Engine Company. An observer reported of one engine, "Those who looked upon the somewhat cumbrous and uncouth monster, with its complication of cylinders, and pulleys, and pipes, and wheels, pronounced it, in advance, an utter abortion." Events confirmed this harsh judgment: one of the most promising of the monsters threw a piston rod on its maiden voyage, was abandoned where it stood, and in time found ignominious service as a chicken coop.

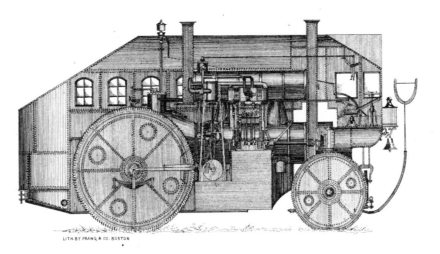

OVERLAND TRACTION ENGINE CO.

LITH BY PRANG & CO. BOSTON

LONGITUDINAL VIEW OF ENGINE UNCOVERED.

When this steam-driven "prairie motor" was touted as the perfect replacement for draft animals, people scoffed, jeered and were soon proved right.

tween himself and the terror behind him." In an instant all the cattle in the extra herd — except Old Dan — stampeded. As they raced past the wagons, the oxen in the traces broke into full gallop. Eighteen wagons were wrecked, three steers and a man suffered broken legs and stock was scattered for 15 miles. When order was at last restored, the wagonmaster asked Wright what he thought had started it all. Wright replied that it was probably a wolf.

The terrain was an implacable foe of the wagon trains, and river crossings in particular gave trouble. Some of the most treacherous crossings were on the Platte. That river was a half mile wide and three and a half or four feet deep at the fords, with a bottom of gravel and quicksand. The channel changed so constantly that men fording it never knew when they might find their cattle swimming and their wagons sinking from view. Along some rivers there were ferries — often no more than plank decks lashed atop three canoes or rowboats — operated by enterprising frontiersmen. But the ferrymen charged from four to five dollars a trip, and for a train of 26 wagons, the fare would have come close to a month's pay for a wagonmaster. And so wagon trains rarely used the ferries, devising their own methods. Some bullwhackers took the wagon boxes off the wheels, secured buffalo hides and tallow from the supply wagon, wrapped the boxes in the hides, waterproofed them with a coat of tallow and ashes and floated them across. More often a less time-consuming approach was used. The men stripped off all their clothes except their shirts and hats, hitched 12 pair of oxen to a single wagon and prodded, whipped and cursed the timid beasts into and across the water. Dr. E. A. Tompkins, a California-bound emigrant, described a freight-wagon crossing he witnessed:

"As we neared the spot where we designed to cross, we observed 400 waggons on the bank and at least 3,000 oxen. The shouting and hallooing combined with the bawling of cattle made a confusion of stunning sounds. The water was high. Ox teams were thrown into confusion, some would become unyoked or get the chains over their heads in the wrong direction. The waggons would swing about in deep water. Often they would upset and thus destroy all they contained or float away to parts hitherto unexplored." For all the chaos, wagon somehow followed wagon across; from bank to

bank the river was filled with vehicles going one way and ox teams going straight back for still more wagons to pull until the entire caravan had crossed.

Beyond the rivers lay the mountains, where grades in steep canyons were frequently brutal. Sometimes teams had to be doubled or tripled on the ascent, and sometimes wagons had to be partly unloaded and several trips made to get all the cargo to the top. On the descent down the far side, regular shoe brakes and chains locking the rear wheels were inadequate for braking. To deal with this problem, the rear axle was raised and a long log or tree trunk was lashed to the center pole just in front of the axle, jacking up the wagon's rear wheels; as the wagon descended, the log, bearing the weight of the rear of the vehicle, served as an effective drag. Once at the bottom, the log — called the "Mormon brake" after its popularizers — was simply discarded.

Sometimes no braking devices helped. On the Chihuahua Trail in the Sierra Madre, where the slopes were especially precipitous, wagons with rear wheels almost six feet in diameter occasionally pitched over the teams that were pulling them, killing men and animals alike. Mountain trails were often so narrow that it took heroic work by a bullwhacker to keep his wagon from plunging into an abyss, sweeping him along with it.

Adding to the natural hazards was the constant possibility of Indian attack. Every wagonmaster and every bullwhacker had heard tales of Indian butchery; vigilance was rarely relaxed. But usually the Indians hesitated to attack trains well manned with heavily armed bullwhackers, and if the trains had had time to corral, they were just about impregnable.

So Russell, Majors & Waddell caravans went unscathed for the most part, although in 1857 Pawnees did raid the firm's oxen while they were grazing. Majors recounted the incident in this bleak passage from his memoirs: "In 1857, the Indians attacked the herders who had charge of about one thousand head on the Platte River, west of Fort Kearney, killing one of the herders and scattering the cattle to the four winds. These were a complete loss."

Lesser freight operators suffered more, since the Indians were bolder about tackling small wagon trains. A bullwhacker named Garrett told of the two Gordon brothers, who were hauling cargo to the government agency that had charge of the Utes in Wyoming. John

Mule-drawn wagons bring supplies to railroad workers extending the Union Pacific's tracks westward through Utah in 1869. Ironically, completion of the transcontinental line ended the heyday of the wagon men.

Gordon's wagon train was ox-drawn, but his brother's was drawn by horses — always a temptation to Indians. "As they were nearing the agency," Garrett wrote, "John Gordon stopped his train for the horse teams to pass. Just as they were passing, the Indians jumped them. George Gordon and all his teamsters were killed. John Gordon and one bullwhacker escaped."

Most wagon trains got through safely to their destinations. The terminus of a trip might be Santa Fe, or Denver, or Salt Lake City, or Helena, or a lonely town with only one street, or a fort, or an Indian agency. Wherever it was, the squeak of the wagon wheels heralded the train's coming, for the bullwhackers had by then exhausted their axle grease; some townsfolk insisted that even before they could hear or see the wagons they could detect the train's approach — if the wind was right — by the scent of scores of sweat-covered oxen. Cattle bawling, drivers cracking their whips to impress onlookers, the train would pull to a halt. Amid still more sound and fury, the stock would be pastured and the freight unloaded.

What typically happened next was recorded by a girl named Marian Russell. In 1852 Marian and her mother somehow managed to wangle a trip to Santa Fe by freight caravan, though passengers were rarely taken along. "As soon as our freight was delivered at the customs house," she recalled, "our drivers began eagerly to sign up and draw their wages. They washed their faces and combed their hair. There was a great hunting for clean shirts and handkerchiefs — a *baile* was forming." The dancing at the ball lasted into the wee hours. One bullwhacker recalled that during his four days in Santa Fe he and his fellows tripped the light fantastic every night. "Those Mexican girls were not such good lookers when seen on the street," he said, "but they were dolls when rigged out in the dancing costumes." Jesse Brown, who bullwhacked from Nebraska City to Fort Laramie and Fort Reno and back — a mission prolonged

On the West's most grueling freight run, a so-called 20-mule-team rig hauls 45,000 pounds of borax—a salt used as a cleansing agent—from a Death Valley lake bed across scorching California desert to a railhead. Such teams had in fact only 18 mules plus two strong horses as wheelers.

80

Montana's Overland Freight Line used an earlier owner's diamond-R brand on wagons, stock, and even a portrait of new owners *(from left)* C. A. Broadwater, Matt Carroll, E. G. Maclay and George Steele.

to eight months because of an unexpected Army-supply emergency — described the aftermath: "The men were paid off, and after visiting a barber shop, a clothing store and taking a sip of 'Oh-Be-Joyful' it was difficult to recognize some of the men with whom we had associated for eight months."

The "Oh-Be-Joyful" often led to trouble. Arriving in Salt Lake City in 1858, some of Russell, Majors & Waddell's bullwhackers comported themselves like men just freed from prison. One of them reported: "Within three days, three of my train comrades were dead. Antonio was stabbed in an affray over a bar-maid; Johnny Bull was shot at a gaming table; and Red, the Missourian, was murdered in a saloon brawl." When the wagon trains pulled in at Army posts, there was always a chance that the commander of an understrength unit would impress bullwhackers into uniform. Even if they were not thus forcibly enlisted, or killed in brawls, many bullwhackers made only a one-way trip. Because there was usually no cargo for the return journey, freighting firms in most cases sold off as many wagons and oxen as they could, once they had delivered their cargoes. So they required fewer bullwhackers on the way back and encouraged those not needed to quit by giving them a bonus equivalent to a third of the wages they had earned on the trip out, if they did not insist on returning home. Most bullwhackers seemed to like the arrangement: the money made a neat little stake for gold prospecting or starting a farm.

For such entrepreneurs as Russell, Majors & Waddell, the end of one freighting season simply whetted the appetite for the next. Having done handsomely in their first two years of operation for the military, the partners looked forward to repeating their success. But the new contract they acquired in 1857 was to prove costly indeed. In June of that year the Fort Leavenworth quartermaster informed the partners that they would have to haul three million pounds of supplies for the Army expedition the government had sent to Utah to quell the Mormons' defiance of federal authority. The partners protested; the shipment would exceed the maximum freight required for the year by their contract. But the Army insisted. It did make one crucial concession; though ordinarily contractors paid for any losses they suffered en route, in this case the partners would be reimbursed — by Congress, the Fort Leavenworth

quartermaster assured them. No written agreement was made of this arrangement.

Russell, Majors & Waddell rounded up additional oxen, wagons and men at premium prices. Their first two wagon trains reached South Pass, Wyoming, in August. But then, 75 miles farther along, hostile Mormon action halted all trains. On two successive nights a Mormon party attacked the caravan, capturing three Russell, Majors & Waddell trains. The Mormon commander, Major Lot Smith, sent the teamsters, including young Bill Cody, on their way. But Smith's men burned the wagons and 300,000 pounds of supplies and drove off more than 1,200 animals. The trains untouched by Smith and his forces ran into other trouble. Mormons made off with 900 more oxen, and Cheyenne Indians stole 800 head of beef cattle. Hundreds of other oxen perished in the deep snows.

The total loss to the partners, as figured by Russell, amounted to $493,762.61, far exceeding their first two years' profits. They billed the government and waited for payment. Three years later, in 1861, they were advised that the government would not honor the claim — on the ground that no written agreement had been made to cover this supplementary venture. By then, the decision was just another bitter pill for the partners to swallow. In the intervening period they had branched out into running a stagecoach line and the Pony Express, and both ventures had proved financial failures. The firm of Russell, Majors & Waddell was floundering and close to collapse.

Still, other freight entrepreneurs persisted, sometimes making a lot of money and sometimes losing a lot. There was always risk, but always the chance — if everything went for the best — of riches. Nor did one have to be a giant in freighting to cherish this belief. One small operator, whose name is lost to history but whose story was recorded in an 1863 frontier newspaper, perhaps epitomized the spirit of the whole business. He assembled a flock of turkeys in Iowa and Missouri to freight to the fledgling city of Denver. He loaded a six-mule wagon with shelled corn, hired two boys as drivers and made the fowl walk. With a tail wind to help them along the 600-mile trek, they achieved 25 miles a day, eating grasshoppers when there were any and corn from the wagon when there were not. In the best tradition of freighting, the man got his birds to Denver.

A tandem wagon rig blocks traffic in Last Chance Gulch
—more formally known as Helena, Montana—in 1874.
Gold strikes in nearby hills had brought in swarms of prospectors and lured settlers away from farming, so wagons had
to haul in food and other necessities from long distances.

The mixed memories of a novice bullwhacker

One of the least likely bullwhackers ever to drive a freight wagon across the plains was William Henry Jackson, a polished 23-year-old New Englander who would later win fame as a painter, photographer and memoirist of the frontier. In 1866, after a quarrel with his sweetheart, Jackson hired on with a wagon train outbound from Nebraska City, figuring to forget his sorrows and at the same time see the country. On the nearly six-month-long journey to Salt Lake City, he kept a diary and made a series of sketches on which he based the scenes shown here.

"I have never used profane language," Jackson confided to the diary, "but since I have commenced driving Bulls I have gone somewhat astray." That was not surprising, considering his first attempt to yoke 12 half-wild longhorns: he spent eight hours wrestling them into submission.

After a few weeks, he got the knack of yoking and driving, but the aggravations of the bullwhacker's life seemed to be endless. "What we have drank in the way of water would astonish a person used to pure water," Jackson wrote. Of one of the many assaults of Western weather, he solemnly observed: "An Eastern person has hardly an idea of a thunder storm."

By the time he reached Salt Lake City, Jackson had mellowed into a true bullwhacker. His hands were callused, he had a scraggly beard, and he simultaneously wore two pairs of trousers whose rips were luckily located in different places. "Taken as a whole," he concluded with ill-concealed pride, "you have a very seedy individual."

Bullwhackers begin the day by yoking oxen in a wagon corral. Jackson was initiated into the process by being "thrown head over heels and stepped on most plentifully."

A belligerent bull, lassoed and secured to a wagon wheel, angrily awaits the yoke.

While one teamster fuels a campfire with bull chips, another fries a panful of bacon that, with bread and coffee, will serve as breakfast.

Jackson's self-portrait with bull whip

3 | The fabled Pony Express

For a year and a half, from April 1860 on, Americans east and west thrilled to the exploits of an elite band of daring horsemen who sped the mail across the wildest miles of the continent, between Missouri and California, on a punishing timetable of 10 days flat. Along with letters, the Pony Express carried important financial and government documents. Even Great Britain's Royal Navy relied on the service; its China fleet communicated with London via San Francisco and the Pony Express.

In their brief period of glory the Express riders transported 34,753 pieces of mail and pounded out a total mileage equal to 24 times around the globe. Only one man fell into the hands of Indians, and his horse escaped and finished the run on its own. By the end of 1861, telegraph wires had spanned the continent, and with the suddenness of a rider reining in for a change of mounts, the Pony Express era came to a halt.

By a scalp-tingling margin, a Pony Expressman on a fleet mustang outruns a hostile Indian band in this painting by artist H. W. Hansen.

Pounding hoofs that were heard around the world

It was early afternoon in St. Joseph, Missouri, and not yet noon in San Francisco, when excited crowds began to collect in the two cities on April 3, 1860. Though nearly 2,000 miles separated them, the people of St. Joseph and San Francisco were turning out to witness the same spectacular ceremony — the start of the Pony Express. Vigorous advance publicity had billed the venture as "The Greatest Enterprise of Modern Times," and certainly in its aims it deserved superlatives, for the Pony Express was intended to carry mail across the West in less than half the fastest time ever before recorded.

The scheme verged on the incredible. Before the inaugural day was out, a mail-bearing daredevil rider in San Francisco and another in St. Joseph would begin hurtling toward each other, galloping full tilt for 35 to 75 miles, then passing the mail to the next relay rider. Speeding through daylight and darkness without halt, the mail from San Francisco would reach St. Joseph, and the mail from St. Joseph would reach San Francisco, in just 10 days — or so the Pony's astonishing schedule claimed. No allowance had been made for the caprices of weather, failures of muscle or nerves, or unpredictable Indian attacks. The 10-day runs were slated to start from each terminus once a week, and to continue the year round.

Whether or not all the promises would be kept, everybody in the two gathering crowds knew that the inauguration of the Pony Express was a historic event — something to observe closely so as to be able to describe it to one's grandchildren. The better-informed spectators also understood the political and financial issues that rode on the Pony Express along with the mail. Russell, Majors & Waddell, the giant freighting firm that had foaled the Pony, was out to demonstrate that the overland route across the center of the continent was superior to the southern route used by the Butterfield Overland Mail Company. John Butterfield's line had been carrying most of the transcontinental mail since 1858, making semimonthly deliveries both ways for a yearly compensation of $600,000. The operation had a glaring deficiency, however: the stages traveled between Missouri and San Francisco by the most roundabout way imaginable, swinging as far south as El Paso, and the journey each way took at least three weeks and usually longer.

Butterfield owed his contract to the partisan maneuverings of Southerners in Congress, who continued to protect their interests by blocking all proposals for a major mail subsidy for the central overland route on the grounds that mountain snowstorms would prevent regular year-round deliveries. If the Pony could prove otherwise — in such dramatic fashion that Congress could not close its eyes to the truth — a huge government subsidy, perhaps as much as one million dollars, might be forthcoming for Russell, Majors & Waddell.

But as the Pony's inaugural day wore on, the crowd in St. Joseph began to wonder if the venture would get underway at all. By 6 p.m., an hour after the announced starting time, people were impatiently milling about, muttering at the unexplained delay. To mollify them, the horse that was to carry the first rider was put on display in the town square. The animal's special equipage drew appreciative glances; it consisted of a light, streamlined saddle and a blanket-like leather mail pouch, or *mochila*, both crafted by the famous St. Joseph saddle maker Israel Landis. As for the animal itself, so many of its hairs were yanked out by souvenir hunters that the reporter for the St. Joseph *Weekly West* observed,

The toll exacted by a perilous occupation appears in the weathered faces of these Pony Expressmen. In fact, none of the four had yet reached the ripe old age of 30.

"The little pony was almost robbed of his tail." The reporter should have looked more closely before the animal was led back to the stable to prevent further torment. It was *her* tail, not "his." She was a fine bay mare, obviously tough, strong-willed and fleet.

The crowd had already heard too many speeches by the assembled dignitaries. But now it listened with more than polite interest to the remarks of William H. Russell, founder of the Pony Express and the most talked-about man in America that spring. Russell, locally popular in spite of his cosmopolitan dress and manner, was the senior partner and financial wizard of Russell, Majors & Waddell; newspapers called him "The Brains of the Border" and "The Napoleon of the Plains." The speech Russell made was just about what one might expect from such a big-time operator: breezy, unrevealing and tastefully brief.

To kill more time, the rider himself put in an appearance. The *Weekly West* subsequently identified him as "Mr. Billy Richardson, formerly a sailor, and a man accustomed to every description of hardship, having sailed for years among the snows of the Northern ocean." But other eyewitnesses at the Pony's inauguration insisted that the first rider was Johnny Fry, a Kansas ranch boy who had won several local horse races and at least as many girls' hearts. The subsequent loss of Russell, Majors & Waddell's records kept the dispute alive for many years—until Richardson himself disclaimed the honor in his memoirs. The first rider from St. Joseph was Johnny Fry.

But this honor for Fry could, in fact, be claimed only for the westbound route. The first eastbound rider, James Randall, had already received a tumultuous farewell from San Franciscans and was three hours along his route before things finally began to stir in St. Joseph. Around seven in the evening, a whistle sounded from the railroad depot, announcing the arrival at last of the mail that the Pony's promoters had collected from all over the East for the first ride westward. It turned out that the special messenger bearing the mail pouch had suffered a frustrating delay. Starting in Washington, he had gone by rail to New York and thence to Detroit —where he missed, by two hours, the connection that was to take him, via Chicago and the eastern Missouri town of Hannibal, to St. Joseph. Though he had hopped the next train out, that did not satisfy the superinten-

dent of the Hannibal & St. Joseph Railroad. He ordered a special train—consisting of an engine and one car—to be kept waiting under steam at the Hannibal station, with the rails to St. Joseph cleared of all other traffic, so that the messenger could be rushed onward to his ultimate destination.

St. Joseph was pretty proud of this feat, and well equipped to pull it off. The town was then the westernmost terminus of rails from the East—one good reason why Russell had decided to base the Pony there instead of at Leavenworth, Kansas, the headquarters of Russell, Majors & Waddell. Another good reason was that St. Joseph had paid well to get the Pony, deeding large tracts of land to the company in return for the fame —and business—that the Pony would bring.

The mail for the maiden run consisted of 49 letters, some copies of Eastern newspapers specially printed on tissue, five private telegrams and numerous telegraphic dispatches for California newspapers. The inclusion of the telegrams and dispatches—wired to St. Joseph from various parts of the East—was another of William Russell's shrewd touches. Though telegraph wires already reached from St. Joseph almost to Fort Kearney, Nebraska, and from San Francisco to Carson City, Nevada, a 1,600-mile gap still existed between Nebraska and Nevada—a gap the Pony could neatly fill.

Together, all of the items in the first batch weighed less than 15 pounds, and even the high delivery charge of five dollars for a half ounce would not begin to cover the cost of the service. But Russell did not expect the Pony Express to make an immediate profit. He did not even expect it to have the telegraphic portion of the business for long. No matter. Rapid transmission of letters, newspapers and business documents would still be needed. If Congress granted the mail subsidy for the central route, it might specify delivery by stagecoach as well as by the Pony Express, or even by stagecoach alone, ignoring the Pony service. In either case, Russell confidently regarded himself as certain to be the beneficiary—if his monumental publicity stunt worked.

By 7:14 in the evening, the mail had been stowed and locked in three of the four pockets of the *mochila;* the fourth pocket was kept empty for mail to be picked up along the way. At 7:15, to the boom of a brass cannon and a great shout from the crowd, Johnny Fry shook hands with William Russell, bounded into the

ST. JOSEPH DAILY GAZETTE.

PONY EXPRESS EDITION.

ST. JOSEPHh, Mo., APRIL 3rd,---6 O'CLOCK, P. M.

JOSEPH, MO.

AY, APRIL 3, 1860—5 P. M.

Through the politeness of the Express Company, we are permitted to forward, by the first Pony Express, the first and only newspaper which goes out, and which will be the first paper ever transmitted from the Missouri to California in eight days The nature of the conveyance necessarily precludes our making up an edition of any considerable weight. It, however, contains a summary of the latest news received here by telegraph for some days past, from all parts of the Union. We send it greeting to our brethren of the press of California.

Municipal Election in St. Joseph.

The result of the City Election here yesterday was the choice of A. BEATTIE Mayor. The vote stood:

Beattie 748
Corby 583

The Pony Express Starts To-day.

Mr. W. H. RUSSELL, the President of the Central Overland California and Pike's Peak Express Company, and Mr. MAJORS, a Director in the Company, arrived in this city yesterday morning, to be present this afternoon to witness the starting of the first pony from the office of the Company. The fame of these gentlemen for intelligent enterprise is as wide as the West, and is now about to be associated with a movement which will extend it from one ocean to the other.

The first pony will start this afternoon at 5 P. M., precisely. Letters will be received for all points up to 4:30 P. M.

A special train will be run over the Hannibal & St. Joseph Railroad for the purpose of bringing the through messenger from New York.

The following is the Time Table which has been adopted. From this city to

Marysville .... 12 hour
Fort Kearney 34
Laramie 80
Bridger 108
Salt 124
Camp Floyd 148
Carson City 188
Placerville 226
Sacramento 232
San Francisco 240

The second Carrier will leave St. Joseph Friday, the 13th, at 9 A. M.

CARSTANG vs. SHAW—VERDICT FOR DEFENDANT.—By private advices, we learn that the verdict in the great breach of promise case, which has been going on in St. Louis for some weeks, was rendered on Saturday night, within a few moments from the retiring of the jury, who found for the defendant. Alas, poor EFFIE! but yesterday and a world of suitors were at your feet, now none so poor to do you reverence. A motion was immediately filed for a new trial.

Foreign News.

NEW YORK, April 1.
The steamship Bavaria arrived this evening from Southampton the 18th ult., and brings a London paper of that date.

ROME, March 16.—This morning a great manifestation in favor of the Pope had taken place at the vatican.

PARIS, Saturday.—The Patrie publishes a letter from Turin, stating that the question of the annexation of Savoy to France had been definitely settled.

The Patrie also states that negotiations in regard to Tuscany are in a fair way of conclusion. The Emperor had received a deputation from Savoy.

NAPLES, March 14.—The Neapolitans who had been sent into exile and others, were informed that they might remain in Naples.

Austria had disapproved of the service measures intended. An Austrian General had arrived. Ambassadors from the Western Powers had given advice to the King.

A Turin letter of the 13th says the Sardinian Parliament will not meet till the 12th April.

The King intends, when the expression of the wishes of the population of Romagna are made known to him, to deliver a speech, declaring that he postpones the acceptance for the present, adding that the negotiations are opened for the purpose of recommending these wishes with respect for the rights of the Holy See.— Unfortunately, the negotiations only postpone the crisis for a few days.

The annexation of Central Italy to Piedmont is accepted everywhere with great enthusiasm.

At the end of the week the King will start on a tour in the provinces which voted for annexation.

One of the first acts of the government, soon an annexation is decided, will be to open a loan of 150,000,000 francs, half to be negotiated abroad and the rest subscribed for at home.

The Paris correspondent of the Times says Prince Corrigran will be Gover.

nor General of Tuscany unless the Imperial idea of a separate step be carried out.

There is great wrath here against the Pope. I am told his Holiness has issued another circular, still stronger than the encyclical on the Romagna affair. The remark is said to have been made in a very high quarter; that the Pope would, from the manner he is going on, make the pamphlet la Pope et Le Congress, a truth. This means that of all his States only Rome would be left to the Pope.

Letters from Rome say that agitation is so great that it is doubtful whether the French army will be able to restrain it much longer The second warning which precede excommunication is said to have been sent to Turin.

Connecticut Election.

HARTFORD, April 2.
The excitement is very great this morning and the voting is progressing rapidly, the vote will be the largest ever given in the State and both parties are confident of victory.

NEW HAVEN, April 2.
Weather splendid, and the voting larger than ever has been known at this hour It is generally quiet except in the Third Ward, where the German Republicans are being driven from the polls. The Democrats are ahead about 200.

WATERBURY, April 2.
The election is quietly proceeding and there is but little excitement at the polls. The whole number of votes polled is 660. The Republicans are leading by 29. The other towns in this vicinity are not yet heard from.

NEW LONDON, 1 P. M.
The vote thus far stands Republican 581, Democratic 416.

GUILFORD, 1 P. M.
The votes here are not counted till P. M. The probability is that the town will be strongly Republican.

WATERBURY, April 2—2 P. M.
The excitement is increasing at the polls. Whole number of votes are 1,200, the Democrats still lead 68 up this hour. Nothing has been heard from the adjoining towns.

NEW BRITON, 2:30 P. M.
Democratic ticket 50 ahead in this place.

NETOWN, 2 P. M.
Average estimates of the two parties is 80 Democratic majority.

NORWICH, 2 P. M.
Republicans 250 ahead.

BRIDGEPORT, 1 P. M.
Immense excitement here. Both parties out in full force. No disturbances yet Bands are parading the streets, and banners flying in every direction. It is impossible to give any definite estimate of the vote. In those Wards, we have been able to hear from the Republicans are slightly ahead, but several Wards are still unheard from.

SECOND DISPATCH.
The vote now stands, 1st Ward about 250 Republican majority. In the 2d and 3d Wards the Democrats are ahead from 140 to 200.

NEW LONDON, 2 P. M.
Vote now stands, Republican 684 : Democrat 562.

NEW HAVEN, 2 P. M.
The election proceeds slowly without any incidents to notice. The Democrats still lead almost 200.

WATERBURY, 2 P. M.
Whole number of votes polled at this hour, 915. Democrats lead by about 51. The voting proceeds slowly in consequence of the crowd at the polls

WINDSON LOCKS, 2 P. M.
Mr. Seymour about 60 ahead, as far as heard from.

MERIDEN, 2 P. M.
The votes not yet counted; it is estimated that the Republicans are about 50 ahead. There is considerable excitement

MIDDLETON, April 2—9 P. M.
Election is over and the vote polled is the largest ever known.
Middleton sends two Democratic Representatives to the Legislature, and Gov. Seymour, Democrat for Governor, 260 maj: Dunham gives 19 majority for Buckinham, Republican, for Governor : Cromwell, 69 majority for Seymour : Portland, 379 majority for Seymour : Chatham, 9 majority for Seymour : and two Democratic Representatives.

HARTFORD, 9 P. M.—Few towns and cities heard from. Democratic gain 1,300 on Governor.

From New York.

NEW YORK, April 1st.
The Herald correspondent says the President was served with all the testimony taken before the Carode Investigating Committee having any personal reference to himself before he prepared his protest message to the House.

The Harper's Ferry Committee decided at their meeting yesterday, not to subpoena Gov. Wise, he having placed in their possession all the facts connected with that affair. They have not decided what action they will take towards Jno. Brown Jr., who refuses to obey their summons.

Congressional.

CHICAGO, March 30.
Lake Pepin is open ; steamer Milwaukee arrived at Prairie du Chien yesterday, from St. Paul.

Washington News.

WASHINGTON, March 29.
The managers of the principal telegraph lines, in connection with the pony express, have agreed upon the following prices for private dispatches to and from California :

For ten words from any Atlantic city or any other telegraph station, or vice versa to dollars forty-five cents ; for a similar number of words from the first station on the California telegraph line to any part of California, and vice versa, two dollars ; while the charge for expressing the message, without regard to length, will be $2 each, making the sum total from any station in the Atlantic States to any states to any station in California, $6 90 for ten words. The charge for each additional word above that number will be 20c each. The understanding is that the telegraph companies will refund the entire tolls to parties forwarding any message which fails to reach California, or vice versa, in advance of any other route, and that they will also return to the lender any moneys paid for dispatches filed in season to overtake the express at St. Joseph, which through any reason may fail to reach that place before the departure of the express.

The House bill, authorizing publishers to print on their papers the date when subscriptions expire, and reducing the postage on town and city drop letters to one cen, passed both Houses of Congress.

WASHINGTON, March 30.
Private letters from Arizona, state that Delegates have been elected to a Convention, to be held at Tucson, on the 1st Monday in April, to organize a provisional Government for the Territory. All connection with New Mexico is severed.

R. Owens, two years ago a member of the Legislature of Arizona, will probably be elected Governor of Arizona, under provisional Government

The same advices state that the disturbances in Chihuhua will probably destroy the trade of El Paso, and prevent the exportation of specie. Most of the specie used by the United States Government and Overland Mail Company, has heretofore been drawn from Chihuhua

WASHINGTON, March 31.
In response to the report of the House Committee on Territories, which asserts that the acceptance or rejection of the admission of a State rests entirely in the discretion of Congress at the time of such application.

Mr. Clark, of Missouri, and the Minority, will present the following points :
The Constitution of Kansas was not formed and presented to Congress in accordance with law, meaning the English bill, but in derogation thereof that it does not appear that there is within her limits a sufficient population as required by law, and further, the proposed area embraces the Cherokee Indian Territory, which Congress in 1854 formally decided should constitute no part of the Territory of Kansas, but be excluded from its boundaries. These reasons form the ground of the objection, on the Democratic side, to the admission of Kansas, under the Wyandotte Constitution.

The Post Office Committee of the House had Mr. Gwin's Pacific Telegraph bill up this morning, and referred it to the Sub-Committee, consisting of Messrs. Colfax, Craig of North Carolina, and Allen. While there was a general agreement in favor of some such enterprise, and of extending Government and rewards its construction, it was thought proper to examine the details of this particular project more fully

The majority of the Harper's Ferry Committee have again decided to summon Gov. Wise, and it is probable the question will be submitted to the Senate.

The Post Office Committee have invited John Cochrane and Mr. Corwin to appear on Tuesday evening, in behalf of Carlos Butterfield's Mail Route along the Gulf of Mexico. The feeling in the Committee is very favorable to this scheme.

Col. Charles E. Smith only retains command in Utah until Col. Cooke, who succeeds Gen. Johnston, shall reach there, when he will occupy the second rank to him.

Petitions from all parts of New York are pouring in praying that the Reciprocity Treaty with Canada may be amended or rescinded ; hostility about it is growing most bitter daily, so ruinous is it to the interior of Western New York. Mr. Hatch's report will not only be strongly condemnatory to the treaty but will urge that it be abrogated at the earliest possible day. President Buchanan will lay the report immediately before Congress.

Union Convention.

BOSTON, March 29.
The Constitutional Union Party Convention was held in this city to-day. 212 towns were represented. Hon. Nathaniel Silsby was elected President, and addresses were delivered by the Great Marshal, P. wilder, G. S. Hillard, Leverett Saltenstall and Geo. A. Curtis. Resolutions, calling on the conservative and patriotic men of all parties to unite for putting down agitation and sectional differences, to check government extravagance ; to protect home industry and for a thorough change in the political affairs of the State were adopted.

A foreign letter says : Meanwhile, Rome is quiet. Folks stick knives into each other on the Corso in broad daylight, quite peaceably and with noise.

Congressional.

WASHINGTON, March 30.
HOUSE.—On motion of Mr. Colfax, the amendment providing that if any person endorses on a letter that it is to be returned to him in thirty days, if not called for, it shall be so done instead of being sent to the Dead Letter office, was passed.

A number of private bills were passed. Adjourned.

SENATE.—The Chair laid before the Senate a message from the President, in reply to a resolution of inquiry relative to the action of the navy in Mexico, and the authority therefor. Ordered to lay on the table and be printed.

Mr. Mason, from the Committee on Foreign Relations, reported a bill relative to the assembling of a convention of commissioners from the United States and Paraguay, to consider the claims on the Rhode Island Company; said commissioners to meet in Washington and sit three months, to be paid jointly by both Governments. He asked for the present consideration of the bill. Laid over.

The bill to carry out the promises of the 15th section of the treaty between the United States and Mexico, concluded February 2d, 1848, was taken up. It provides for the Commissioner to adjudicate private claims under the treaty, there being a special fund in the treasury for paying them. After a debate, it was laid over

The private calendar was taken up, and bills upon it discussed the balance of the day.
Adjourned.

WASHINGTON, April 2.
HOUSE—Mr. Hickman, from the committee of Judiciary, reported a bill to extend the right to appeal from decisions of the Circuit Court to the Supreme Court of Utah.

Mr. Elliott introduced a bill for the removal of the obstructions at Hurlgate, and a bill for the improvement of the Harlem River, which were referred to the Committee on Commerce.

Mr. Morse ineffectually endeavored to introduce a bill prohibiting the Chinese Coolie trade in American vessels.

Mr. Burnett objected.

The bill for the suppression of polygamy in Utah was considered.

The debate was lengthy.

Million, Pryor, Ethridge and others spoke in favor of the bill. Adjourned.

SENATE—Mr. Hunter, from the Finance Committee, reported back the Indian Appropriation bill, with amendments.

The bill for the final adjustment of private land claims in Florida, Louisiana, Arkansas and Missouri passed.

The bill to authorize the location of certain warrants for bounty lands, was passed.

Mr. Davis' Territorial resolutions were called up, when Mr. Soulsbery made a speech in opposition to the Republican party and its prospective nominee for the Presidency, Mr. Seward.

Mr. Ten Eyck argued against the extension of slavery into the Territories, contending that no one had a right to interfere with it in the States, and saying it would have been abolished in many places had it not been for unwarrantable interference with it. He regarded the fugitive law as constitutional, and said New Jersey would stand with the Middle States in repelling ultraism and extravagance, and urge upon her sister States to preserve the Union.
Adjourned.

Destructive Fire.

INDEPENDENCE, March 30.
A fire broke out here last night at 12 o'clock, and destroyed all of the eastern side of the square, including Beckham's drug store, Coyle's grocery, A. B. Tamirer's tin shop, M. Sampson's store, Keecher's saloon, Thomas' livery stable, besides several small buildings.

CLEVELAND, March 30.
The store of H. Comstock, at Bedford, was destroyed by fire last night. Loss $5,000.

NEW YORK, April 2.
Isaac Townsend, a retired merchant and one of the governors of the Alms House, died yesterday.

Evidence has been produced in the mysterious case of the sloop Spray that the horn of the murderer was heard on a vessel off Norwalk Island, in the Sound, and subsequently the report of a pistol was heard. This corresponds with the statement that the Spray was at anchor in that vicinity. The Sound in that neighborhood is to be dragged for the murdered men.

Bank Statement.—Increase in loans, $874,728 ; do specie, $134,553 ; do circulation, $102,000 ; do deposits , $414,512

From Mexico.

NEW YORK, March 30.
The official dispatches from Capts. Jarvis and Turner, detailing the engagement and capture of Miramon's steamers, crats the point are published ; they contain, however, nothing of importance, in addition to was given has already been stated.

John Cummings was hung this morning—all he trouble paid, for murder. He died calmly, expressing sorrow for the crime for which he had been condemned, and commending his wife and children to the charities of them

The Arabia, from Liverpool, arrived this forenoon to the 7th

Washington Correspondence of St. Louis Republican

WASHINGTON, March
The most interesting and important subject now under consideration by the American Congress is our Territorial policy.— The blundering statements in the N. Y. Herald, as regards this policy, do great injustice to the parties having direct charge of these great national questions. The story in the Herald has just enough of truth in it to give currency to its errors, which greatly annoys the committees and induces me to state the true position of the Territorial policy, as about to be recommended by the Senate Committee.

This committee have had, and will have no conference with the Committee of the House, but will act upon their own judgment. They have already authorized three bills to be reported, viz :

1. A bill to organize the Territory of Arizona. The name of this proposed Territory is thus changed from Arizona, at the suggestion of Gen. Jeff. Davis the the latter is a corruption of the former name. It was at one time thought the better course to give this region only a District Court, Marshal and Surveyor-General, but subsequent examination demonstrated the propriety of organizing a Territorial Government complete.

2. A bill to organize the Territory of Jefferson, (Pike's Peak) and without any of the contest as to the name detailed in the correspondence. The name of Jefferson being suggested, I am informed by the Committee that no objection was made, and the name adopted without a word of opposition.

3. A bill amendatory of the act organizing the Territory of Utah—by which the seat of government is to be removed from Salt Lake City to Carson Valley, and the name of the Territory changed from Utah to Nevada. The bill also makes the sole population the sole basis to citizens of the including realized by the of the Valle to the the second in con discontent attracted in the he an the representation from Salt Lake region in the legislature.

The amendments proposed in the organic act will not, as represented in the Herald, interfere with the present delegate in Congress, or the present political status of the Territory. The change proposed are all prospective, and will be brought about by a steady operation of the proposed policy. The change of the name of the Territory is designed to break the charm which "Utah" seems to have acquired over a certain portion of the degraded population of Europe, and arrest, if possible, at least in some degree, the immigration of foreign Mormons. The Senate's Committee have taken a large amount of testimony on the subject—brought before them during the consideration of this last bill—and if published, this testimony would be highly interesting to the country, but the proceedings of a committee being confidential, these facts will not be made public. Captain Hooper was not consulted as to the policy proper to be pursued relative to Utah, but he was before the Committee several times, giving information, and by his ready and clear responses, and his gentlemanly and ingenuous manner, made upon every member of the Committee, the best impression of his most favorable impression. It is but simple justice to Captain Hooper to say that by his modest and conciliatory course since a member of Congress, he has made many warm friends even of those bitterly opposed to the peculiar institution of his Territory.

The Senate committee have proposed any change in the boundary Kansas and Nebraska, as the Herald's correspondent, as several Senators are Kansas admitted boundary was established which the the

For admission tain so far as though I have port it by a the Territori dorsed by the crats the point ories"—and bills, which will all also gentle men of Un silent of the appoint the new good. Legislature, as was the e This, it is admitted, now evils complained of, but with discrimination be a fair and honorable which may admit of

The first mail packet carried west by the Pony Express included a special lightweight-paper edition of a Missouri daily.

Always concerned for the spiritual health of his employees, Alexander Majors issued every Pony Express rider a Bible — using up a stock of specially bound copies he had ordered for his company's wagon-train crews.

saddle of the fast bay mare, galloped down Jules Street to the banks of the Missouri River and clattered aboard a waiting ferryboat. In about half an hour he was on the far shore, in the hamlet of Elwood, Kansas, and spurring his mount westward. The route was easy to follow, even in the dark. Blazed by emigrants who knew it as the Oregon Trail, it had since been turned into a broad, grassless strip by the tremendous traffic of forty-niners and the freight wagons that followed them across the rolling prairie.

About 45 minutes beyond Elwood, Fry pulled up in Troy, Kansas, switched himself and his *mochila* to a fresh horse in about two minutes, and galloped off once more. He changed mounts again at Kennekuk and yet again at Kickapoo. At 11:30 p.m. he reached the little settlement of Granada and turned the *mochila* over to the next relay rider, Don Rising, who was saddled up and waiting for him. Rising galloped on for more than eight hours, changing mounts at 15-mile intervals and arriving in Marysville, Kansas, at 8:15 a.m. on April 4.

So far the mail had traveled 112 prairie miles in 13 hours. At 5:15 a.m. on April 5, after it had been passed on to three more relay riders, the mail reached Fort Kearney — 230 miles out.

Beyond Fort Kearney, the terrain changed; the relay riders pounded through a dreary landscape — dry, dusty and brown except for narrow green strips along riverbanks and streams. On April 6 — 61 hours and 45 minutes out — a rider passed Chimney Rock, the towering emigrant landmark 535 miles from St. Joseph.

Relay by relay, the mail was rushed on to South Pass, the broad opening in the Rockies that marked the Continental Divide. From there to Fort Bridger and on to Salt Lake City, the route was rugged, arid and dangerous. But the *mochila* arrived safely in the Mormon capital on the evening of April 9, not quite six days after it had left St. Joseph.

Westward from the Great Salt Lake to Carson City, the Pony riders relayed the mail through one of America's worst desert regions, sparsely populated by the Paiute and Gosiute tribes. The desert crossing took three days. When the rider arrived on the outskirts of Carson City, a telegrapher took the telegrams and wired them ahead to Sacramento, along with a message that the rest of the mail was on the way.

Then came the last phase of the journey, a tortuous course through Carson Pass in the Sierra Nevada and downslope to Sacramento. The mail reached Sacramento at 5:25 p.m. on April 13, about two hours less than 10 days. The final relay rider, William Hamilton, was welcomed to California's fast-growing capital with a cannon salute, marching bands, clanging church bells and flag-waving crowds, and the state legislature adjourned to join in the celebration. One of the many signs displayed in store windows would have brought special satisfaction to Russell, Majors & Waddell. "Hurrah for the Central Route!" it read.

A telegrapher sent on to San Francisco the news of Hamilton's arrival, and another celebration awaited the rider when, at 12:38 a.m. on April 14, he — and horse — put in there on the steamer *Antelope (page 96)*. In all, more than 30 relay riders had brought the mail through; but, as the San Francisco *Bulletin* noted, credit was also due to their mounts. "The little fellow who came down in the Sacramento boat this morning had the vicarious glory of them all. . . . He was the veri-

A wild-eyed mount and exhausted rider battle snow and winds to cross the Sierra between Nevada and California. In winter this 85-mile stretch became the worst obstacle of the whole 1,966-mile Pony route.

A Sacramento River paddle steamer completes the last leg of the Pony Express route to San Francisco. On the first Express run, rider William Hamilton trotted his horse aboard so that he could deliver his packet personally in the city. Later relay riders entrusted their saddlebags to the skipper.

table Hippagriff [the winged horse of fable] who shoved a continent behind his hoofs so easily; who snuffed up sandy plains, sent lakes and mountains, prairies and forests, whizzing behind him, like one great river."

By the time San Francisco started celebrating, the last eastbound relay had reached St. Joseph and set off another outburst of rejoicing there. To be sure, some of the riders had been held up in the Sierra Nevada by an unusually fierce blizzard that piled up 30-foot drifts; but riders farther along made up the lost time. And already two more mails were on their way from the opposite ends of the route. It looked as though William Russell had a winner.

Newspapers everywhere, even in Europe, were unstinting in their praise. The paper that offered the sweetest music to Russell's ears was Denver's *Rocky Mountain News,* which combined acclaim for the Pony with a blunt attack on the Southern opponents of its route. "The Express Company deserves great credit," said the editorial, "for concentrating public attention on the central route, and it is hoped that their enterprise will *shame* Congress into legislation in favor of the opening of a daily or tri-weekly mail route to Denver, Utah and California."

As far as Russell was concerned, government action could not come too soon, for he was in dire financial straits. Russell's troubles — and the idea for the Pony Express — dated back to the winter of 1857-1858 and the Army's disastrous campaign in Utah to quell Mormon defiance of federal authority. In freighting the Army's supplies, Russell, Majors & Waddell had incurred losses of $493,000. When the firm demanded compensation, the War Department declared that it had overdrawn its 1857 appropriation and could make no payment whatsoever. The company's credit, up to then virtually unlimited, was gravely impaired; it was never, in fact, to be repaid for its losses in Utah, on the further ground that no formal agreement had been drawn up for this special supply assignment.

Still, the Utah debacle had yielded one very useful bit of information. The two men in charge of the wagon trains — Russell's nephew, Charles R. Morehead Jr., and a former Army captain named James Rupe — had returned to the firm's Leavenworth headquarters under abominable weather conditions, but nevertheless had made the trip with remarkable ease. As Morehead summarized the journey: "We traveled about 1200 miles, as the road then ran, in thirty days, in the dead of a severe winter, through hostile Indians and ravenous wolves, in snow every foot of the way, without a change in animals and without grain."

William Russell was delighted at his nephew's report. It meant that the central overland route, pronounced impassable in winter by partisans of the southern route, could be traveled year round, no matter how bad the weather. Russell, the incorrigible optimist, had already been thinking of ways to make up for the Utah freighting fiasco and now concluded that a handsome government subsidy for transporting mail over the central route might well be the answer.

True, mail was already being carried over the route, between St. Joseph and Placerville, California. George Chorpenning, the pioneering mailman, still held a government contract for deliveries west of Salt Lake City. The eastern end of the run, first operated by Samuel Woodson, was now in the hands of one John M. Hockaday. But deliveries took six weeks and transport was still by pack mule on an inadequate bimonthly schedule. The route's potential for speedier and more efficient service remained to be demonstrated.

Out of these ruminations by Russell came the concept of the Pony Express. Other men would claim credit for the idea, and indeed precedents abounded. Relays of mounted couriers had delivered letters in colonial times; and in 1853, an important Presidential message, arriving in San Francisco by ship, had been raced on to Portland, Oregon, by a series of horsemen. The general idea was in the public domain — but no application of it had approached the sweeping scheme conceived and actually undertaken by Russell.

For the nonce, he put the plan aside and attended to more pressing business problems. In early March of 1858, amid the credit difficulties posed for his firm as a result of the ill-starred Army campaign against the Mormons, he finally managed to finance the freighting operations required for the following months under the terms of the Army contract. Russell resolved the problem, characteristically, by going straight to the top. In Washington he called on Secretary of War John Floyd and asked for an advance on his company's future earnings from its Army contract. Floyd could not oblige, since his department had yet to receive its 1858 ap-

propriation. Still, he was amenable to suggestion and he agreed instead to endorse $400,000 worth of acceptances, or credit vouchers, which Russell then used as collateral to secure a matching sum in loans from four banks. The transaction was the only way that both men could get an essential job done. But it was also illegal, and it would haunt them for the rest of their lives.

If Russell had been as prudent as his partners William Waddell and Alexander Majors, he might have chosen to let the freighting firm recoup its losses from the Utah disaster by the slow but sure method of fulfilling subsequent contracts with the Army. But Russell was Russell — a man who had no patience for small, hard-won gains, who reveled in taking big risks for big profits in the shortest time possible. On his own, he

A torchlight parade and honor guard greet
William Hamilton, first Pony rider to reach
San Francisco, as he arrives past midnight
on April 14, 1860. A brass band struck
up "See, the Conquering Hero Comes."

plunged into costly new ventures inspired by recent gold strikes in the Pikes Peak region of Colorado, then known as western Kansas.

Some time in 1858 Russell helped to found the town of Denver as a central depot for the gold fields; his share in the enterprise brought him 30 acres of prime land on the town site. Then, to capitalize on the expected influx of prospectors, he decided to start a stagecoach line from Leavenworth to Denver, and offered partnerships in it to Majors and Waddell. They turned him down and advised him against the venture, but Russell, put on his mettle by their opposition, stuck to his decision.

Organizing the stage company and building relay stations on its 687-mile route across Kansas proved to be a longer, costlier job than Russell had calculated, requiring an outlay of at least $250,000. Despite the refusal of Majors and Waddell to join in this enterprise, Russell borrowed repeatedly on the credit of their mutually owned firm and at the same time sought new partners for the stage company. In February of 1859 he incorporated the firm as the Leavenworth & Pike's Peak Express Company; his co-owners included a freighting veteran named John S. Jones and one Luther R. Smoot, who was already Russell's partner in one of his earlier ventures—a Leavenworth bank. Stagecoaches began running between Leavenworth and Denver—the terminal points of the line—in April. But the Pikes Peak strikes proved to be sadly inferior to the riches found in California and passenger revenues never came close to matching operating expenses. However, Russell had caught stagecoach fever and he stubbornly intensified his efforts to make the new firm a success.

In May he pulled off a stunning coup. For a mere $120,000 in promissory notes, he acquired John Hockaday's contract to deliver mail from St. Joseph to Salt Lake City by way of Fort Kearney, Fort Laramie and Denver. Now Russell had a vested interest in almost two thirds of the central overland route, and he formulated his master plan: he would gain a monopoly on mail service over its full length. His dream came true the following year, when he acquired the Salt Lake City-to-Placerville route from the original contractor, George Chorpenning.

In late June of 1859, Russell's stagecoaches were no longer plying between Leavenworth and Denver only, but over the much more extensive route he had acquired by buying out Hockaday: from St. Joseph all the way to Salt Lake City. The stage line, refurbished at great cost (on loans and credit, of course) with additional way stations and elegant Concord coaches, was soon providing exemplary service and was a success by every measure but dollars and cents. By mid-October, the Leavenworth & Pike's Peak Express had debts totaling $525,532 and Russell was being hounded by anxious creditors.

He took the only course he saw open to him: he dumped his predicament in the laps of Alexander Majors and William Waddell. As always conservative, they were tempted to let Russell sink or swim, but realized that if they did not rescue him they might endanger their own company's reputation. So they agreed to have the firm take over the bankrupt stage line and refinance its debts. The resilient Russell drew up

PONY EXPRESS AT CARSON CITY.

[SPECIAL DISPATCH TO THE ALTA CALIFORNIA.]

TEN DAYS LATER.

St. Louis Dates to 12th April.

Eight Days and Nineteen Hours on the Way.........
Rhode Island Democratic.........Row in Congress
.........American Vessel Stopped by a Spanish
Steamer......Siege of Vera Cruz Abandoned......
Eight Days Later from Europe.........Liverpool
Dates to March 29th......The Two Annexations
Finished......Excommunication of Victor Emanuel......An Occasion of National Rejoicing......
End of the Moorish War.

[Prepared by our Special Correspondent, at St. Louis, thence by Express to St. Joseph's, thence by Pony Express to Carson City, thence by telegraph to San Francisco, for the *Alta California*.]

[PER ST. JOSEPH, PLACERVILLE AND ALTA LINES.]

CARSON CITY, APRIL 22, 1860.
The Overland Pony Express, from St. Joseph, Missouri, arrived here at 4:10 this morning, with dates from St. Louis to the 12th inst. The Express was detained six hours at Roberts' Creek, by reason of the horses having been driven off by the Indians.

The Pony Express in St. Joseph.
ST. LOUIS, April 12, 1860.
The departure of the last Pony Express was an important event in St. Joseph. The Express was detained two hours and a half by the failure of the New York messenger to make the connection. The ceremony of inaugurating the event was performed by the Mayor of the city, who put the letter-bag on the horse, and accompanied the act with a speech.

papers incorporating the new stage company under the more geographically appropriate, if long-winded, name of the Central Overland, California & Pike's Peak Express Company—which common usage soon shortened to the C.O.C.&P.P., or simply the C.O.C.

It was to no avail. Not even the pinchpenny bookkeeping of Waddell and the field experience of Majors could turn the line into a money-maker. The only hope was a big mail subsidy, and that demanded a big gamble. Russell pulled from his mental file the best means of dramatizing the virtues of the Central Overland route—the Pony Express. On January 27, 1860, he sent a fateful telegram from Washington, where he was at the moment, to Leavenworth, where his son John was headquartered as secretary of the C.O.C. line. The message was brief and to the point:

"Have determined to establish a Pony Express to Sacramento, California, commencing 3rd of April. Time 10 days."

Whatever prompted Russell to choose April 3 as the starting date —and few men ever professed to understand the workings of his mind —he certainly could not be faulted for dawdling. He had allowed little more than two months for a host of complicated preparations. The key employees in Russell's various companies had to march to get the job done.

In Salt Lake City, A. B. Miller, Russell's partner in yet another of his ventures, a local merchandising business, advertised for 200 sturdy mustangs to be used on the western end of the line. In Leavenworth, John Jones, one of Russell's partners in the C.O.C., advertised for 200 mares, "warranted sound, not to exceed 15 hands high, well broke to the saddle," for use on the eastern

An envelope intended for a Denver paper
trumpets its contents—news of Lincoln's
first election. The Pony Express added an
unscheduled, extra-fast mail run to rush this
major story to the West in eight days.

end of the line; most of these 200 were selected from
trail-hardened Army stock at Fort Leavenworth. All
along the line, purchasing agents sought out choice horses and paid top dollar for them. The average price paid
for some 500 animals was $200, about four times the
rate for an average mount.

Benjamin Ficklin, the skillful field manager of the
C.O.C., took charge of route preparations, with five capable division superintendents working under him. The
superintendents hired crews to build new relay stations
and modify the old ones the stage line had used. In all,
190 stations were needed: 25 "home" stations for
changes of riders and 165 smaller, intervening "swing"
stations for quick changes of mounts. The stations were
to be equipped and provisioned by local merchants,
among them R.B. Bradford, Russell's partner in still another enterprise, a large Denver store.

In choosing sites for the stations, the superintendents
used only one criterion: the distance a horse could cover at top speed in each area's terrain before the rider

needed a fresh mount. At that very point the station
was located. If the site was near water, so much the better; if not, water would be shipped in along with food.
The builders used whatever local materials came to
hand—the plentiful timber at both ends of the route,
sod in Nebraska, adobe bricks in desert areas. In several
barren places, workmen made swing stations by goug-
ing a cavity in a hillside and roofing it over with logs
hauled in from elsewhere. Most of the home stations,
too, were spartan affairs, with rough bunks and primitive kitchen facilities for the off-duty riders who rested
there between runs.

The division superintendents also conducted interviews and tryouts for hundreds of would-be Pony riders, many of whom were lured from routine jobs by the
chance for glory, excitement and the good pay of $50 a
month plus board and keep. In Sacramento, the street
in front of the St. George Hotel was turned into a
rodeo ground as local youths showed off their riding
skills to the plaudits of bystanders. Mormon lads were

similarly tested in Salt Lake City. Riding prowess was but one qualification. The candidate also had to be young (20 was considered ideal) and light (about 125 pounds), with unusual strength and stamina, as well as an adult sense of responsibility. It was taken for granted that the applicants were courageous. If not, one dangerous trip would send them packing.

Initially, 80 riders were hired; about 40 more would eventually serve, most of them as eager replacements for boys who found the job too punishing. Each proud new recruit was immediately required to sign the famous Alexander Majors pledge of honesty, loyalty to the company, sobriety, decent speech and gentlemanly conduct—"so help me God."

All of these preparations, masterfully coordinated by William Russell, got the Pony off to its flying start on the scheduled date of April 3, 1860. More than a month later, sensational stories of that first trip were still appearing in the newspapers. The Pony was an ongoing story of thrills, speed and lone daring. Few reporters actually saw a Pony rider in action, but one who did, Mark Twain, never forgot the stirring sight. He happened to be traveling by stagecoach through Nevada in 1861 when the passengers were alerted by the driver's cry, "Here he comes!" As Twain wrote years later: "Away across the endless dead level of the prairie a black speck appears against the sky, and it is plain that it moves. Well, I should think so! In a second or two it becomes a horse and rider, rising and falling, rising and falling—sweeping toward us nearer and nearer—growing more and more distinct, more and more sharply defined—nearer and still nearer, and the flutter of the hoofs comes faintly to the ear—another instant a whoop and a hurrah from our upper deck, a wave of the rider's hand, but no reply, and man and horse burst past our excited faces and go swinging away like a belated fragment of a storm!"

The sense of invincible self-confidence and devotion to duty conveyed by that Pony rider was affirmed by dozens of his fellows in hundreds of acts of casual heroism in the face of floods, snowstorms, buffalo stampedes and Indian attacks. "Pony Bob" Haslam, waylaid by some Indians in Utah Territory, completed his 120-mile run with his jaw broken by an arrow and with one arm shattered by bullets. Howard Egan, finding that his path through a narrow canyon was blocked by an Indian encampment, refused to make a long detour; he spurred his horse straight through the camp, scattering the warriors in all directions. Worse than the Indians —worse than anything, the riders said—was a mountain run through a blizzard in sub-zero cold with snowdrifts higher than a man's head. Warren Upson spent more than a day blindly struggling through a white maelstrom to a station he normally reached in a couple of hours. But all the riders brought the mail through.

Such heroics made the riders riveting figures not just to newspaper readers at home and abroad but to the people who lived along their route. Young women adored them, especially the first westward rider, Johnny Fry, whose professional prestige was no doubt augmented by his handsome features. Girls would turn out to watch and wave as Johnny galloped past on his run from St. Joseph. One lucky girl, who made a playful grab at Johnny as he flashed by, tore off a piece of his shirttail and sewed it into a patchwork quilt.

There was nothing special about Johnny's shirttail except that it was his; the riders wore anything they pleased on the job. The usual dress consisted of a buckskin shirt, cloth trousers tucked into knee boots, and a slouch hat. Although a ceremonial outfit had been ordered by William Russell himself, the only riders obliged to use it were the few whose run started and ended at St. Joseph with the crossing of the Missouri River. Jack Keetley, who often rode that leg, later recalled the ridiculous regalia and how the boys gave it short shrift: "We always rode out of town with silver mounted trappings decorating both man and horse, and regular uniforms with plated horn, pistol, scabbard and belt, etc., and gay flower-worked leggings and plated jingling spurs, resembling, for all the world, a fantastic circus rider. This was all changed, however, as soon as we got on the boat. We had a room in which to change and to leave the trappings until our return."

The plated horn mentioned by Keetley was originally intended as standard equipment; the riders were supposed to blow it as they approached a relay station, in order to alert the stock tender to saddle up a fresh mount. But the horn was discarded when the pounding of hoofbeats proved to be warning enough. It also had been planned to arm the riders heavily against Indian attack. But a carbine and two revolvers made a cumbersome load, and the rider's armament dwindled to a knife and a revolver, sometimes with an extra bullet-loaded cylinder tucked away for emergencies.

Actually, the Pony riders' best defense was sheer speed. Their horses could outrun any Indian pony, and for a reason that had nothing to do with the animals themselves. Nick Wilson, who had lived with the Shoshoni Indians as a boy, knew the reason well and saw it work when a band of Indian riders jumped him between Shell Creek and Deep Creek, Utah. "I looked back over my shoulder," Nick said, "and saw them coming, about thirteen of the devils, as hard as they could ride after me, yellin' and shootin'." But his horse had the advantage of superior feed. As Wilson put it, the horse's "grain-fed muscles got me out of the danger of their arrows and the few old guns they had. Their grass-fed ponies couldn't keep long within gunshot."

One Indian tribe, the 6,000 Paiutes of Utah and Nevada, always posed a threat of trouble, in large part because their poverty fostered a spirit of violence. A Paiute eruption did occur in May 1860 (page 109). The Pony Express, having just completed eight once-a-week trips in both directions, was forced to suspend operations for the first and only time; when service was restored a month later, it was on a twice-a-week basis — a typical Russell reaction to adversity.

Paiute depredations cost Russell about $75,000 in stock and equipment, took the lives of 16 station hands — and accounted for one valiant feat that, alone, would have been enough to confer mythic stature on the Pony Express. Amid the first Paiute raids, "Pony Bob" Haslam made what was probably the longest one-man run in Pony history, skirting death most of the way.

Haslam, a fearless rider who joined the Pony at its inception and stayed on to the end, was assigned to the Nevada run between Friday's station at the foot of Lake Tahoe and Fort Churchill, 75 miles to the east. When he began his celebrated ride from Friday's on May 11, he may not have known that trouble lay ahead; if not, he soon learned the hard way. Twenty miles out, he reached Carson City, expecting to get a fresh mount there. But all the stock in town had been commandeered by a mob of local residents bent on killing some Paiutes. It turned out that the Paiutes had launched their war on the white man four days earlier, attacking a number of stations between Carson City

and Fort Churchill, killing some of the occupants and stealing or scattering the stock. Thus Haslam had to whip the same tired horse past one abandoned station after another, all the way to Fort Churchill.

There his relief rider, Billy Richardson, refused to risk taking the mail on to the next home station, Smith's Creek, 115 miles further east. So Pony Bob grabbed a fresh horse and made Richardson's run himself. Changing mounts at Sand Springs and again at Cold Spring, he finally reached Smith's Creek early on May 12. So far Haslam had ridden 190 miles in about 18 hours.

At Smith's Creek Pony Bob handed his eastbound mail to a relay rider named Jay Kelly and knocked off about eight hours' sleep. Awakening, he found that a relay rider had arrived with the westbound mail. Haslam took it and headed back toward Fort Churchill. At Cold Spring, he discovered that the Paiutes had burned the station since he passed it the day before, killing the keeper and stealing the horses. At Sand Springs, he picked up a fresh mount and also a traveling companion, the stock tender. Pony Bob had decided that it was too dangerous to leave him — and he was right. Next day the Paiutes descended on Sand Springs; the man would almost certainly have been killed.

At Carson Sink, Haslam left the stock tender, changed horses and sped on to Fort Churchill, where he rested for an hour, then went on to Carson City. There he found the townspeople in mourning for 46 members of the Indian-chasing posse; they had blundered into a Paiute ambush at Pyramid Lake and it was only by luck that the 60 other possemen had escaped with their lives. Without further incident, Haslam arrived back at Friday's station on May 13. He had covered 380 miles in some 36 hours of riding.

Haslam's round trip had been interrupted by his eight-hour nap at Smith's Creek and his hour of rest at Fort Churchill; and even if his ride was the longest one, it left unsettled the question of who made the longest continuous ride. One claimant to that laurel was Jack Keetley, who said he had ridden 340 miles nonstop in about 24 hours. Keetley started east with the mail from Big Sandy station in Nebraska; rode it to Elwood, Kansas, just across the Missouri River from St. Joseph; and then retraced his path as far as Seneca, Kansas. Why Keetley made the trip remained unclear; someone said it was on a bet. In any case, Keetley was only

SPECIAL SADDLERY FOR HIGH SPEED

The unique lightweight saddle kit shown in replica below was designed especially for the Pony Express — reportedly by one of its riders, W. A. Cates. The entire assembly weighed less than 13 pounds, or about one third as much as an ordinary Western saddle. Over the stripped-down saddle went a leather rectangle *(right)* called a *mochila* (Spanish for knapsack) with four mail pouches called *cantinas,* and cutouts that fit around the pommel and cantle of the saddle. The *mochila* could be yanked off one horse and thrown across another in well under the two minutes allotted in the Pony Express schedules for a rider's change of mounts.

human: he ended his ride sound asleep in the saddle.

Buffalo Bill Cody, the most famous courier of them all, claimed—somewhat less credibly—to have surpassed both Haslam and Keetley without the aid of any sleep, in or out of the saddle. Cody, who had first served Russell, Majors & Waddell as a wagon-train messenger at the age of 10, was hired for the Pony as a 100-pound stripling of 15. He was entrusted with the 116-mile run between Red Buttes on the North Platte River and Three Crossings on the Sweetwater River in Nebraska. After completing his regular westbound run to Three Crossings, Cody found that his relief rider had been killed the night before in a drunken fight; and since no replacement was available, he rode on for 76 miles more to the next home station, Rocky Ridge. There he passed on the westbound mail and received the eastbound mail to take all the way back to Red Buttes. Cody recalled the episode rather grandly: "I pushed on with the usual rapidity, entering every relay station on time, and accomplished the round trip to Red Buttes without a single mishap, on time." The total distance of this trip was 384 miles, four miles longer than Haslam's. Cody boasted that "this stands on the records as being the longest Pony Express journey ever made." But he did not report his ride until after he had become Buffalo Bill, the renowned showman and self-promoter, and his stories were known to be less accurate than his uncanny marksmanship.

Through the summer and fall of 1860, the dazzling performance—and acclamatory newspaper coverage—of the Pony Express was William Russell's sole source of pleasure. Things were rapidly going from bad to worse throughout his shaky corporate empire. In the expectation of a big mail subsidy for the C.O.C., he had spent so lavishly on coaches, horses and relay stations that the line was losing upwards of $1,000 a day. Perhaps events would prove his optimism justified, but there were other grave problems threatening Russell, Majors & Waddell. The firm's preparations for the 1860 freighting business were based on the work load of the year before; thousands of men had been hired and thousands of oxen bought to haul Army supplies. Then the partners learned belatedly that they had been underbid for a large part of the Army's business by another freighting company. To make matters worse, the Army was slow in sending delivery instructions for the part of the supply business that Russell, Majors & Waddell still retained. This meant that the company would have to pay many of its hired hands for standing around doing nothing. It also meant an even longer than usual wait for payment from the War Department once the deliveries were completed.

All in all, the situation was dismal. With loans and credit growing ever harder to get, cash was in such short supply that from time to time Russell failed to meet the payroll for both the freighting firm and the stagecoach line. The plight of the stage line became a grim public joke when some sardonic employee made a play on the initials of its name—the Central Overland, California & Pike's Peak Express—and dubbed the company "Clean Out of Cash & Poor Pay."

Sheer desperation forced William Russell to spend more and more of his time in the East trying to raise money. Several times during the summer and fall of 1860 he called on Secretary of War Floyd and dunned him for overdue payments on freighting services. On one occasion, Floyd was able to make a partial payment of $161,000, but the money was immediately swallowed up by monstrous indebtedness. In place of further payments, Floyd continued to endorse Russell's acceptances against future company earnings. But by now bankers knew that these credit vouchers exceeded Russell's ability to repay and he could no longer get loans using them as collateral.

On the verge of bankruptcy, Russell blurted out his problems to Luke Lea, an old banker friend. Lea suggested that a certain Godard Bailey might be of assistance. It turned out that Bailey was a law clerk in the Interior Department and the custodian of a fortune in bonds being held in trust for various Indian tribes. Russell quickly entered into discussions with him.

Bailey happened to be married to Secretary of War Floyd's second cousin, and when he learned that Floyd might have to resign if his illegal endorsement of Russell's credit vouchers became known, he agreed to help. According to the plan that emerged, Russell would "borrow" some Indian bonds from Bailey, use them as collateral for bank loans and return them just as soon as he could pay off the loans. Pending the return, Bailey would hold new credit vouchers signed by Russell; presumably they would mitigate the crime, if it were discovered, by proving that the intention was only to bor-

A former Pony Express station near Echo Canyon, Utah, still in use as a stage stop in 1868, shows signs of technological progress. At left, photographers from the Union Pacific survey the site for the advancing railroad, and behind them soar the tall poles of the transcontinental telegraph.

English fans of the Pony Express enjoyed this 1861 *Illustrated London News* sketch despite its errors. The rider is much too portly; his rifle should be a pistol, and the bulging mail sack a flat-lying *mochila*.

row, not to steal, the bonds. The two men were indeed scrupulous about exchanging bonds and acceptances. When bonds worth $870,000 were found to be missing in December 1860, vouchers in exactly the same amount balanced them out. But this fact was to prove a pitifully weak defense against numerous accusations of wrongdoing.

On December 24, Russell was arrested in his New York office on three charges of receiving stolen property and one charge of conspiring to defraud the government. He was shipped to Washington and clapped into jail. Bail was set at $500,000, a figure that outraged Russell because Bailey, arrested on three charges of theft, was released on only $5,000 bail. Russell's friends in the East raised $300,000, and his friends out West rallied to his defense with pledges of two million dollars in securities. After a few days in jail, he was released on reduced bail of $300,000.

In January of 1861, the House of Representatives set up a Select Committee to investigate the whole mal-

odorous mess. In hearings that went on through February, 46 witnesses were examined and cross-examined. Russell testified on four occasions: he was alternately evasive and frank, and frequently confused as to dates and sums of money involved.

The Select Committee, having weighed the huge mass of contradictory testimony, then produced a report. One of its conclusions was that Secretary of War Floyd, who had since resigned and fled to Virginia — by then a state of the Confederacy — had illegally approved acceptances not only from Russell but from several other businessmen. The report also noted that President Buchanan had known of and forbidden Floyd's traffic in acceptances, but had not pursued the matter. Another conclusion by the committee was that Secretary of the Interior Jacob Thompson, a second Cabinet member who had resigned under fire, was guilty of "neglect" in guarding the stolen Indian bonds.

Bailey, who had confessed his crime, was never brought to trial; he avoided summonses until the whole

108

The month blood flowed across the Pony's path

Only once in the history of the Pony Express did the mail not go through. That was in May 1860 during the Paiute War, a clash whose principal hero was a peace-loving Indian.

Some 6,000 Paiutes in Nevada had suffered a winter of fierce blizzards, "freezing and starving to death by scores," according to a Carson City paper. The Paiutes blamed their woes on the white man, who committed such acts as hacking down trees from which the Indians gathered nuts. By spring, the whole tribe was spoiling for war—except a chief named Numaga. For three days Numaga fasted and argued for peace. But on May 7 a few hotheads stole away and raided the Williams Station of the Pony Express, killing five men.

Over the next weeks other isolated whites in Paiute country were ambushed and slaughtered. The Pony Express was a special target; in all, seven of its relay stations were razed, 16 employees were killed and 150 horses were driven off.

Through all this, Chief Numaga tried to restrain his tribesmen. One day, when Paiute warriors decoyed a pursuing party of whites into ambush, Numaga burst out of the Indian lines waving a white handkerchief, hoping to make peace on the spot. The whites' response was to open fire, and a pitched battle ensued.

By early June the Army accomplished what Numaga could not: an end to the war that had taken more than 75 lives. The Pony resumed operations; as for Numaga, he resumed leadership of his people, a chieftain whose wisdom stood sadly confirmed.

Paiute chief Numaga holds a symbol of the warring spirit he tried to control in his tribesmen.

matter was forgotten in the heat of civil war. Russell was brought to trial before the Criminal Court in Washington late in January 1861, after he had testified before the Select Committee. And it was on that technicality that Russell's clever lawyer appealed for the dismissal of all charges. A law on the books since 1857 exempted witnesses before Congressional committees from criminal prosecution on matters involved in their testimony. Russell's case was dismissed.

Though no charges against him had been proved, he did not get off scot-free. Almost at once he paid the ultimate price for the bond scandal: bankruptcy.

Even as the Select Committee was holding its hearings that January, Congress began its annual debates over mail contracts for the year. The Pony Express had proved that the central route was superior to the long southern route, and the first order of business was a postal appropriations bill that called for daily mail service across the central part of the continent. The bill passed the House early in February, and it was on the Senate floor when news came that Confederate forces had cut Butterfield Overland Mail's stage line, halting transcontinental movement of mail by the southern route. Endangered by imminent warfare, the line had to be provided for somehow—and the provisions were hardly to Russell's liking.

An amendment to the bill was introduced, requiring that Butterfield Overland Mail switch its operations northward to the central overland route. Moreover, the amendment also eliminated competitive bidding for the mail contract on that route. There was a wry irony in this outcome for John Butterfield himself; only the year before he had been ousted from his own company for failing to pay large debts he owed a major creditor, Wells, Fargo & Company. If anyone stood to gain from the switch north, it was Wells, Fargo, by now in full control of the Butterfield operation.

For Russell, the measure passed by Congress was an even worse blow. Few Congressmen cared. With the bond scandal echoing through Washington, they were not about to trust him with a huge mail subsidy, which turned out to be one million dollars a year.

The bypassing of the C.O.C. sealed the doom of Russell, Majors & Waddell. The three old partners had realized as much when the bond scandal broke. Their known liabilities now exceeded their assets by around two million dollars and they had no choice but to go into bankruptcy.

For a time, Russell deluded himself with forlorn hopes of making a comeback. While no freight wagon of the firm of Russell, Majors & Waddell would ever roll across the plains again, the C.O.C. had relay stations, coaches, livestock and employees that the Overland Mail Company—now divested of Butterfield's name—needed badly. In March of 1861, Russell worked out a brilliant deal that breathed new life into the bankrupt C.O.C. He relinquished the western half of the route to the Overland Mail Company—a meager gift since Congress had already awarded it the whole route. Overland and C.O.C. would share the million-dollar mail almost equally, and each would pay for and control Pony Express operations on its segment of the route. For the first time, the Pony's deficit was funded by government subsidy instead of by Russell himself.

Yet these arrangements were a hollow triumph. Although Russell still held the title of president of the C.O.C., the creditors of the company understandably wanted a steadier hand at the helm. On April 26, 1861, the board of directors forced Russell to resign.

The man elected to replace him was a perfect link between the past and the future. He was a lawyer, Bela M. Hughes, an old friend of Russell's who had managed his affairs in St. Joseph. Hughes was also a cousin of Ben Holladay, an upstart freight operator who had quietly been extending credit to the Pony Express and thereby building up a claim on the parent C.O.C. When Hughes mounted the throne of the bankrupt stagecoach empire, it was only as regent; Holladay became the power behind the throne. In March of 1862, he was ready to take power himself. By then the C.O.C. had conclusively failed to pay off the debts due him. So Holladay got a court order to have the firm sold at auction and he acquired it for only $100,000. With the com-

---

After Wells, Fargo became agent for the western half of the Pony Express, letters that went by Pony bore not only government postage but the company's own stamps, placed at or near the top left corner of the envelopes. The one dollar denomination on the upper envelope paid for a half-ounce letter; the "garter stamp" on the lower envelope means payment due. This envelope reached San Francisco in the final Pony pouch, which arrived on November 20, 1861.

Pony Expressmen made perfect subjects for pulp epics, and none more so than ex-rider Buffalo Bill Cody, who graced the cover of this tome after he had gone on to become the impresario of his "Wild West Show."

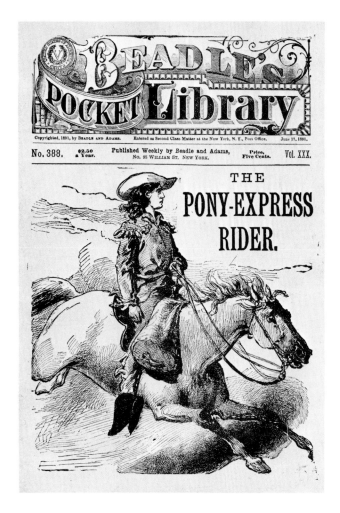

pany, Holladay also inherited Russell's title—"The Napoleon of the Plains."

After Russell's ouster as president of the C.O.C., he quickly passed from the national scene. Henceforth, it was all downhill—not only for him, but for his two former partners. Waddell weathered bankruptcy best; he sold his spacious home in Lexington, Missouri, to his son for one dollar but continued to live there. Alexander Majors started all over again in freighting, but after a few poor seasons gave up the business for good. Soon he drifted into prospecting, and that didn't work either. Then he disappeared from sight for many years, and was rediscovered as an old man, living alone in a shack near Denver, writing his memoirs of the frontier years. The man who found him was none other than Buffalo Bill Cody, whom Majors had hired to ride for the Pony Express. Cody paid to have Majors' manuscript edited and

published, but it was a financial failure. By that time, few people remembered Alexander Majors, and those who did remembered him not for his great freighting firm, but for a sideline Russell had forced him into against his will—the Pony Express.

Russell's fall was perhaps even steeper than Majors'. For a little while, friends still listened to his seductive visionary schemes and even lent him sums for speculation; in Colorado, he organized two road-building companies and incorporated two towns. But the projects soon petered out. Russell then moved to New York and acquired a partnership in a brokerage house that specialized in speculative mining stock. In this role, he went broke again, and his splendid home at 686 Broadway was sold out from under him. Before he died of a stroke in 1872, he suffered what must have been, for him, two bitter humiliations. He was reduced to selling Tic Sano, a patent remedy for neuralgia. And he had to write a humble letter to Waddell, begging for —and receiving—the $200 he needed to file yet another petition for bankruptcy.

The Pony Express galloped on after Russell was removed as its guiding spirit, but its life began to ebb measurably through the summer of 1861 as work speeded up on the East-West telegraph line.

By late August, one wire-stringing crew had advanced westward 90 miles beyond Fort Kearney, and the Pony soon abandoned service east of that point. Another crew made rapid eastward progress from Carson City, sometimes advancing 25 miles a day. The fast-dwindling gap between the telegraph poles was finally closed in Salt Lake City on October 24, 1861.

Five days later, after some throat-clearing local messages, the first coast-to-coast telegram was ceremoniously dispatched. In it, California Chief Justice Stephen Field congratulated President Lincoln on the completion of the line and pledged his state's continuing loyalty to the Union in these sad days of civil strife.

Soon autopsies were being performed on the Pony in the public prints. Calculations indicated that it cost the Pony about $16 for each of the nearly 35,000 pieces of mail it had delivered; and it had received, on the average, $3 per letter in delivery charges. The net losses for 18 months of operation, including the four-week hiatus during the Paiute War, were estimated at anywhere between $300,000 and $500,000. Set against

this deficit, the Pony had conclusively proved the superiority of the central route, roughly marking out the path later to be followed by the transcontinental railroad, and it had provided countless stories of dedication and courage for a people badly in need of such relief and reassurance. The Pony had profited no one, but it had immeasurably enriched the whole country.

But the Pony did not die immediately after the telegraph gap was closed on October 24. Here and there, riders continued to make short local runs — almost as if the habit were too strong to break. On November 20, 1861, the last rider on the last run handed over the mail in San Francisco and began looking for a new job. By then, the death of the Pony had been a foregone conclusion for so long that no one noted the rider's name.

Newspapers had already done their mourning for the Pony. The California *Pacific* said it as well as anyone:

"A fast and faithful friend has the Pony been to our far-off state. Summer and winter, storm and shine, day and night, he has traveled like a weaver's shuttle back and forth til now his work is done. Goodbye, Pony! No proud and star-caparisoned charger in the war field has ever done so great, so true and so good a work as thine. No pampered and world-famed racer of the turf will ever win from you the proud fame of the fleet courser of the continent. You came to us with tidings that made your feet beautiful on the tops of the mountains; tidings of the world's great life, of nations rising for liberty and winning the day of battles, and nations' defeats and reverses. We have looked to you as those who wait for the morning, and how seldom did you fail us! When days were months and hours weeks, how you thrilled us out of our pain and suspense, to know the best or know the worst. You have served us well!"

Telegraph lines strung from East and West met in 1861 at this Western Union office in Salt Lake City. Though the telegraph was incomparably faster than Pony Express, rates were so high—as much as 75 cents a word—that frugal spenders had special cause to mourn the Pony's passing.

Ex-jockey Johnny Fry, who rode the first leg of the first westbound Pony Express run, later met death as a Union scout.

A proud band of men who rode into history

They were special and they knew it. The self-assurance in the faces of the Pony Expressmen pictured on these and the following pages reflects a certainty that they did a demanding job, and did it well. Many, though young, had already proved themselves as bullwhackers or broncobusters before signing on with the Pony. "They were looking for something exciting," said Bill Cates of his fellow couriers, "and the Pony was just what they wanted."

Charley Cliff called his occupation "the lonesomest kind of a job" and William Campbell admitted "it was strenuous work at any time." But the challenges rarely fazed the Pony Expressmen. Richard Erastus Egan once rode 330 miles, about twice his scheduled distance, simply to oblige another rider who wanted to take time off to visit his sweetheart.

These lusty bachelors in their late teens and early twenties snatched romance on the run. The dashing Johnny Fry so charmed the girls along his route that they were said to wait by the wayside to proffer cakes and cookies they had baked just for him. One of these girls, according to legend, invented the doughnut so that Johnny could spear the snack on one finger at full gallop.

Fry did not have long to enjoy the adulation. When the Civil War broke out he enlisted in the Union forces and soon fell a casualty. A number of other ex-Pony riders died young, victims of frontier crime or of vigilante justice. But sturdy physiques sustained many more into ripe old age. Some had successful careers in business, ranching, politics and the professions. Four became Mormon bishops. All of them wore their memories of the Pony as pridefully as medals. Bill Campbell, who had carried the text of Abraham Lincoln's first inaugural address westward in his saddlebag, cherished one of the most satisfying memories of all. Every one of his fellow couriers, Campbell recalled, felt that he was "helping to make history."

A Pony Expressman at 13, David Jay lived to 83.

On a bet, Jack Keetley rode 24 hours nonstop.

117

Charley Cliff ended up in freighting and once repulsed an Indian band singlehandedly with two arrows in him.

Here a mature-looking 20 or so, John Burnett later carved out a career as a Wells, Fargo agent in Salt Lake City.

Richard Erastus Egan, a devout Mormon, survived many close calls with Indians to become a bishop of his church.

Irish-born Patrick McEneaney, pictured at age 19, rode five months for the Pony and 10 years as a U.S. dragoon.

4 | A stagecoach empire

By the 1860s, the stagecoach reigned as the most popular means of carrying people, mail and valuables across the West. But the choice of stage lines was limited: sooner or later, most travelers found themselves paying their fares at offices such as the one at left — one of many in a far-flung stage network owned and imperiously operated by a single individual, Ben Holladay.

For five years, from 1862 through 1866, Holladay enjoyed a virtual monopoly of the eastern half of the central overland route, an advantage he maintained by piratical methods against his rivals. Expectably, his critics were many. To Denver's *Rocky Mountain News* he was "a nuisance to be abated by Congress." A competitor branded him "wholly destitute of honesty, morality and common decency." On the other hand, no less respectable a journal than *Harper's Weekly* rated Holladay as "the greatest organizer of transportation the West has produced." Both his critics and admirers were right.

One of Holladay's myriad coaches prepares to depart from his Denver office.

123

Ruthless ruler of the Western roads

One night, at the summit of his career in the mid-1860s when idolators were describing him as the Stagecoach King. Ben Holladay was traveling eastward from California enthroned in his private Concord coach. It was a glittering rig with gold scrollwork around the doors and silver-encased side lamps, and out in the darkness, racing along at the ends of the ribbons, were six matched dapple-gray horses, as famous for their speed as for their stylish appearance.

No journey the proprietor made on the Holladay Overland Mail & Express lines ever spared the horses, but on this occasion he had more reason than usual for haste. His wife, Ann, whom he had brought West with him on a business trip, lay opposite him in a corner of the coach, sleeping; she was ill, and he wanted to get her back to the comfort of their opulent mansion in Washington, D.C. They still had a way to go; the coach was only then nearing Denver and it would be several days more before they reached the outermost railhead in Kansas and the relief of a sleeping car.

Ann did not stir even when the grays suddenly reined up so short that Holladay was nearly pitched out of his seat. And she slept on when the coach door was wrenched open and her husband found himself looking into the muzzle of a double-barreled shotgun.

According to his own later account, Holladay instantly thought of a number of things. His coat was buttoned high, but he wasn't certain it was buttoned quite high enough to conceal the gleam of the emerald stickpin for which he had paid $8,000 the week before in San Francisco. He thought of the $40,000 in gold hidden in a money belt around his waist. Most of all,

Owner of a transportation empire, luxury-loving Ben Holladay sports a suit tailored in France and a watch fob made of a tiger claw—an apt symbol of his combativeness.

he wondered if the robber knew who his victim was.

"Come on! Shell out!" demanded the voice behind the gun. Cringing back from the light of the reading lamp inside the coach, Holladay fumbled in his pockets and brought out his loose money—a few hundred dollars. Then, still trying to keep light away from the emerald, he unhitched his watch and handed it over, along with its five-pound chain forged from gold nuggets.

Outside he heard another voice demanding that the driver "throw down the box"—the repository in which valuables were stored and shipped. Holladay's nose began to itch abominably, and his hands instinctively reached toward it.

"Keep 'em up or I'll blow a hole in your head big enough for a jackrabbit," advised the man with the gun.

"But I've got to scratch my nose," Holladay protested in desperation.

"Keep 'em up. I'll scratch it for you," the voice said. Thereupon the muzzle of the shotgun came forward the few remaining inches and scraped back and forth across the nose to soothe its suffering.

When the highwaymen left at last, Holladay was caught somewhere between relief and indignation. He still had the emerald and the $40,000, and his wife slumbered on; on the other hand, he was undeniably irked at the bandits' failure to recognize the nobly caparisoned stagecoach of the most famous—or perhaps most notorious—businessman between the Missouri and San Francisco.

Despite the loss of his loose money and watch, the incident was not without profit to Holladay. The story of the holdup became his favorite anecdote. He found it useful for regaling Wall Street bankers, state legislators, United States Senators and Postmasters General, whose support was essential to keeping all his enterprises afloat. Moreover, even if Ben Holladay had suffered the loss of his stickpin and his money belt, he

Shops on Commercial Street in Atchison, Kansas, prominently advertise their wares to catch the eye of travelers in transit. Ben Holladay's choice of the town as his eastern terminus in 1862 swelled the influx.

would not have been grievously injured except in pride.

At the time of the holdup, he probably had no precise measure of his net worth, but it was a lot. His Holladay Overland Mail & Express Company (more modestly called the Overland Stage Line during its early years) operated 3,145 miles of stagecoach and freight lines in Kansas, Nebraska, Colorado, Nevada, Utah, Oregon, Idaho and Montana. As sole owner, Holladay had at his command 15,000 employees and 20,000 vehicles, including 110 of the world's finest stagecoaches built by the Abbot-Downing Company of Concord, New Hampshire. In his stables and corrals were 150,000 draft animals: oxen, mustangs, durable Missouri mules and swift, magnificently sturdy Morgan horses. The United States Post Office was paying him $365,000 a year to carry mail on the central overland route; and he was grossing up to $350 a seat on the run between Atchison, Kansas, and Salt Lake City.

Yet overland transport was only one of Holladay's enterprises. He also owned 16 steamers that plied the Pacific Coast and ventured as far as China. And he owned slaughter houses, grain mills, packing plants, whiskey distilleries, general stores, thousands of acres of land, and gold and silver mines.

A man of such means could afford to indulge his penchant for creature comforts — as well as his wife's yearning for entree into high society — so Holladay also maintained a number of lavish residences. His home at 1131 K Street in northwest Washington, conveniently near the White House, was guarded at the portal by two seven-foot-high bronze lions, purchased in Italy for $6,000 each. Inside, in addition to crystal chandeliers and old masters, was a library of the classics, beautifully bound but never opened except by maids with feather dusters and an occasional insomniac house guest.

In New York City, Holladay also kept a brownstone mansion on Fifth Avenue, not far from the Wall Street office where he dealt shrewdly with the barons of finance. North of the city, near White Plains, sprawled his premier residence, Ophir Farm — a million-dollar, 200-room palace surrounded by 1,000 acres stocked with deer, antelope and genuine prairie buffalo. Measured against that estate, the first house Holladay had built in the town of Weston, Missouri, seemed a trifle constricting. Still, it was better than a shack, being made of stone with 16 rooms and — a Holladay trade-

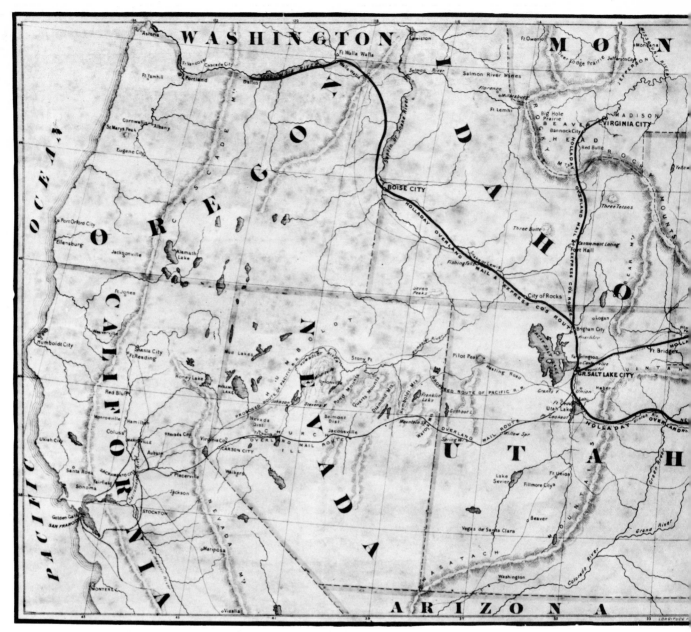

A transportation map produced in the mid-1860s charts the Holladay line's main routes from the Missouri River through Denver to Salt Lake

mark — a central hallway wide enough so that a Conestoga wagon and a six-horse team could have been driven through it from front door to back.

Ben Holladay owed all this power, pelf and circumstance to himself alone. He was born in 1819, one of seven children of a hardscrabble Kentucky farmer. He grew up sturdy and muscular — topping out finally at six feet two — and conscious of his swarthy good looks. Even as a youth, he was full of fire and soaring ambition, no candidate for the menial striving required by life on a farm. Adventure, he knew, lay westward. At 16 he ran away and found a job in a general store in Weston, across the Missouri River from Fort Leav-

enworth. But working for somebody else did not fit Ben's vision of the future. While still in his teens he was running his own tavern, mainly serving explosive frontier whiskey to soldiers from the fort. By the time he was 21 he had a drugstore and a dirt-floored hotel and began sending for his brothers to help him.

While acquiring these worldly goods, Holladay ingratiated himself with some important, if unlikely, friends. Missouri was then in a ferment of animosity toward a group of Mormons who had founded a new town called Far West and who appeared to crave ever more autonomy in their local affairs. Late in 1838, Governor Lillburn Boggs mobilized the state militia

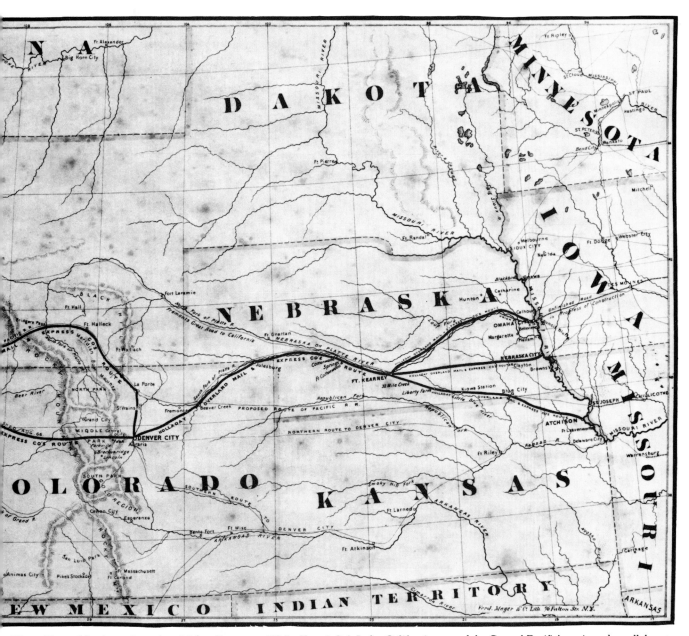

City, with two Northwest branches. Lighter lines trace Wells, Fargo's Salt Lake-California run and the Central Pacific's projected parallel route.

and ordered Colonel Alexander Doniphan to drive the Mormons out of the state. The assignment was a case of spectacularly poor judgment on the Governor's part: Doniphan, a lawyer in civilian life, had represented the Mormon prophet Joseph Smith and sympathized with the plight of Smith's followers.

Having sized up Holladay's zest for action, Doniphan made the young man his unofficial courier and sent him on a series of visits to the town of Far West carrying forewarning of the Governor's strategy and advice for Mormon leader Brigham Young. Young was grateful to Holladay as the bearer of useful intelligence and came to trust him. Years later, 1,200 miles to the

west in the valley of the Great Salt Lake, Holladay would cash in on Young's high regard.

In the meantime, Holladay began to perfect the straightforward philosophy that was to guide him all his life: when a man saw what he wanted, he took it with no more ceremony than necessary. He was 21 when he fell in love with a beautiful red-haired schoolgirl, Ann Notley Calvert. Ann's father was a judge and her mother a woman of great social pretensions. When they objected to Holladay's suit, he borrowed a fast mare, rode to Ann's school outside Weston, plucked her from the classroom and swept her off to the home of her uncle, a man of more romantic spirit than her parents.

A local magistrate was waiting to marry the couple.

Six years later, in 1846, Holladay came to grips with the destiny that was to make him master of a transportation empire. He mortgaged his holdings, bought 14 wagons and 60 mules, took on a cargo of trade goods and set out for Santa Fe, where he unloaded 28-cent tea for $1.50 a pound and garnered comparable profits on other commodities.

Three years after that trading expedition—the first of many—Holladay came up with a scheme that promised even higher returns. He thought of the service he had rendered the Mormons, who by now were firmly entrenched in Utah, and decided that they were very likely in sore need of manufactures from the East. A Weston merchant, Theodore Warner, supplied the goods—$70,000 worth of clothing, implements and window glass—and Holladay provided the wagons.

Hoping the Mormons remembered him favorably, but aware of their antipathy toward all nonbelievers, he took the precaution of obtaining a letter of recommendation from his old mentor, Alexander Doniphan, to Brigham Young. When Holladay's freight-wagon train reached Salt Lake City, the letter achieved its intended effect. Young read it and thought back from this tall, powerful man before him to the youth who had sneaked through Missouri militia lines to the town of Far West 11 years before. In church the following Sunday, before his assembled people, the Mormon leader bestowed his blessing: "Brother Holladay has a stock of goods for sale and can be trusted as an honorable dealer."

The next year Holladay doubled the size of his cargo to Salt Lake City—and disposed of it as handily as before. This time, however, he did not return to Missouri. Beyond the Sierra the gold rush was on and Holladay scented the chance for a killing. In trading his goods to the Mormons he now decided to ask not for cash but for Mormon cattle at six dollars a head. Despite predictions of disaster, he drove the herd over the Sierra Nevada into California and put the stock out to pasture in the Sacramento Valley to fatten up after the exhausting journey. Holladay knew he would be bankrupt if he failed to sell the cattle, but he maintained an air of cool unconcern. When the Pacific Mail Steamship Company sent word that it might consider buying some of his beef, he replied that he was too busy to come and bargain, but airily added that he might be will-

As a gold-smelting center for nearby mines, Black Hawk Point, Colorado, rated daily service by a Holladay stage from Denver. Below this 1862 view is the town seal, with a Latin motto—"Let It Be Saved."

A receipt for shipment via Overland Stage of $87,000 in Treasury notes and gold dust limits — in fine print — Holladay's liability for loss. The shipping fee was slightly more than 1 per cent of the value — $930.

THE OVERLAND STAGE LINE,

FOR CARRYING THE

GREAT

Through Mails

Ben Holladay.

FROM THE

ATLANTIC

TO THE

Pacific States

Proprietor.

Denver City Dec 6th 1864

Received from *Mess Clark & Co*

in apparent good order, *One Letter with two Packages.* said to contain

Gold Dust valued at Twenty five Thousand ($25000.00) Gold or Sixty two thousand ($62000.00) Dollars in Treasury notes.

MARKED "

Northrup & Chick. Nassau Street New York city

IT IS AGREED, and is a part of the consideration of this contract, that the OVERLAND STAGE LINE are not to be held responsible for any loss or damage except as forwarders only; nor for any loss or damage by the dangers of railroad, ocean or river navigation, leakage, breakage, fire, or from any cause whatever, unless the same be proved to have occurred from the fraud or gross neglect of ourselves, our agents or servants, or unless insured by us, (in no case do we insure against leakage or breakage,) and in no event is this Company to be liable beyond their route as herein receipted. VALUED UNDER FIFTY DOLLARS, unless otherwise herein stated. ALL KINDS OF FRAGILE WARE AT SHIPPER'S RISK.

For the Overland Stage Line,

Charges 930.00   *C S Dahler* AGENT.

ing to discuss the matter if the company officials came to him. For the rest of his life, he remembered that gambit with pride. Pacific Mail paid 30 cents a pound for stock that had cost him less than a penny a pound.

At this point, Holladay was comfortably rich. He could have scaled down his speculative maneuvers and joined Ann in her principal preoccupation — social climbing. But the gentle life was not for him; he was harnessed to a runaway imagination and a craving for power. In the next few years he dealt aggressively in distilleries, packing plants and freighting — making work for his brothers — and bought into Nevada's fabulous Ophir Mine, which was to bestow its name on his grandiose farm in New York. Then, in 1859, Holladay joined forces with perhaps the only other man in the West who could match his own breadth of vision and artful dealing: William Russell of Missouri.

No love was lost between them. Russell, as senior partner of the great freighting firm of Russell, Majors & Waddell, had refused to lend Holladay money at a time

when Ben was trying to get started in freighting. But although Holladay had a long memory for injury, he saw no objection to Russell's making a profit so long as he himself could profit even more handsomely.

Holladay initiated the alliance. When Russell casually confided to him that the Army had given his company a special contract to haul 843,000 pounds of flour all the way from Missouri to its posts in Utah — at $22.50 a hundredweight upon delivery — Holladay had a proposal. Given his friendship with the Mormons, he suggested to Russell, there was a better way. Instead of hauling in Missouri flour, let Holladay buy Mormon flour at seven dollars a hundredweight on the spot in Salt Lake City and deliver it to local Army posts.

Russell pointed out that the Army had already purchased the flour — a superfine variety — from millers in St. Louis. To Holladay this was no problem; he proposed that the St. Louis flour be hauled to Denver, where it could be sold at $40 a hundredweight. Though this arrangement was a flagrant violation of the Army contract, Russell found it irresistibly attractive; without a qualm, he said he knew someone who could help stave off trouble with the Army. Russell paid a call on Secretary of War John Floyd in Washington and won his consent to the plan — by offering him, it was later alleged, a share of the illegal profits. The deal went through without a hitch. But Holladay's cut was far greater than Russell or Floyd knew, for he was reportedly able to procure the Mormon flour for the Army at only one dollar a hundredweight — six dollars less than he told the others he had to pay.

There seemed to be no limits to Secretary Floyd's willingness to cooperate with his friends. That same year the Army decided to auction off some mules it had in Utah, along with wagons, sets of harness and other items. Curiously, there was no urgent need for this auction to be held; none of the items could be described as surplus. Somehow the Army failed to publicize the auction dates in the East. But Holladay showed up and successfully bid on 782 mules, which had cost the Army $175 a head, at $75 each. Added to this bargain, he picked up 21 wagons, which had cost the Army $130 apiece, at $20.

Two years later, in 1861, Holladay closed in on his erstwhile collaborator, William Russell. Though he had never forgotten Russell's original refusal to lend him money, he had ostensibly turned the other cheek. Now, however, he found himself, no doubt to his relish, in the role of Russell's creditor.

From time to time he had been lending Russell, Majors & Waddell sums of money as two of the firm's major ventures — the Pony Express and the Central Overland stage line — sank ever deeper into debt. In July 1861, Holladay had been given a deed of trust to Central Overland's properties as collateral on loans totaling $208,000. Presumably for fear of alarming other creditors of the line, Holladay had not registered the deed; but he held it over the heads of Central Overland's directors as a kind of Damocles' sword.

In November they issued a $400,000 bond in his favor, together with a mortgage on the company. But the Central Overland was in a fatal spiral. Two weeks later Holladay declared the bond forfeit and called on the trustees to seize the property and advertise a sale of its assets. Its other creditors — small men certain to be grievously hurt by what, for Holladay, was simply a

business deal — obtained an injunction to block the sale, but a Kansas judge, apparently a Holladay admirer, quickly dissolved the injunction.

On March 21, 1862, with nobody else appearing to bid, Holladay bought the stage line's assets for just $100,000. In one last effort to head him off, two directors of the defunct company sued in U.S. Circuit Court in Kansas to have the sale declared illegal. They won, but to no avail; the federal marshal for Kansas reported that he could not enforce the court order because he could find no officer of the company on whom to serve a summons. The statement was probably accurate, since Holladay — by this time Central Overland's sole owner and officer — was usually in New York, Washington or San Francisco and seldom appeared in Kansas except for brief visits.

The system Holladay took over, extending 1,200 miles from Atchison to Salt Lake City, constituted slightly more than half of the central overland route to California; the western leg was handled by the Overland Mail Company, formerly of the Oxbow Route and much experienced in long-distance staging. Very little in Holladay's freighting experience had prepared him for stagecoaching — a far different and more complex pursuit. For one thing, staging meant passengers, and passengers were somewhat more delicate and a lot more demanding than sacks of flour. For another, staging implied speed — matters of days and hours instead of the months a freight-wagon train could take. Stagecoaching also meant meeting the delivery schedules of the express companies and the U.S. postal service.

But stagecoaching, as defined by Holladay's shrewd, rapacious mind, also meant big money, and he had every intention of making it. To begin with, the drivers he hired were the best in the business. Handling six fast horses in the hitch — or mules where the terrain was muddy or sandy — they were expected to maintain an average speed of five miles an hour. This called for a steady trot on the trail but usually — in keeping with the owner's flair for showmanship — a race-horse start and a headlong finish. The run between Salt Lake and Atchison generally took 11 days. As if to demonstrate the relative ease of meeting this schedule, Holladay once raced his own coach a greater distance — from San Francisco to Atchison — in just 12 days and two hours. The trip cost him $20,000 in dead or ruined horseflesh. ◉

A pair of New Englanders who helped win the West

Because the Concord coach proved itself a superb performer for its arduous job, the New Hampshire factory that built it became internationally famous on the strength of that one product. The success and fame of the Concord were attributable to the lofty standards of the factory's owners, Lewis Downing and J. Stephens Abbot. They were such diligent day-to-day managers of their plant in Concord (for which their product was named) that no coach ever left the shop without the proprietors' personal inspection.

The Concord's virtues were speed, splendor and extraordinary durability. Downing and Abbot were so careful in choosing and seasoning their timber —basswood for cabin panels, elm, oak and hickory for running gear— that the wood often outlasted the ironwork. Stage men said of the Concord, "It don't break down; it only wears out" —and even the wearing out was debatable. One coach, shipped around the Horn, sank with the vessel near San Francisco. Raised after a month under water and dried out, it was still in service 50 years later.

Each vehicle was gleamingly painted —the colors varied— and each carriage exterior was decorated with an original landscape or other artwork. So impressive were the results that a veteran driver, William Banning, declared the Concord was "as tidy and graceful as a lady and had, like the lady, scarcely a straight line in its body."

The collaboration that made this achievement possible began in 1826 when Downing, an ambitious wheelwright, hired Abbot, an expert coachbuilder. The partnership, with names in alphabetical order, was formed two years later and lasted until 1847. For the next 18 years the two craftsmen were rivals, but after Downing retired, his son re-established the old partnership, and the Abbot-Downing Company survived into the 20th Century.

An engraving of the Concord coach factory in the 1880s reveals its success under the heirs of Abbot and Downing *(right)*. The six-acre plant employed almost 250 craftsmen producing 2,000 vehicles per year.

J. STEPHENS ABBOT

LEWIS DOWNING

ABBOT DOWNING COMPANY

THE GREAT CONCORD COACH

Concord coaches, including this model owned by Wells, Fargo, weighed more than a ton, stood eight feet high and cost from $1,200 to $1,500. They could accommodate as many as 21 passengers—nine seated inside on three upholstered benches and a dozen more on the roof. The driver's seat, or box, was shared by an express messenger riding shotgun over precious cargo. The boot, a leather-covered receptacle under the driver's seat, held mail and a strongbox of valuables. Express parcels and personal baggage went into a bigger rear boot.

The teams that drew the Concords—four or six horses—had their task made easier by the sturdiness of the vehicle itself. The most ingenious design feature was the suspension of the carriage on two thoroughbraces, three-inch-thick strips of leather that served as shock absorbers. The rocking motion created by the thoroughbraces bothered some passengers, but moved Mark Twain to lovingly describe the Concord as "a cradle on wheels."

Rear Boot

Brake Shoe

136

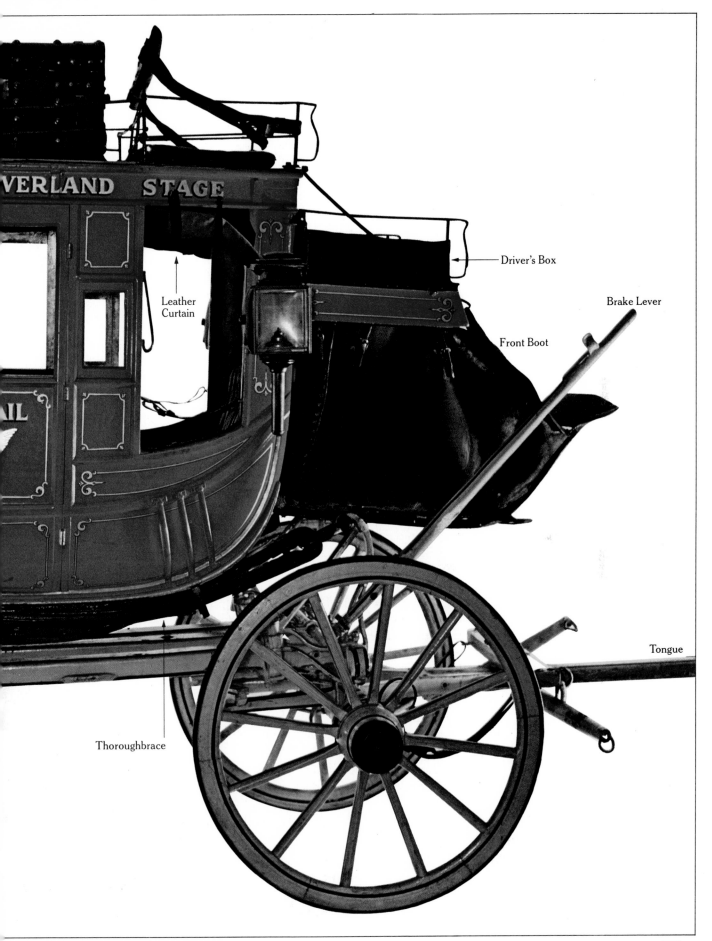

Driver's Box

Brake Lever

Front Boot

Leather
Curtain

Thoroughbrace

Tongue

olladay dressed his stage drivers like dandies, in wide-brimmed sombreros, high-heeled boots and velvet-trimmed corduroy uniforms. In winter he furnished them with overcoats of Irish wool lined with blue flannel. They were a proud and haughty lot, equipped with nine-foot-long whips as their badge of office. Holladay, although a lusty bottle man himself, would permit no drinking on duty; but off duty his drivers contrived to impress the *Rocky Mountain News* as a "drunken, carousing set in the main." They could afford to carouse, for Holladay paid them handsomely: $100 a month in normal times, $200 when Indians were on the warpath.

Holladay's coaches were as eye-arresting as his drivers, painted in bright red and lettered in gilt with the legends "Holladay Overland Mail & Express" and "U.S. Mail." All this glitter may have given a passenger the impression that he was about to set out on a festive journey, but he paid well for the experience. The fare from Atchison to Salt Lake City was $150—paid in advance—and it sometimes rose as high as $350 when Holladay could credibly cite the risk of encountering hostile Indians somewhere along the way west. Travelers were often regaled en route with verses, some unprintable, of the Holladay *Driver's Song,* which expressed the company's *esprit de corps,* and perhaps helped relieve the sting of that fare. One of the more decorous verses went:

You ask me for our leader, I'll soon inform you, then;
It's Holladay they call him, and often only Ben;
If you can read the papers, it's easy work to scan;
He beats the world in staging now, or any other man.

At the peak of Holladay's staging operations in the mid-1860s, passenger revenues often grossed $60,000 a month; in addition, the company harvested sums of $90,000 to $140,000 each month from shipments of gold dust, bullion and other valuable cargo, which the Holladay stages carried for 50 cents a pound under contracts with the nation's three leading express agencies: Wells, Fargo; American Express; and United States Express. Carrying the United States mail ensured further profits. Although it was not the largest source of revenue, the mail subsidy guaranteed a steady income that offset fluctuations in the company's other sources of revenue. Over the course of Holladay's five years in

staging, the Post Office Department paid him almost two million dollars.

Holladay never denied, and his compatriots never doubted, his ruthless instincts; and no notions of fair play ever interfered with his prosecution of business for profit. He had no sooner taken over William Russell's old company than he moved against a small-fry stage operator who happened also to be sheriff of Denver. As a sideline, the sheriff was running a feeder stage line between Denver and Central City, a distance of only 30-odd miles, for a charge of six dollars per passenger. When the very first Holladay stage left Atchison, it carried the proprietor's personal instructions to his Denver agents to put a competing stage on the Central City trail, at a cut rate of two dollars per passenger. After the sheriff's modest operation expired as expected, Holladay jacked up his fare to $12, jammed some of his passengers not in stagecoaches but in double-decker omnibuses and slowed the running time by half.

The same competitiveness was demonstrated when the gold strikes of 1862-1863 in Montana and Idaho created an urgent new demand for a stage line north from Salt Lake City, and a few courageous entrepreneurs set out to fill the need. The Alder Gulch strike in Montana caused the overnight growth of Virginia City, whereupon three stage lines—respectively run by men named Oliver, Peabody and Caldwell—immediately began to serve the new Golconda, each charging $150 a seat per passenger and one dollar a letter for mail on the 400-mile run from Salt Lake. At first Holladay was satisfied with doubling the fare on his route from Atchison to Salt Lake, but the new route proved irresistibly attractive—particularly since he knew he had the weight to drive the others off.

While the three entrepreneurs got the public used to the route, Holladay visited Postmaster General Montgomery Blair in Washington and discussed the situation. Out of this mission came two mail contracts. One of them was for $186,000 a year to carry mail between Salt Lake and Walla Walla, Washington Territory, by way of the gold-rich Boise Basin in Idaho. The other, at $13,271 a year, was for an offshoot of the first route, providing service to Virginia City and Bannock City in Montana.

In September 1864, Holladay set his fare between Salt Lake and Virginia City at $25—$125 less than

The murderous career of Captain Jack Slade

In a grim scene re-created by artist Charles Russell, Jack Slade blasts away at the bullet-ridden body of Jules Reni, slumped against a corral post.

Shrewd as he was in acquiring other people's properties, Ben Holladay suffered considerable chagrin when, in 1862, some 200 miles of stage line extending from Julesburg, Colorado, westward into Wyoming became part of his domain. He soon found that the Sweetwater Division, as this part of his central overland route was called, hardly constituted a good buy. Crooked employees were making off with its cash, and horse thieves with its stock; attacks by bandits and Indians were throwing coaches off schedule.

Still, the Sweetwater line had one notable asset—the division superintendent, Joseph Alfred ("Captain Jack") Slade. A soft-spoken, short, roly-poly fellow, Slade was in fact a fugitive from a murder charge in Illinois, and the suspected perpetrator of as many as 26 killings in all. With Holladay's blessing, Slade imposed so forceful a

stewardship that Sweetwater Division coaches steadily improved their record of punctuality and security. "True," wrote Mark Twain, "in order to bring about this wholesome change Slade had to kill several men —some say three, others say four and others six—but the world was the richer for their loss."

One victim was Jules Reni, who had been stationmaster at Julesburg before the Slade era. After Slade reclaimed some stage horses Reni had stolen, Reni caught Slade unarmed one day and emptied a revolver into him. But Slade survived, and after recovering he had Reni hunted down and brought to him by company agents. He lashed his prisoner to a corral post overnight in the cold, then in the morning began using him for target practice. Between pistol shots, Slade gulped whiskey and gleefully

told Reni where he was going to hit him next. Reni died with 22 holes in him. Slade cut off his ears and carried them around as souvenirs.

So pleased was Holladay with Slade's protective prowess that within a few months Slade was given another 400 miles of stage line to supervise. But liquor proved his eventual undoing. After one drinking bout in which he shot up an Army warehouse, the Army prevailed on Holladay to fire his prized employee. Slade then moved to Virginia City, Montana. But one night at the theater he outraged solid citizens by calling upon the leading actress to strip. Next day Slade was still raising hell. Their patience exhausted, the town's vigilantes meted out justice of Slade's own brand; they hanged him for disorderly conduct. His wife buried him in a zinc coffin filled with alcohol.

Reflecting Holladay's unabashed ego, his laurel-wreathed studio portrait dominates an 1864 advertisement for his company, dwarfing the pictures of four of his aides and of a typical coach used on his line.

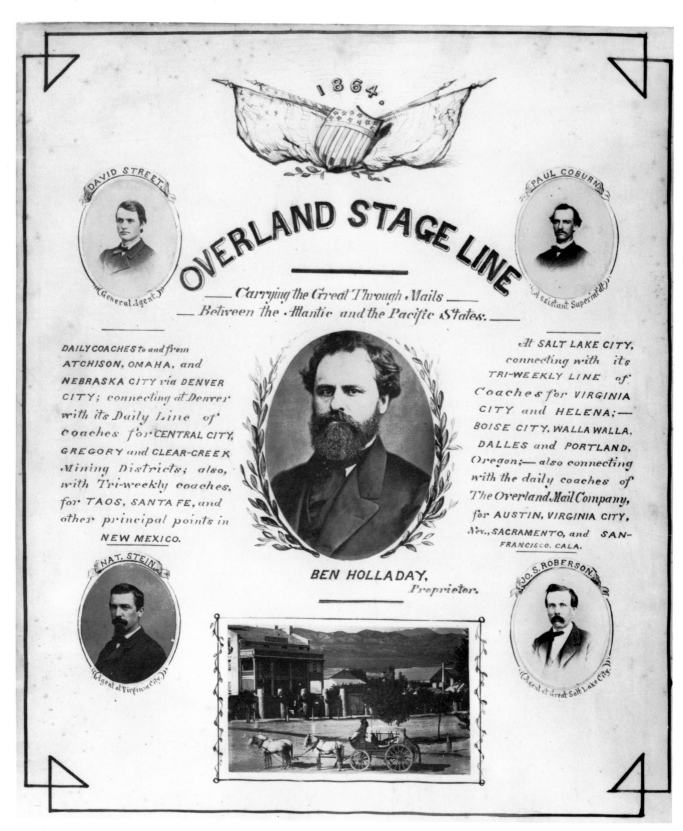

the fare his rivals charged. It took only three months to kill off the competition. Peabody and Caldwell sensibly gave up and sought other means of livelihood, but Oliver was a doughty fellow. In May 1865 he made an attempt to get beyond Holladay's range by opening a new 120-mile line northward from Virginia City to Helena. Charging a modest tariff of $25 and furnishing the line with new coaches, Oliver hoped to be able to hold on to his customers. He hoped in vain. Holladay permitted him to suffer through a bitter and difficult winter. Then, with the spring thaw, Holladay put his own coaches on the same run, charging a fare of $2.50. This time it took only two months to break Oliver for good. Once that was achieved and Holladay was firmly in the driver's seat in Montana, he followed up with a by-now familiar maneuver: he raised the passenger fare to $37.50, took his new Concord coaches off the line, replaced them with 20-passenger wagons that were far less comfortable and, as a final touch, reduced the frequency of departures.

"There was of course no rebate to passengers who had paid for first-class travel and had to put up with any conveyance Holladay chose to thrust upon them," one victim wrote. "Nor did Holladay ever rebate any fare to passengers, who found that they also had to push, or at least get out in the boggiest part of the road and wade through gumbo so that the vehicle could move." Another outraged passenger wrote to the *Montana Post* after a ride in a Holladay wagon, "If the earnestness and deep sincerity with which my maledictions are uttered could insure their taking effect, I would not stand in Ben Holladay's shoes for *two* mail contracts." The curses were wasted; Holladay was never impressed by damnation emanating from his customers—or, for that matter, from the populations of whole cities that had no other recourse but to rely upon him for their mail and transport.

He had one celebrated encounter with the town of Marysville, Kansas—a Holladay stage stop—over his suggestion that the community build a good road as well as a bridge on the outskirts, across Spring Creek. When residents argued that Holladay's company ought to build its own roads and bridges, he cut their town off the stage schedule and had his coaches bypass it altogether, incidentally saving about 35 miles of the run. Marysville retaliated by burning Holladay in effigy and

cutting adrift the ferry that he had built across the Big Blue River. When this stratagem failed to bring Holladay around, a Marysville posse dug a trench across the Holladay route; a night coach fell into it, injuring several passengers and so disabling some of the horses that they had to be shot. An Army officer happened to be along, and as a result Holladay was able to get troops from nearby Fort Leavenworth to escort later stages through the Marysville combat zone.

Seeing the light, the people of Marysville finally took up pick and shovel, and voluntarily built the road and bridge that Holladay wanted. Even so, his wrath toward the impudent locals was slow to subside. He waited another five months to let the town back into his good graces and onto his schedule.

The town of Fort Kearney likewise felt his displeasure as a by-product of manipulations designed to dispose of a competing line called the Western Stage Company. Western Stage, originating at Omaha in Nebraska Territory, terminated at Fort Kearney, there depositing its mail, express shipments and passengers to be reloaded on Holladay's east- and westbound stages. But Holladay coveted this feeder line, and Fort Kearney was soon compelled to accommodate coach-loads of unhappy would-be through passengers for whom, by evil chance, there were never seats available on connecting Holladay stages in either direction. The difficulty was ironed out in the customary fashion when Western Stage sold out to Holladay at the price that Ben was prepared to pay.

Intolerant as he was of any kind of interference, Holladay found that there was one kind of trouble from which not even his roughshod tactics could buy his stages immunity. In 1863 there was a general Indian uprising that reached a peak of virulence after Colonel John Chivington's infamous massacre of peaceable Indians at Sand Creek in eastern Colorado. The tribes, in a rare show of unity, rose in fury all across the plains and in the mountains. At one point Holladay himself came close to a confrontation with the raiders. Traveling eastward from California, he was stopped in the Wasatch mountains by a report of hostile Indians ahead; a large force of them had attacked a wagon train and its 40 well-armed men at Bridger Pass, killing one man and making off with some of the draft animals. Holladay got to a telegraph station and wired the details to his New York office, prudently concluding: "I return to San Francisco tonight. Uncle Ben takes the backtrack for the first time in his life."

Having taken it, he then took ship to the East Coast. There he undertook the urgent business of appealing —all the way up to President Lincoln—for troops to guard his line against the Indians, meanwhile keeping his customary coterie of Senators and Congressmen persuasively wined and dined at his mansion on K Street.

There was little doubt—despite the cynical accusations of California Senator John Conness that the Indian attacks were a put-up job engineered by Holladay —that the stage line was now in very serious trouble. Frank Root, one of Holladay's express messengers, reported in the summer of 1864 that "between Big Sandy and Thirty-Two Mile Creek, every station but one was burnt by the Indians. This was a terrible visitation and the company was obliged for several weeks to abandon the route for fully 500 miles."

Robert Spotswood, Holladay's tough young superintendent on the line east of Denver, worked out a convoy system to cross Indian country: several coaches at a time traveled together under an escort of soldiers. Even this strength was not always secure if the convoy came under heavy attack. On one occasion, reported by Frank Root, Spotswood and "his caravan having been taken by storm, he got the vehicles in as close order as he could under the harassing flight of arrows and he and his men fell back. The stagecoaches were brought around on the double quick into this barricade. Hostilities began early in the morning, and it was evening when the redskins drew off. The fight was a bitter one and few men engaged in it came out without being hit. Two were stretched out; one, Alex Hardy, a hostler, dead, and Jim Enos with an Arapaho arrow protruding from his abdomen. The dying man was carried up to Cooper Creek station, where stood an old blacksmith shop. Accompanying the party was a surgeon who, being unable to pull out the arrow by hand, found it necessary to use a pair of the blacksmith's tongs. In an instant after the arrow left the wound there was a single convulsion and poor Enos was dead."

When the Indian uprising finally began to subside —after the end of the Civil War had freed Army troops for duty on the plains—Holladay tendered Congress an itemized bill for $526,739 to cover losses he incurred through Indian attacks. Eleven years later, after much hemming and hawing, Congress finally offered to settle for $100,000. However, Holladay, who by that time was down on his luck and desperately in need of money but still given to theatrical gestures, grandly refused to take it. If the country could not afford to pay its honest debts, he declared, then far be it from him to squeeze the nation's taxpayers.

Before Holladay played out his epic role, he scored one last coup with all the canniness and flair that he could muster. This final triumph came, ironically, even as he recognized that the transcontinental railroad would soon put an end to the great days of stagecoaching. Holladay was ready to go out of business as audaciously as he went into it.

A former Denver merchant, David Butterfield—no relation to John Butterfield of the old Oxbow Route and the Overland Mail—had decided to challenge the Holladay line's monopoly between the Missouri and Denver. He organized his company, the Butterfield Overland Despatch, with three million dollars in capital—some of it supplied by Wells, Fargo; by American Express; and by United States Express. Though the three agencies had long been Holladay customers, they had become increasingly disgruntled by his highhanded system of rates. Butterfield settled on a route that was shorter than Holladay's by 61 miles, running his stages along the Smoky Hill River.

Almost as soon as Butterfield's stages started to roll, he began to have serious Indian trouble. The numerous persons who habitually suspected Holladay of dirty tricks in any matter of competition were immediately convinced that Butterfield's Indian tormentors were, in effect, Holladay hirelings in war paint. Certainly the warriors who began ambushing Butterfield's stages in October 1865 were notably different in their methods from other war parties on the plains; while they burned the stages, ran off the stock and robbed the passengers, they inexplicably abstained from the common Indian practice of killing and scalping all the males.

Raids continued along the Smoky Hill trail the rest of the year. Finally, two employees at one of Butterfield's relay stations were killed, and his passenger business began to dwindle. In this sort of competition Butterfield was at a distinct disadvantage since he did not, as Holladay did, have a troop escort as well as

hired toughs like Jack Slade *(page 139)* to protect his vehicles from Indians or robbers.

Butterfield's business was also suffering from a post-war depression in mining activity, and by January 1866 he was in deep trouble. That month his company was reorganized under a Colorado territorial charter, with Butterfield retained as general manager. There was little doubt that Wells, Fargo was behind the reorganization, for immediately thereafter the giant agency — again joined by American Express and United States Express — made it plain to Holladay that unless he carried their express shipments on their terms, a Wells, Fargo stage line would be set up between Salt Lake and Denver to connect with the Butterfield line, effectively outflanking Holladay's monopoly.

The only reaction a challenge of that sort could evoke from a man like Holladay was fury. From New York, he ordered two of his trusted employees to serve as spies, inspect the reorganized Butterfield operation and report to him in detail. When the private intelligence came in, he bragged to his chief Western agent, "Now I am going to take the bull by the horns!"

Holladay sent a note inviting David Bray, a New York banker who served as the president of the Butterfield line, to a luxurious luncheon that was catered by Delmonico's, New York's finest restaurant, and served in Holladay's private office. It is doubtful if his guest really enjoyed the meal. As soon as the banker — a man of diminutive stature — arrived, the huge and domineering Holladay began to harangue him: "I want to see you about your Despatch line. You are out over a million dollars, and that is not the end. You can never get your money all back. But I can get you out of it better than anyone else."

Bray may have been persuaded as much by his host's overbearing presence as by his argument. In any event, he had to eat hastily, for Holladay had given him only until 3 p.m. to summon his board of directors and come to a decision. The decision went as Holladay expected. Before sundown the Butterfield Overland Despatch had been sold and Ben Holladay was its new owner.

Holladay polished off this eminently successful March day in 1866 by instructing a secretary to send a telegram to Wells, Fargo and its affiliates, advising them to start their threatened line between Salt Lake and Denver, "and be damned." Having newly acquired another 585 miles of stage lines — giving him 3,145 miles in all — he raised express charges on gold shipments to 5 per cent of the mint value and raised the passenger fare for the Atchison-Salt Lake run from $150 to $350 — an extortionate amount he had previously charged only in ostensible emergencies.

Holladay was now at the climax of his career. He knew that Union Pacific rails were pushing well into the Western plains and that a matching set was climbing the Sierra from the Pacific. He could see — painful though it may have been — that his coaching empire was facing its doom. On November 1, 1866, only eight months after he had consolidated his empire over the fiscal corpse of Butterfield Overland Despatch, Holladay suddenly sold out to Wells, Fargo for $1.5 million in cash, $300,000 in Wells, Fargo stock and an honorific seat on the board of directors.

But this was scarcely enough to satisfy Holladay's appetite. Almost at once he turned his back on coaching and launched himself into river steamboating and railroading in the burgeoning Northwest, acquiring, among other properties, the Oregon & California Railroad. Holladay's dealings in his new domain were as unscrupulous as ever, his personal style as crude, and his relations with his customers no more obliging than before. "What are the people of Oregon to do?" asked a Willamette newspaper plaintively. "Will they rise in their might and strike down this monster monopolist?"

Holladay, as usual, scorned such barbs. He built a handsome new mansion in Portland, entertained lavishly and bribed state legislators by the dozen. He seemed to have succeeded in transferring his enormous power intact from stagecoaching to newer means of transport — but it soon developed that he harbored yet another ambition. He wanted — as he revealed to his retinue of hangers-on — to be a U.S. Senator. The poet Joa-

The stern-wheeler *Dayton,* seen moored on the Willamette River, was one of nine steamboats that Holladay acquired to form a river-going fleet in Oregon. The venture postdated the sale of his staging empire.

quin Miller, whose family had settled in Oregon in the 1850s, wrote letters and newspaper columns, probably for a fee, assiduously promoting Holladay's candidacy: "I do not say that Ben Holladay built the city of Portland or brought all the wealth and ready money that now floods the state," Miller conceded, "but I do venture to say that he has done more in that direction than any other one individual."

But neither Miller's prose nor Holladay's bribes could make him a plausible candidate. Ben then decided that if he could not have the Senate seat for himself, at least he could control the man who did win it. In 1872 a suitably pliable candidate was found in the person of John H. Mitchell, and a campaign was launched to woo the support of the state legislature, the body then responsible for electing U.S. Senators. There were some tense moments during the campaign when Oregon papers reported Mitchell's simple political credo: "Whatever is Ben Holladay's politics is my politics, and whatever Ben Holladay wants, I want." But $100,000 spread among the state's legislators neutralized the caviling of the Holladay-haters, and Mitchell in due course was elected and went to Washington.

To finance his rail and steamship ventures as well as his aborted political ambitions, Holladay had floated a complex structure of bonds and debentures. The stratagem was not new for him; occasionally in the past, when he had found himself overextended—when, for instance, he was using his capital to buy out competitors —he had thought nothing of launching a new bond issue and using the proceeds to pay the interest on the old. This time, however, Holladay sold his bonds and debentures not only on Wall Street but also in the money markets of Europe—a logical extension of his philosophy that the farther away his investors and backers were, the better.

As long as distant bankers and speculators retained faith in the Holladay magic, the philosophy worked.

The first train of the Oregon & California
Railroad—Holladay's last speculative venture—chugs along track built in 1868 and
1869. He lost this remaining vestige of his
empire in the financial panic of 1873.

Even those men of finance suspicious enough to make the long journey to the Northwest to double check their investments in person tended to succumb either to Holladay's dazzling performances or his browbeatings or his bribes. His most important backers consisted of a consortium of German bondholders. When the disturbing rumors of Holladay's fiscal manipulations reached this group at last, it dispatched a representative, one Baron de Lasley, to investigate. But the Baron's English was flawed, and Holladay managed to fast-talk his guest into producing a favorable report on the results of his inquiry.

Then, on September 18, 1873, the New York stock market plummeted. In the panic that ensued one of the earliest collapses was that of the Holladay empire. On this occasion, with money scarce and scared as well, there was no floating a new bond issue to pay off an old one. Holladay had no choice but to default. From Europe and Wall Street his creditors swooped in

like vultures to pick over the carcass of his railroad and various other properties.

It fell to the German bondholders to bring some order out of the financial chaos. They appointed an American journalist of German birth, Henry Villard —son-in-law of the famed abolitionist editor, William Lloyd Garrison—as their agent to guard the dwindling assets. On a visit to the Northwest, Villard soon discovered the magnitude of Holladay's recklessness and the inaccuracy of his accounting. Where Holladay had assured the Germans that 375 miles of Oregon & California railway track would be laid, Villard found only 250. Where the Germans had been led to believe booming towns flourished along the right of way, Villard found sparsely populated settlements and undeveloped tracts of forest. Finally, Villard made a bitterly realistic assessment of the great man himself. Holladay, said Villard, was "illiterate, coarse, boastful, false and cunning." Moreover, he was through. After an inter-

regnum during which Holladay was reduced to a pow-
erless name on the letterhead, Villard personally took
control of the railroad.

When Holladay's luck ran out at last, it ran all the
way out, in his personal life as well as business. His beloved wife, Ann, who had slept through that coach robbery years earlier and whose hard-won social status was
Holladay's only claim to respectability, died at Ophir
Farm in New York on the same day her husband de-
faulted on the Oregon & California's bonds. One after
another, their four grown children fell away. Ben's favorite daughter, Jennie, who had married a worthless
European nobleman at her mother's behest, died in
childbirth after a visit to her father in Oregon. Son Joe,
a lifelong wastrel, drank himself to death in Hong Kong.
Daughter Polly, who like her sister had married a European and fallen on evil times, died aboard a ship
bound for New York. Holladay's surviving child and
namesake, Ben Jr., bitterly contested with his father for
title to the few properties remaining in the family, and
died, like his brother, an alcoholic. None of the children
lived to middle age.

Holladay himself remarried a year after Ann's death,
taking as his second wife young Lydia Esther Campbell, daughter of an Oregon pioneer. Portland gossips
were outraged at what they felt to be a mismatch between a sweet innocent and a reprobate 30 years her senior, but the marriage proved happy and enduring. The
second Mrs. Holladay gave him two children, a new
family and renewed zest. He tried for a comeback with
the fragmentary properties that still remained, only to
be stopped this time by one of his brothers, Joe, who
claimed title to them. There was more battling and dis-
appointment until, in 1887 in his 68th year, Holladay
died in Portland. His longtime friend and attorney, a
man named John Doniphan (evidently a relative of Colonel Doniphan), summed up for the late Stagecoach
King. "I regard Ben Holladay as one of nature's gifted
children," Doniphan wrote in a letter some time later
to the *Catholic Tribune* of St. Joseph, Missouri. "Had
he been on the same theater, he was capable of playing the role of Napoleon, as I think he resembled him
in many characteristics. He believed results justified
means, and he trusted in his star too far." It was surely
as fair an epitaph as Holladay could have expected—had
he been the kind of man to care about such things.

148

Holladay played out the finale of his career, including a vain bid to become a U.S. Senator, from this stately residence in downtown Portland. He hung the walls with fine art and reportedly stocked the cellar with enough wine "to float the Navy," but Oregon voters only resented the ostentation.

A stagecoach races out of Golconda, Nevada, in 1887, speeding to make a connection to San Francisco.

5 | Rocky roads to adventure

For several decades in the mid-19th Century, almost anyone who had to go anywhere in the West went by stage. Some travelers had a relatively easy time of it. A mere 24-hour journey, for example, confronted passengers on a coach of the Pioneer Stage Company, which covered the fairly short run between California and Nevada. Pioneer's was a bullion-rich territory, and the line served it well with Concord coaches

(below) and high-stepping teams. But even here lurked danger and discomfort. When one Pioneer coach upset, riders were brickbatted by a ton of silver bars that had been piled on the carriage floor.

If the traveler undertook a full cross-country journey from the Missouri to the Pacific, he faced hundreds of hours of cramped, sleepless, dust-choking anguish. True, there were interesting fellow passengers and magnificent vistas,

but there was also the nerve-fraying possibility of a runaway team, flash flood or savage gust of prairie wind that might bring a coach to ruin in the middle of nowhere.

Even if no calamity occurred, the traveler was certain to be thoroughly exhausted at the conclusion. One survivor described his trip as "the hardest two weeks' work I ever did," and then stumbled off to a solid 20 hours in bed.

A rifle-toting guard stands by as miners in Dolores, Colorado, board Concord coaches in 1893 for the 35-mile run to the gold camp of Rico. This local stage line provided transport services for such colorfully named mines as Yankee Boy, Hoosier Girl, Millionaire, Trout and Johnny Bull.

En route from Deadwood, South Dakota, to mines in the Black Hills, a pair of "mud wagons" — so-named for their ability to handle the worst roads — pause on a mountainside trestle. These canvas-topped vehicles were lighter in weight than Concord coaches and were built closer to the ground.

The arrival of the stagecoach in Cripple Creek, Colorado, in 1892 draws a crowd, and for good reason. The stage often brought fascinating strangers in the newest city attire, and it carried away another kind of exciting cargo: bullion from the fifth richest gold-producing area in the world.

157

OVERLAND MAIL ROUTE
TO CALIFORNIA.

Through in Six Days to Sacramento!

CONNECTING WITH THE DAILY STAGES

To all the Interior Mining Towns in Northern California and Southern Oregon.
Ticketed through from PORTLAND, by the

OREGON LINE OF STAGE COACHES!

And the Rail Road from Oroville to Sacramento,

Passing through Oregon City, Salem, Albany, Corvallis, Eugene City, Oakland,
Winchester, Roseburg, Canyonville, Jacksonville, and in California—
Yreka, Trinity Centre, Shasta, Red Bluff, Tehama, Chico,
Oroville, Marysville to SACRAMENTO.

TRAVELERS AVOID RISK of OCEAN TRAVEL

Pass through the HEART OF OREGON—the Valleys of Rogue River, Umpqua and Willamette.

This portion of the Pacific Slope embraces the most BEAUTIFUL and attractive, as well as some of the most BOLD, GRAND and PICTUERESQUE SCENERY on the Continent. The highest snow-capped mountains, (Mt. HOOD, Mt. SHASTA and others,) deepest ravines and most beautiful valleys.

Stages stop over one night at JACKSONVILLE and YREKA, for passengers to rest. Passengers will be permitted to lay over at any point, and resume their seats at pleasure, any time within one month.

FARE THROUGH, FIFTY DOLLARS.

Ticket Office at Arrigoni's Hotel, Portland.

H. W. CORBETT & Co.,
Proprietors Oregon Stage Line.

PORTLAND, July 19, 1866.

[W. D. Carter, Printer, Front St., Portland, Oregon.]

"We bowled away and left the States behind"

No one stagecoach journey across the West was ever like another; too many imponderables lurked along the route. A mechanical breakdown, a passenger's illness, an unseasonal blizzard, a sudden, lethal onslaught by bandits or inflamed Indians — any of these and more could turn a trip into a nightmare. On the other hand, the time might pass without incident and the travelers arrive at their destination on schedule. No one could predict. For good or ill, a journey by stagecoach was an adventure into the unknown, to be approached with either trepidation or calm, but always with a tingle of anticipation.

Westbound departures from the towns along the Missouri offered an added measure of excitement. The stages that left from St. Joseph or Leavenworth or Atchison were no mere local runabouts, carrying people on short hauls, but long-distance conveyances traveling the classic overland route: across the open rolling prairie to Fort Kearney, Nebraska; along the Platte to the Denver turnoff at Julesburg, Colorado; from Denver into the Rockies at Fort Bridger, Wyoming; down the dry, dusty Wasatch mountains into Salt Lake City; across the most desolate stretch of desert in America and through the lofty passes of the Sierra Nevada into California. For those going all the way it was the longest stagecoach ride in the world: from Atchison, Kansas, to Placerville, California — 1,913 miles; advertised traveling time, 17 days.

Just the prospect of such an odyssey was enough to stir the blood, but there also was the element of novelty. Most outbound travelers converging on the Missouri River towns were Easterners or Midwesterners

who had never before ventured beyond the Big Muddy. They might be anonymous folk planning a new life in the West — farmers, schoolteachers, merchants, miners and other fortune seekers, an occasional wife with children in tow going out to join a husband who had already settled in. Or they might be bankers, government officials, indefatigable Englishmen on round-the-world tours, such veteran journalists as Horace Greeley and such budding writers as young Sam Clemens, later to be better known as Mark Twain. But even the most urbane traveler was likely to turn into a tenderfoot on the banks of the Missouri, as eager to plumb the mysteries of the vast lands on the far side as any fellow passenger.

A typical stage departure from Atchison — say, on a crisp spring day in 1864 — had something of an air of ritual. At 7:30 in the morning the westbound stage pulled up before the Planters' House hotel on Commercial Street. The team of six glossy Kentucky trotters, in loosened harness, stamped and flicked their tails impatiently. A stock tender kept a watchful eye on them as he helped the stage conductor with the loading. Leather pouches crammed with mail — brought by an early-morning train from St. Joseph to the east bank of the river, and ferried across by the steamer *Ida* — went into the front boot, a storage compartment below the driver's seat. On top of the mail in the boot went an iron strongbox, locked against robbers, containing the most valuable items going West. Lumpy canvas bags of printed matter and express packages were stowed in a second, larger boot behind the carriage, with the overflow placed inside the coach itself. Passenger baggage (limited to 25 pounds per traveler, with a stiff charge of a dollar for each pound over) also went into the rear boot as well as on top of the carriage.

As the loading proceeded, the nine passengers, fortified by a hearty hotel breakfast of bacon and eggs, came out into the cool morning air for a look at the rig

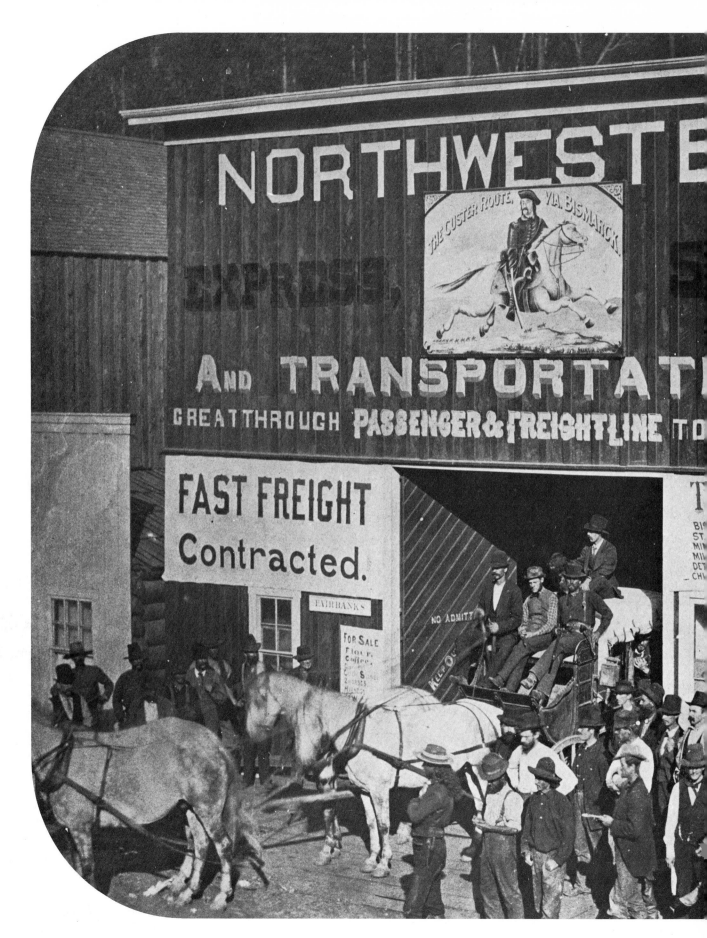

that would be their transport and, indeed, most of their world for days to come. Those going through to California had paid as much as $600 for their passage. Some of them certainly looked as if they had that kind of money; their tailored suits and white linen bespoke more fashionable haunts back home. All of them, stylish or not, had the jocular, somewhat self-conscious manner of people on the brink of an act of great daring.

As usual, a few Atchison residents were on hand to see the stage off, and travelers and townsmen exchanged pleasantries. A local wag tried a well-worn joke, suggesting that the passengers get short haircuts "so's the Arapahos can't scalp you," and causing one or two wry faces among his listeners. An Easterner carrying bologna, cheese, crackers and some tins of sardines and herring was congratulated on his foresight: the food at the stage stations en route, an Atchison man had heard, left a lot to be desired.

Now and then a ticket holder cast an admiring glance at the glistening coach that stood waiting. It was a Concord, universally considered the finest stagecoach ever built, with a carriage not quite eight feet long and five feet wide. That may have seemed rather small for holding nine passengers — not to say an overflow of mail and packages — but if the traveler had any qualms he was reassured by a glimpse of the interior, with its fine leather upholstery, wood paneling and fittings of polished metal. Leather curtains at the windows served in lieu of glass; leather, the ticket agent explained to a questioner, was less hazardous and better able to absorb the dust, wind, rain and possibly snow that might be encountered along the route.

Finally the last of the mail and baggage was stowed. The driver emerged from the stage line office and climbed onto his lofty perch — called the box — just forward of the carriage. Next to him settled the one company employee who always went along: the express messenger, whose functions included looking after the passengers, packages and mail, and guarding the strongbox in the front boot. His double-barreled shotgun was prominently displayed.

The driver shouted "All aboard!"; the passengers hastily clambered into the carriage and the stock tender tugged on the cinches that drew the harness firm. In all the flurry of activity, it did not seem possible that only a half hour had passed since the horses had pulled up to

161

A 377-mile journey from Nevada to Utah cost the bearer of this ticket $96. Fares varied widely, based on the traffic — and competition. The price of meals, as much as two dollars at stage stops, was extra.

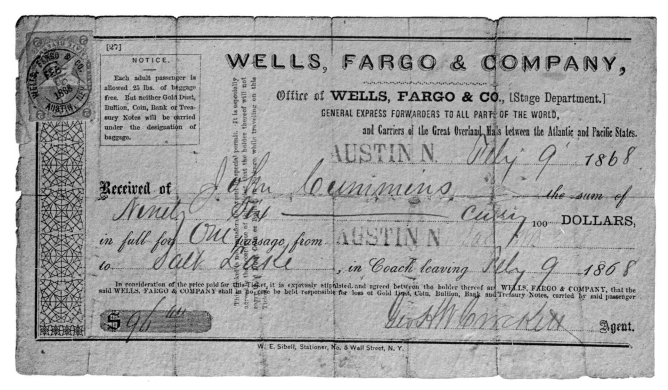

the hotel. Yet the stage rolled out at 8 o'clock sharp.

On this particular journey the feelings of the passengers as they set out were unrecorded. But Mark Twain expressed the sentiment of all stage travelers when, in *Roughing It*, he looked back at his own departure from St. Joseph in 1861. Twain was only 25 at the time, and traveling with his brother Orion, who had been appointed territorial secretary in Nevada.

Their arrival in St. Joseph had been marked by a bit of unpleasantness. Neither had known of the 25-pound baggage limit imposed on stage passengers, and not wanting to pay the extra tariff for overweight, they had gone through the onerous process of unpacking their trunks, throwing a hasty selection of clothes, canteens, blankets, pipes and tobacco into a valise, and having the nonessentials shipped back to their home in St. Louis. But not even this mishap dampened Twain's spirits. He was exhilarated at the prospect of the adventure that lay before him, and well aware that he was about to enter a whole new world. "The driver cracked his whip," he wrote of the moment of departure, "and we bowled away and left 'the States' behind us."

The first hour or so for passengers out of Atchison was a time of getting acquainted with one another and learning something of the routine of the long ride. The average speed of the coach would be eight miles an hour. About every 12 miles there would be a stop at a swing station, for the purpose of changing horses; such stations consisted of little more than a stable and a granary, presided over by a couple of stock tenders. Stops would be longer at home stations, which were 40 to 50 miles apart.

Here the transients would find a dining room, a stage office, sometimes a telegraph office, and bunks for sleeping. But these, the travelers were cautioned, were not for them; if a storm, a threat of Indian attack or other emergency forced an overnight stop, they would have to bed down on the station's earthen floor. The bunks were for stage drivers, conductors and express messengers changing shifts; drivers, in particular, changed after every home station. This news was somewhat disquieting to novice passengers; not only would they have to catch whatever sleep they could while sitting bolt upright in the coach, but they would find an unfamiliar figure at the reins at just about the time they were getting to know his predecessor.

Even as they digested this information they were becoming aware of more immediate discomfort. The

162

An 1877 column in the *Omaha Herald* offers stage travelers a crowded compendium of tips on safety, comfort and rules of etiquette on a journey — with a final warning that the experience is no "pic-nic."

coach, they began to realize, was horribly cramped. True, the seats were upholstered, but each person had only about 15 inches of space. The three passengers in the front row and the three in back had a wall of the carriage to lean against. But the only means of support for the unfortunate trio on the center bench was to clutch leather loops suspended from the ceiling. The company was jammed hip to hip, knee to knee, with no place for legs except atop bulging sacks of cargo. One English traveler, William Tallack, recalled his agony in his memoirs. "I felt doubtful," he wrote, "as to how far I might endure a continued ride of five hundred and forty hours, with no other intermission than a stoppage of about forty minutes twice a day, and with only such repose at night as could be obtained whilst in a sitting posture and closely wedged in by fellow travelers and tightly filled mailbags."

Besides the closeness of the quarters — never emphasized in advance by the stage companies — there was the ceaseless rocking of the carriage. This shiplike motion was due to the fact that the coach rested on a suspension system of two thorough braces — long leather straps — sewn or wrapped to a thickness of three inches and anchored to the carriage at the front and rear axles. The thorough braces served as shock absorbers; they prevented the horses from feeling the jolts that came when ruts were struck, and permitted a speed that otherwise would have jarred the whole rig apart.

Passengers with queasy stomachs tried not to think of days and nights ahead on steep roads with little grad-

Hints for Plains Travelers.
B H.:Pioneer.

The best seat inside a stage coach is the one next the driver. You will have to ride with back to the horses, which with some people, produces an illness not unlike sea-sickness, but in a long journey this will wear off, and you will get more rest, with less than half the bumps and jars than on any other seat. When any old "sly Eph," who traveled thousands of miles on coaches offers, through sympathy to exchange his back or middle seat with you, don't do it. Never ride in cold weather with tight boots or shoes, nor close-fitting gloves. Bathe your feet before starting in cold water, and wear loose overshoes and gloves two or three sizes too large. When the driver asks you to get off and walk, do it without grumbling. He will not request it unless absolutely necessary. If a team runs away, sit still and take your chances; if you jump, nine times out of ten you will be hurt. In very cold weather abstain entirely from liquor while on the road; a man will freeze twice as quick while under its influence. Don't growl at food at stations; stage companies generally provide the best they can get. Don't keep the stage waiting; many a virtuous man has lost his character by so doing. Don't smoke a strong pipe inside especially early in the morning, spit on the leeward side of the coach. If you have anything to take in a bottle, pass it around, a man who drinks by himself in such a case is lost to all human feeling. Provide stimulants before starting; ranch whisky is not always nectar. Be sure and take two heavy blankets with you; you will need them. Don't swear, nor lop over on your neighbor when sleeping. Don't ask how far it is to the next station until you get there. Take small change to pay expenses. Never attempt to fire a gun or pistol while on the road; it may frighten the team and the careless handling and cocking of the weapon makes nervous people nervous. Don't discuss politics or religion, nor point out places on the road where horrible murders have been committed, if delicate women are among the passengers. Don't linger too long at the pewter wash basin at the station. Don't grease your hair before starting or dust will stick there in sufficient quantities to make a respectable "tater" patch. Tie a silk handkerchief around your neck to keep out dust and prevent sunburn. A little glycerine is good in case of chapped hands. Don't imagine for a moment you are going on a pic-nic; expect annoyance, discomfort and some hardships. If you are disappointed, thank heaven.

ing and no paving, when the carriage would heave and plunge like a storm-tossed ship at sea. For the moment at least, riding the level stretches west of Atchison, the motion of the coach was almost lulling. And there were diversions to combat the germs of worry. Fascinating conversation was one. If a returning Westerner happened to be aboard, his tales of the new land left his audience wide-eyed. When storytellers paused, word games were played and, by a little ingenious shifting of positions here and there, even whist or euchre might be attempted, with the level surface of an express package as a surrogate table. Poker, too, was a common pastime, but company officials kept watch for sharpers who rode the stages and cleaned out unsuspecting victims.

Early in the journey, however, nothing was likely to be as interesting as the terrain itself. No more than an hour and a half out of Atchison, the stage left the rolling cornfield country and set out across the plains, which stretched ahead for 700 miles. People from east of the Missouri River were always struck by the immensity of the prairie and most of them liked what they saw. Twain remembered "fresh breezes, vast expanses of level greensward, bright sunlight and an atmosphere of such amazing magnifying properties that trees that seemed close at hand were more than three miles away." A Boston newspaperman, Albert Richardson, wrote: "I wonder if the Almighty ever made a more beautiful country than Kansas."

Richardson was one of the rare travelers who made the overland trek more than once, and he prob-

Unbroken and unruly lead mules rear under the driver's whip as the pair behind them in the team pitches over in a tangle of harness.

Overland on the Oxbow: a personal portfolio

From the back of the moving coach, a passenger's rifle fells an antelope *(center, foreground)*.

A trip on the Butterfield Overland Mail offered passengers a few diversions and all too many discomforts, encountered in harnessing a refractory team of mules, fording a river of unknown depth, or any number of similar misadventures. One passenger who experienced his share of both good moments and bad was William Hayes Hilton. In the fall of 1858, Hilton booked passage from San Francisco to St. Louis on the Oxbow Route. He traveled mostly on celerity wagons, light stagecoaches with roller flaps on the sides, which were especially suited to use on rough roads. During the trip Hilton covered a sketch pad with scenes of the high points, some of which are shown here. Hilton's mustache and goatee make it easy to identify the sharpshooter *(left)* and the night guard *(opposite, top)* as the artist himself.

In the early days of the line, some stages halted at night. Here a passenger watches over sleeping companions and grazing animals.

Crossing a Texas river, passengers clamber for dry perches as the stationmaster *(foreground)* from a nearby depot guides the animals.

ably based this comment on a journey blessed by unusually fine weather. There were times in summer when the wind gusted almost visibly across the prairie, rattling coaches, staggering horses and blowing baggage away. Hail beat like bullets and teams turned tail to the storm. Sheets of rain blasted through the coaches' leather curtains and drenched everyone inside. "Kansas brags on its thunder and lightning," Horace Greeley reported, "and the boast is well founded." He was assured, probably by someone describing a tornado, that at times the wind blew so hard it snatched the iron tires from coach wheels. Under the summer sun the grass turned to straw

and prairie fires might sweep over thousands of acres. When that happened, coaches ran through choking smoke and soot; and when the wind shifted suddenly, horses bolted for their lives.

At Fort Kearney — 253 miles out of Atchison — the westward trail met the Platte River, which the route would follow for several hundred miles. The Platte was a central landmark that produced divergent reactions in those who saw it for the first time. A Pennsylvania newspaperman named Alexander McClure was unimpressed. "The river Platte is wide, shallow, muddy, treacherous and apparently useless," McClure wrote.

A way-station manager leads out a fresh team of horses for an incoming stage, as his aproned wife stands by the door to greet the hungry driver.

"It does not even skirt its own banks with timber." When he did see trees, he amended his notes only slightly: "Occasionally it presents a pretty growth of cottonwood for a few miles, but they are mere apologies for trees and make the general view, if possible, more cheerless by their deformed and stunted growth."

The veteran stage messenger Frank Root, whose regular run was between Atchison and Denver, and who thus had ample opportunity to study the terrain as he rode on the box beside the driver, saw the Platte in almost poetic terms, "fringed here and there with miniature forest belts and the rich, dark soil was covered with tall, luxuriant native grasses." He particularly enjoyed moonlit summer nights, with "silvery rays being reflected in the waters of the beautiful stream."

Everyone agreed, however, that the landscape was more austere than the countryside just west of Atchison, and that the passage through it was more demanding. "The Platte mosquitoes lacerated me through the sleeves of two woolen shirts," Richardson reported, adding that dust covered his companions so thoroughly that "for several minutes I did not know them."

Richardson's complaints were mild by comparison with the annoyance expressed by McClure, an invet-

The name of this particular station at a river crossing in eastern Wyoming might have given nervous passengers pause; it was Robbers' Roost.

Because stage drivers were charged with the custody of the U.S. mail they hauled, all were required by Congress to swear to this oath. Its loyalty provisions were aimed at weeding out Confederate sympathizers.

CERTIFICATE OF THE OATH OF MAIL CONTRACTORS AND CARRIERS REQUIRED BY LAW.

I, *Charles McDonnell* , being "employed in the care, custody, and conveyance of the mail" on Route No. *14782* , from *Oroville* to *Tehama* , State of *California* , do swear that I will faithfully perform all the duties required of me, and abstain from everything forbidden by the laws in relation to the establishment of Post Offices and Post Roads within the United States; and that I will honestly and truly account for and pay over any moneys belonging to the said United States which may come into my possession or control; and I further solemnly swear that I have never voluntarily borne arms against the United States since I have been a citizen thereof; that I have voluntarily given no aid, countenance, counsel, or encouragement to persons engaged in armed hostility thereto; that I have neither sought nor accepted, nor attempted to exercise the functions of, any office whatever under any authority, or pretended authority, in hostility to the United States; that I have not yielded a voluntary support to any pretended government, authority, power, or constitution within the United States, hostile or inimical thereto. And I do further swear that, to the best of my knowledge and ability, I will support and defend the Constitution of the United States against all enemies, foreign or domestic; that I will bear true faith and allegiance to the same; that I take this obligation freely, without any mental reservation or purpose of evasion; and that I will well and faithfully discharge the duties of the office on which I am about to enter: So help me God.

Ch. McDonnell

Sworn before the subscriber, *A Justice of the Peace* for the *County* of *Tehama* , this *4th* day of *August* , A. D. 186*6*; and I also certify that the person above named is above the age of sixteen years, to the best of my knowledge and belief.

G. H. McPherson J P
Tehama Township

☞ The person who takes the oath should sign his name above the Magistrate's certificate. This certificate must have affixed a five-cent revenue stamp, which should be canceled by the person using it writing on it his initials and the date, per act of Congress of July 1, 1862.

One oath to be signed by a contractor, and *one* by each Carrier employed.

erate dyspeptic who toured the West with his wife in 1867. After Fort Kearney, McClure wrote, "there is but one continued plain, parched, whitened with alkalai and altogether inhospitable, bleak and desolate." The fine alkali dust, McClure grumbled on, "keeps a perpetual cloud about the coach and penetrates the eyes, ears, nose, mouth, hair and clothes. Nor do its torments stop with itself. It has an ally of innumerable little sand gnats, so small as to be hardly perceptible, and they get in the hair and under the clothing, and bite much worse than even western mosquitoes."

But there were compensations for these afflictions. Wildlife was still abundant on the Great Plains. Horace Greeley was stunned by the sheer size of the buffalo herds. He knew his readers were tired of the subject, he noted in one of his dispatches, but he had seen—literally, he believed—a million buffalo on a single day! Such volume brought out the hunter latent in nearly every passenger, and people who had prudently brought pistols with them blazed away from the coach. Every one of Greeley's traveling companions fired on "one old bull [that] shambled along. They thought they wounded him fatally, but he vanished from sight." The indiscriminate shooting was simply target practice; real damage to the animals was rare, and even when a marksman managed to succeed, his quarry was left to rot on the prairie.

When taking pot shots at buffalo grew monotonous, passengers turned their attention to smaller animals. Prairie dogs were ubiquitous. Prairie chickens and quail flashed up beside the road, and now and then a pelican alighted on the Platte. Often there were wild turkeys, jack rabbits, deer and antelope within shooting range, and occasionally elk and gray wolves ("prairie lawyers," as Greeley called them). Coyotes made the evenings melodious. This creature endlessly amused Mark Twain: "He is so spiritless and cowardly that even when his exposed teeth are pretending a threat, the rest of his face is apologizing for it."

Human traffic on the plains was less frequent, but invariably a welcome sight. Frank Root always enjoyed the puzzlement of passengers at seeing an eastbound coach come their way every 12 hours, though stage schedules called for only one coach a day in either direction. What they failed to realize, Root said, was that their own coach was simultaneously moving westward at just about the same rate; had it remained stationary, its occupants would have seen an eastbound coach only once every 24 hours. When this space-time phenomenon was explained, Root added with gentle amusement, it "was easily understood by those not too dull of comprehension."

Often the westbound coaches would pass plodding freight-wagon trains, which took five weeks from Atchison to Denver compared to six days for the stage. In the course of one round trip, Root crossed five separate times the path of a bullwhacker friend who was leading an ox team to Denver. Root derived a certain pride from figuring that he had traveled 3,265 miles in the time his friend had walked 653.

About 500 miles into the journey the stage began to climb the rising foothills of the Denver road. The change in the wildlife was evident almost at once. Now there were elk, bears, mountain sheep, mountain lions and, among the lesser creatures, grouse and sage hens; Root, who had been served sage hen at some home stations, observed that they "required a cast-iron stomach to digest." More tempting to the palate were the trout that filled the streams, but there was no time to stop and fish.

Nor was there time to take a dip. Mark Twain managed only one such bath on his entire 1,818-mile, 20-day journey, in a "limpid, sparkling stream" called Horse Creek. Other travelers were seldom even that lucky. Dirty, sweaty and disheveled though they usually were by this point, they pleaded their case in vain. For the stage driver, a stream was there to be crossed —and as expeditiously as possible. Fording it could be a perilous undertaking, and an alternative was rare; though some of the broader streams had flatboat ferries capable of carrying coach, horses and passengers, such conveniences were the exception.

Because of sudden rains or thaws, streams often ran dangerously high. The horses uneasy and stumbling, the wheels striking hidden rocks, the coach would lurch across. Every instant posed the possibility of an upset that could tumble everyone into swift water that often was much deeper just beyond the ford. At one crossing in Colorado, Alexander McClure reported, a coach was swept downstream and whirled over by the current; the lead horses were drowned, but the passengers were

A crusty driver who grumped his way to fame

The bluff, hard-driving, hard-drinking Hank (Henry James) Monk, a veteran reinsman on California stages, was a likely candidate for fame of some kind. And it took only one encounter with Horace Greeley to render Monk a certified legend of Western stagecoaching. He had Greeley, the great New York editor, aboard one day on a downhill run to Placerville, and Greeley asked for haste, fearing he would be late for a lecture. Obligingly, Monk snapped his whip, and soon they were rocketing down the mountain road so wildly that the editor was pitching helplessly around the inside of the coach like a loose mailbag. Greeley called out that he wasn't in *that* much of a hurry. But Monk, now in the spirit of the thing, yelled back, "Keep your seat, Horace, I'll get you there on time."

Years later, Monk's California admirers gave him a gold watch with his admonition to Greeley engraved inside. As for Greeley himself, the experience so haunted him and deflated his ego that he reportedly said of Monk, "He was the only man ever to make me look the fool."

Monk often did as much for others in his three decades as an exemplar of his trade. On one occasion, glimpsing a would-be bandit on the road ahead, Monk poured the last of his whiskey over his head and slumped down in a simulated stupor. When the highwayman incautiously ignored him and turned to rob the passengers, Monk stealthily grabbed a length of iron pipe and laid the robber out cold. Then he bellowed at his astonished passengers, "You and the bullion's safe, but that bastard cost me my last drink!"

Though muffled in winter gear, Monk keeps his hands bare to give him the feel of the reins.

saved "only after almost superhuman efforts to get out of a stream but twenty feet in width."

Traveling in the Rocky Mountains was also perilous — and awe-inspiring. The first sight of the Rockies, often at dawn, dazzled everyone. As familiar as Frank Root was with the spectacle, he always shared the initiates' wonderment. "I shall never forget the event," he was to recall years later. "Long's Peak, towering up 14,271 feet above the level of the sea, its summit covered with a silvery-white mantle, was the finest view I had ever seen. I doubt if any grander scene exists in the whole world."

But a more sober mood prevailed as the roads were encountered. Greeley described one road that was "eaten into the side of a steep mountain, with a precipice of from five to fifteen hundred feet on one side and as steep an eminence on the other. Yet along this mere shelf, with hardly a place where two meeting wagons can pass, the mail stage was driven just as fast as four wild horses could draw it."

A passenger on another coach recalled that, upon sweeping suddenly around a mountain curve, "we found ourselves confronted by nothing but blue sky. We streamed around the curves, at one moment swinging over the abyss and the next, swinging back easily toward the bank. In some places we would lose sight of the [lead horses] around the curves before we would get there ourselves. They were dainty, elegant little animals, those leaders. They danced like wild deer along the verge of the precipice."

Some people quailed at the experience and some enjoyed it, in the retelling anyway. An English traveler, John W. Boddam-Whetham, was one of the enthusiasts. He found the ride "so novel a sensation, so exciting that you cannot help cheering on the horses in spite of a very probable upset on an almost perpendicular rock several hundred feet in height." He was convinced that even the horses enjoyed themselves.

Albert Richardson, the newspaperman, was also an enthusiast — at least in retrospect. Back in Boston, long after it was all over, he conceded that "it is a thrilling

ride six inches from disaster — the blood bounds for weeks at the memory." He might have added that disaster had been averted — for himself and all others riding in his coach — through the skill, and the nerve, of one man only. That was the stage driver, also known variously as the whip, the reinsman or — appropriately enough — Jehu, from the Old Testament passage: "and the driving is like the driving of Jehu, son of Nimshi; for he driveth furiously."

The most important gift a good driver could have was a special way with horses: a delicate yet commanding hand on the reins, an intuitive feel for what the animals might do and the ability to calm high-strung teams. A capable reinsman did not need to lash his horses often, nor did he crack his whip dramatically; he used it subtly to signal and guide his team. He had other means of persuasion.

F. R. Burnham, an addict of stage travel, recalled a brief but pointed chat he once had on the subject. "As a small boy," he wrote, "I saw the eminent reinsman, John Reynolds, having an argument without words with his off leader [right-front horse]. I asked: 'How does the horse know what you want him to do?'

"'I talk to him through the ribbons, sonny,' he answered."

For fear of losing their sensitivity on the ribbons — the reins — drivers wore light gloves of silk or of the finest buckskin, even in winter temperatures so cold they had to be bundled up from head to foot. Frostbite sometimes claimed a finger as a result, but that was a risk drivers took. A skilled reinsman held three pairs of reins wrapped in the fingers of his left hand, keeping the right free for the whip or for handling the friction brake. Most teams were so tightly harnessed that they perforce had to operate as a unit. But a first-rate reinsman could handle pairs of loosely hitched animals separately, sending the leaders into a turn while holding the wheelers — the pair just below his box — steady until the right moment for them to turn too.

If this coordination went awry, instantaneous calamity could follow — animals tangling and falling, the stage

The day after driver Hank Monk put the nervous passenger Horace Greeley in his place with a terse "Keep your seat, Horace," the reinsman (wearing the straw hat on the lead coach below) made amends by allowing Greeley (white trousers) to take the place of honor — up on top, next to him.

172

crashing into them or overturning. But when properly done, the maneuver appeared so effortless that many passengers decided there was little to driving a stage because the horses did it all. An occasional seasoned traveler knew better; one of them remarked that his driver put him in mind of "a skilled musician playing upon a familiar instrument."

Presumably because of the stress of their work, most drivers liked their whiskey and rarely refused, as Frank Root put it, an invitation to "take a smile." And presumably for the same reason they possessed an uncommon capacity for profanity, which they modified to a degree only when ladies were among the travelers. To a preacher who remonstrated, "Don't swear so. Remember Job; he was severely tried; but he never lost his patience," one puzzled driver replied: "Job? Job? What line did *he* drive for?"

Since a new driver came on at every home station, travelers got to know a good many reinsmen en route. Some were genial, outgoing types to whom passengers warmed instantly; others were aloof, regal and silent — until a nerve of loquacity was touched or until the sun dissipated a hangover. Either way, the driver was fully aware that he was regarded as a character, and usually he enjoyed the role he played and took great pains to live up to it.

But generally, behind the façade, stood a capable, experienced, dependable person, who was well aware of his responsibilities. He had to take a costly stage, expensive horses, express shipments that often included gold, and a party of nervous passengers through wild, lonely, dangerous country. More than courage was involved, or steely nerve at the edge of a Rocky Mountain precipice. The driver also had to have sound judgment and a capacity for quick decisions. When a blinding snowstorm suddenly obliterated the road ahead, when a stream was running too full to ford, when a horse went lame at night, it was the driver who decided on the spot what should be done. He had to have confidence in himself, and he had to have considerable knowledge of the country, its routes and landmarks — serving, as one Englishman commented, as a "living road-encyclopedia."

When Indians suddenly appeared along the route, a knowledge of the nature and habits of Indians also came in handy. Most drivers could speak some Indian lan-

guages, like Sioux, Pawnee and Comanche, and some of them had even lived with tribesmen. Many had been buffalo hunters and scouts, and had ridden or driven all over the continent.

A few drivers came from backgrounds that, for one reason or another, they did not care to divulge. Frank Root knew an excellent reinsman who had been educated as a lawyer in Massachusetts; he kept his whereabouts hidden from his family, advising them only that he had gone "on the stage." Then there was Charley Parkhurst of California. Charley handled the reins as well as anyone, fended off a goodly number of bandits and accidents, and even in old age — plagued by rheumatism and the loss of an eye from a horse's kick — continued to drive, chew tobacco, drink moderately and gamble a bit. Finally Charley retired to a small farm near Watsonville, California, and died of cancer in 1879. It was only when friends came to prepare the driver's body for burial that they discovered that Charley Parkhurst was in fact a woman.

The ultimate test of a driver was his ability to handle his passengers. A reasonable amount of tact was required, since stage companies took a dim view of antagonizing people who had paid richly for passage. On the other hand, the very nature of the driver's job required him to give orders and exact obedience. He was, in effect, monarch of his craft and of all he surveyed. Most of his charges quickly learned to treat him with respect, and without condescension; tipping was out of the question, though he might with a lordly nod accept a handful of cigars.

Even important personages were expected to deal with him as a social equal; and if they failed to do so, he was capable of reminding them of the fact, subtly or otherwise. In 1868 when a coach carrying no less a celebrity than the Speaker of the House of Representatives, Schuyler Colfax, arrived at a stage stop well past midnight, the station keeper's wife balked at serving a meal — until the driver himself casually mentioned that he was a mite hungry. Only then, one of the Speaker's fellow travelers later reported, was "breakfast for all forthcoming." A territorial governor received his comeuppance in blunter fashion. Again the scene was at a stage stop, though on this occasion the problem was not hunger but weariness. The Governor asked if he might possibly rest awhile on the bunk the station

Stogie-chomping Charley Parkhurst *(left)* was a hell-for-leather California stage driver for three decades. When Charley died, friends who were preparing the body discovered that Charley was actually a woman.

keeper always kept in readiness for the driver. "Certainly," was the driver's prompt reply, "if you haven't any graybacks [lice] about you."

Any traveler who tried to teach a driver his business was a brash man indeed. Frank Root told of one reinsman, Rodney West, who was known as "Bishop," perhaps for his solemn ways. On a mountain road an Easterner invited himself into the seat next to Bishop and proceeded to entertain him with tales of the superiority of Eastern drivers and coaching. Finally they reached a steep incline, and Bishop locked the rear wheels for the descent, a maneuver that seemed to amuse the Easterner enormously. Bishop kept his silence and the coach started down the mountain, racing just inches away from a cliff. Root elaborated: "The tenderfoot grew more and more paralyzed. His extensive experience had not accustomed him to just that kind of a road. Finally he made one frantic leap and landed on the hillside. 'Bishop' never checked his horses. Some hours later Mr. Tenderfoot followed on foot

and had the pleasure of waiting for the next stage."

The Easterner had committed not one *faux pas,* but two. Snickering at the driver's technique was bad enough; preempting the seat alongside him without consulting him was worse. Deciding who would share the driver's box was the driver's prerogative. If the weather was good and his mood congenial, he might ask the express messenger to yield his place temporarily to a favored passenger. It was an honor travelers seldom refused, precarious as the perch might seem.

There was no experience like it, sitting next to a Jehu decked out in the finery he sported, watching him deftly wield his whip — its stock sometimes aglitter with silver — but best of all, listening to his wit and wisdom.

Occasionally the driver might surprise a cultured seatmate by his familiarity with a foreign language or two or with Shakespeare or Scripture. More often he proved to be a natural storyteller, spinning yarns by the score. An Englishman who on several occasions served as an audience later wryly observed that some drivers "have really such excessive regard for the truth that they use it with penurious frugality." Few other travelers found that a fault.

Inevitably, as passengers reported with relish about such encounters, a stereotype of the stage driver as knight of the road became fixed in the popular imagination. Sadly, however, there were exceptions. Some drivers were arrant show-offs; one of them was so proud of his short, quick turns that he eventually overturned his stage and smashed it. Now and then a driver turned to crime. Frank Williams drove his Montana stage into an ambush and called out, "Here they are, boys." His seven waiting co-conspirators killed five passengers and made off with express valuables worth $70,000. Williams was tracked to Denver, captured and hanged.

There were drivers who were fools or cowards. Alexander McClure and his wife were riding a stage during the Indian wars of the late 1860s when the driver announced that he would take care of himself in the event of attack, even if it meant taking one of his lead horses and deserting his stage and passengers. But McClure and another occupant of the coach were armed, and the driver was soon given to understand that he and his lead horse were to remain with the stage.

Fortunately for Western travel, many more drivers were capable of heroism. A typical example was Hank

An Indian war party, swooping down on a stage in this scene by artist George Simons, encounters unexpected resistance from a security escort of soldiers riding on the roof. The Army could rarely spare men for such duty, and stage lines sometimes had to detour around danger areas.

Harper, who was shot by an Indian sniper in Utah in 1862. He crumpled into the boot below his seat, dying, and gasped for one of the passengers. In response, a corpulent judge clambered up the side of the swaying coach. Harper fitted the reins into his hand and gave him instructions on how to take the road. By the time the judge brought the team to a halt at the next station, Hank Harper was dead.

Bob Emery was driving a coach in Kansas in 1864 when Indians jumped it. The terrified passengers shrieked for more speed; Emery put the whip to the horses. In *The Omaha Bee*'s account: "There were two points at which all would have been lost but for the driver's wonderful presence of mind. There were two abrupt turns in the road where the coach would have been thrown over had he not brought the team to a halt and turned with care. This he did to the dismay of some of the passengers, who saw escape only in speed, but their subsequent praise of his conduct was as great as his courage was cool and calculating. George Constable, who was conducting an ox train over the route, saw the coach about a mile ahead, and at once corralled his twenty-five wagons. The brave driver drove his nine passengers into this shelter and safety."

Emery died of illness within the year; on his deathbed one of the passengers he had saved brought him a gold ring engraved with the group's thanks and slipped it onto his finger.

A time always came on the long journey westward when stage travelers began to wish devoutly for its end. The reasons were many: the critical loss of sleep, the grinding discomfort of close quarters, hours of tedium, hours of terrifying peril either natural or man-made. The worst was the lack of sleep.

The passengers in the coach would doze, drop into deeper slumber, fall against their neighbors, awaken with a start and begin to doze again. They braced themselves when they could, but usually their heads rolled and their necks strained with each jolt of the coach. Their legs swelled, their muscles cramped, their joints began to throb. Each movement pushed someone else and forced him to move; half comatose, the passengers muttered and grumbled. Again they would sleep, and again they would awaken, not sure if they had been asleep for an hour or a minute. A California physician,

The desolation of eastern Utah badlands called the Devil's Playground engulfs a stagecoach whose crew and passenger are bundled up against the chill. The biting winds and dust of such barren stretches were as much a trial to stage travelers as the risk of an Indian attack or an accident.

Dr. Joseph Tucker, fell victim to "the horribly weird feeling that accompanies the effort to resist slumber." He often woke from what seemed like hours of sleep to discover that only minutes had elapsed.

Under such conditions people abraded each other's nerves, and tempers often flared. Passenger friction could be deadly serious. In March 1866, a passenger on the overland route went berserk, stabbed a fellow traveler, then drew a pistol, killed a second passenger and wounded a third before he himself was shot to death —all within the narrow, rocking confines of the coach.

Lacking a doctor to certify a traveler's madness, stage drivers and passengers alike kept a careful eye out for strange behavior. When incipient delirium was detected in a passenger, he was sometimes forced to stay over at a stage station and, despite his protests, take his chances on the next coach. Now and then such passengers wandered away from stations in a daze and disappeared. Journalist Richardson referred to "stage-craziness" as a recognized malady of the West.

Accidents also tended to become more frequent as the miles wore on, not because of driver carelessness, but because of a decline in the quality of the teams that were used. The horses hitched to the stage in front of the Planters' House in Atchison had been handsome and disciplined, inspiring confidence in nervous travelers. But as the stage moved west and left behind settled farms and breeding ranches, half-wild stock was pressed into service. Passengers would watch in barely concealed terror as squealing, kicking, biting mustangs —obviously barely broken—were forced into harness. A stock tender would have to stand by the head of each animal until all was ready; then at a signal the men would jump back. One brace of mustangs fought so hard they broke out of the harnesses, reared straight up and fell backward, with one landing completely underneath the stage, kicking up at the stage flooring. The horrified passengers fled.

Newly broken teams started off so violently that novice travelers inside the coach would assume they were the victims of a runaway. Mark Twain noted that with a team of mustangs "the coach shot out of the station as if it had issued from a cannon." When such teams rocketed out, they were likely to maintain a hard gallop for miles. The coach would rock and jounce, hurtling the occupants about and tempting them to leap out. Passengers were frequently admonished to "stick to the coach," since jumping out, no matter how tempting, was more dangerous than hanging on.

Mules, which were also used on the western end of the stage run, could be as obstreperous as mustangs and as accident-prone. Of one episode that Albert Richardson and Horace Greeley suffered through together, Richardson wrote, "The mules ran down a precipitous bank, upsetting the coach which was hurled up on the ground with a tremendous crash. . . . I sprang out in time to escape being overturned. From a mass of cushions and blankets soon emerged *Greeley*. Blood was flowing profusely from cuts in his cheek, arm and leg." Greeley made only passing reference to this nasty wreck in his own account of his travel experiences, but in fact his leg had been injured seriously and he was to limp for the rest of his life.

Danger to life and limb from Western mustangs and mules was real enough; and so was the damage done to digestive tracts by Western food. Since the meals served at home stations en route were not included in the price of passage but had to be paid for with good hard cash, travelers bitterly resented the steady drop in quality —or its total disappearance—the farther along they went. Nostalgia set in for meals that had been enjoyed early in the journey.

Alexander McClure remembered arriving at Alkalai Station, west of Fort Kearney, at 10 o'clock one night; despite the lateness of the hour, the spread that was laid before him included fried ham, stewed veal, fried potatoes, canned tomatoes, peas, warm rolls and tolerable butter, blackberries, peach pie, coffee and tea. When Greeley stopped in the same area he was highly pleased with a more modest but lovingly prepared repast of bacon and greens, good bread, applesauce and pie. Yet only 50 or so miles to the west his colleague in the fourth estate, Richardson—forced by a flooding stream to stay overnight in a town that had only three buildings —morosely faced up to "the inevitable fat pork, hot biscuits and muddy coffee."

Once, while Richardson and Greeley were traveling together, they thought they saw a way to solve the problem of increasingly atrocious station meals. Their coach was speeding along a stretch of road when, to their utter surprise, they spotted a small tent at the wayside, with the word "grocery" labeled on it in enormous letters. This bonus was too good an opportunity to pass up, and the two men requested the driver to stop so they could buy some food.

As Richardson told the story: "With keen appetites we awake the melancholy merchant who in green spectacles is sleeping soundly between two whiskey barrels.

'Have you any crackers?'

'Nary cracker.'

'Any bread?'

'Any *what?*'

'Bread.'

'No, *sir,*' (indignantly) 'I don't keep a bakery.'

'Any ham?'

'No.'

'Any figs?'

'No.'

'Well, what *have* you?'

'Why, I have sardines, pickled oysters, smoking tobacco and, stranger, I have got some of the best whiskey you ever seen since you was born.'"

A story widely told on the plains summed up the food situation. At one station a hungry stage passenger sat down at the table and the station keeper placed a huge platter of rancid pork and a pot of mustard in front of him. "Is that all?" asked the disappointed traveler. "Thunder," was the reply, "I'd of thought that was enough for six men." "But I don't eat pork," said the traveler. "Oh," counseled the keeper, "then help yourself to the mustard."

By the time Mark Twain had crossed the country, he saw a "dismal plausibility" to the pork-and-mustard story "that took all the humor out of it." Twain himself had better luck with food at one stop on his Western journey. At the Green River, Wyoming, station he enjoyed a big breakfast of fresh antelope steak, hot biscuits and coffee and pronounced it "the only decent meal we tasted between the United States and Great Salt Lake City."

Frank Root, though a loyal employee of the stage line, admitted that the company was "more on furnishing passengers with the substantials than the delicacies." The farther the travelers got from settled areas where farming was taking hold, the more they found themselves subsisting on two pitiful meals a day of fried salt pork of dubious age, corn dodgers (fried or boiled corn-bread cakes), dried fruit and bitter coffee for which there was sometimes sugar but rarely any milk.

One man complained to a station keeper of obvious dirt in the meal served him.

"Well, sir," said the keeper, mustering a Biblical allusion, "I was taught long ago that we must all eat our 'peck of dirt.'"

"I am aware of that fact, my dear sir," said the passenger, "but I don't like to eat mine all at once."

Like the food, the quality of the home stations themselves deteriorated as the stage moved into more desolate and less settled country, plunging the spirits of the travelers even deeper. The first stations out of Atchison were often pleasant log structures with a corral and outbuildings. In the stations between Fort Kearney and the Rockies every building was of adobe—sundried brick—with a sod roof, leading the irrepressible Twain to observe that this was the "first time we had seen a man's front yard on top of his house."

Twain described what the traveler fresh from the East encountered. "The buildings consisted of barns, stable room for twelve or fifteen horses and a hut for an eating room for passengers. This latter had bunks in it for the station keeper and a hostler or two. You could rest your elbow on its eaves, and you had to bend in order to get in at the door. In place of a window there was a square hole about large enough for a man to crawl through, but this had no glass in it. There was no flooring, but the ground was packed hard. There was no stove, but the fireplace served. There were no shelves, no cupboards, no closets. In a corner stood an open sack of flour, and nestling against its base were a couple of black and venerable tin coffeepots, a tin tea pot, a little bag of salt and a side of bacon. By the door on the ground outside was a tin washbasin. Near it was a pail of water and a piece of yellow bar soap, and from the eaves hung a hoary blue woolen shirt—this was the station keeper's private towel."

Crude as adobe may have seemed to an Eastern eye, it actually was a sound building material. Three-foot walls were cool in summer and warm in winter and, as Frank Root pointed out, were fireproof, bulletproof, Indian-proof and would last for centuries. But the stations still looked like hovels to passengers accustomed to Eastern amenities. The very character of the buildings indicated to thoughtful travelers that the journey would probably get worse before it got better. Even

The grim scene of a coach severed in half, its dead horses still in harness, draws spectators after an accident near Redding, California. Careening over on uneven terrain was a constant hazard of stagecoach travel.

Wreck of Weaverville Stage near Redding, Cal.

when there was time for a nap, the only passengers not condemned to stretch out on the earthen floor were women; a woman was allowed to share the bed of the station keeper's wife — if the keeper were gallant enough to yield his place. Bad as the rest accommodations were, the facilities for refreshing oneself were worse. At the least, washing water had to be hauled from a creek; some stations had to cart water a dozen miles.

There was only one redeeming feature to offset the ordeal of coping with the generally primitive conditions, the indescribable filth and inedible food. After the close company on the coach, travelers — especially the journalists among them — were delighted to see new faces and hear new stories. Among the people passing through, or visiting from the ranches and settlements nearby, were buffalo hunters, Indian-fighters, stockmen and assorted adventurers. Twain had the unusual experience of encountering an old boyhood friend with whom he had been on the outs since the time he had dropped a watermelon on the fellow's head from a second-story window in Hannibal, Missouri. His friend hadn't taken this at all well but now, a thousand miles from home, the old animus was forgotten.

Horace Greeley discovered that a station keeper he engaged in conversation was a former Cincinnati lawyer, and his wife a onetime actress in New York City. But they were an unusually polished couple; most of the station people were predictably roughhewn. Twain thought that "from western Nebraska to Nevada a considerable sprinkling of them might be fairly set down as outlaws." The men sported blue homespun pantaloons patched with yellow buckskin and stuffed into high boots. Often protruding from one boot was a horn-handled fighting knife, and many keepers carried a long-barreled Colt's revolver in a belt holster.

The solitude they endured could be punishing. Loneliness explained the pets, usually cats — once even a brace of owls — that travelers found at stations. Sometimes, in the desperate mutual need for companionship, the station people would have the residents of other stations and ranches come in from miles around for a dance. There would be music and whiskey and laughter all night; in the morning the revelers would hitch a ride on a stage back to their stark lives.

Stage passengers could feel the anguish of isolation in the hunger these outlanders had for news and reading material. Richardson remembered an unkempt stock tender who, after hitching up a new team, held up his lantern to the coach and asked the passengers, "Gentlemen, can you spare me a newspaper? I have not seen one for a week and can't endure it much longer. I will give a dollar for any newspaper in the United States not more than ten days old."

In all there were 153 home stations between Atchison and Placerville and ultimately the last of them was passed. By then the original complement of passengers on a coach had been replaced, at least in part, by new travelers. Some of the early ones had gotten off at Denver, others at Salt Lake City — either to change to the California-bound coach, or to stay in the Mormon capital, or to travel on small feeder stage lines to towns and settlements well distant from the main overland route.

An amateur poet on one coach, looking back over his trek westward, produced some lines of doggerel that he thought summed up the venture:

Creeping through the valley, crawling o'er the hill,
Splashing through the branches, rumbling o'er the mill;
Putting nervous gentlemen in a towering rage.
What is so provoking as riding in a stage?

Spinsters fair and forty, maids in youthful charms,
Suddenly are cast into their neighbors' arms;
Children shoot like squirrels darting through a cage
Isn't it delightful, riding in a stage?

Feet are interlacing, heads severely bumped,
Friends and foe together get their noses thumped;
Dresses act as carpets — listen to the sage:
"Life is but a journey taken in a stage."

When finally the last night passed and the last joltings were over, most passengers were not inclined to such philosophizing. Exhausted and dirty as they pulled themselves together, they got off the stage without looking back and headed for a hotel, a bath, a barber and a bed. William Tallack of England, a man of extraordinary good spirits, remembered "leaping off the coach" when it came to a halt; he must have had unusual strength left. Albert Richardson saw the arrival as a kind of triumph: "Our vehicle whirled around the last street corner, ran for several yards poised upon two wheels, while the others were more than a foot from the ground; and with this neat stroke ended our ride."

The long journey was over, and the travelers were glad of it. But inevitably, after the irritation had worn off, the view in retrospect was one of pride of participation in an unforgettable exploit.

Everyone, it seemed, had a special memory, a special story to tell. The foresighted Easterner who had brought some victuals with him recalled how he had saved the day on one stretch of the road when a wheel grew so hot it locked on the axle. Wheels were supposed to be greased at every home station, but sometimes this chore was ignored. Lacking grease, the driver was considering laying blades of grass along the axle for the wheel to turn on when the Easterner produced a piece of cheese. They cut thin slices, wound them around the axle, slipped the wheel back on and rode into the next station.

Demas Barnes, a mining inspector, always got a laugh telling about the day he found himself sharing his coach with a young widow and her four small children. As night fell, Barnes did his best for the children, arranging mail sacks and blankets into beds for them. The children drifted off to sleep, but their mother paled with terror. Barnes, a well-intentioned man, described her anguish: "The woman! — dear me! — not gifted with Eve's gentle confidences, posted herself upright in the furthest corner, and insisted she would not sleep all night; and I think she would have declared she had kept her word had I not had to climb out for her lost bonnet once or twice. The Lord forgive her awful suspicions!"

A preacher remembered riding along the Platte in 1867 when Indians attacked. By a rare chance he happened to be the sole passenger at the time. The Indians' first volley killed the driver, knocking him off the box. The minister described what followed: "I saw the driver keel over and the horses swerve from the road off onto the prairie. My first impulse was to get the lines and fetch the horses back on the road. So I climbed out of the window and got upon the box, but the lines had dropped on the ground. I climbed down to pick up the lines, the Indians popping away all the time, and just then the coach struck a wallow. Down I went into the mud and the stage went on without me." To his surprise and pleasure, the Indians followed the stage and he crawled off to the river and safety.

Alexander McClure's wife also recalled an encounter with Indians that turned out all right, but what she

remembered most vividly was quaking on the coach floor, and clutching a revolver her husband had given her —with strict orders to turn it on herself if the Indians succeeded in their attack.

McClure's own favorite story concerned a day of unbelievable winter weather during a feeder-line ride from Virginia City, Montana, eastward. "The atmosphere was thick with frost," he wrote, "and throughout the day the sun was unfelt. The horses' nostrils were covered with ice and the mustaches of the driver and passengers were all frozen into uniform whiteness. That night the mercury stood at thirty below zero."

The travelers stopped for the night at a station and the next day exchanged their coach for an open sleigh, whose runners could negotiate the snowy roads better than the wheels of the coach. They started at five in the morning, McClure recalled, and "not a face was visible. The driver had a fur mask and the passengers looked like so many blocks covered with robes. Just as day was breaking, the sleigh got off the beaten road and we were tumbled pell-mell into snow up to our waists.

It was a terrible ordeal, for our hands were almost frozen, even in our fur gloves, before we got restored to our places. Three upsets before ten o'clock relieved the monotony of this memorable morning ride."

One of the most spellbinding experiences of all befell Dr. Tucker, the California physician, and he related it at loving length. He was on his way home to San Francisco from St. Louis, and traveling not the central overland route but by way of the south. Perhaps it was the heat that helped kindle the passions of which he told.

Tucker was sitting with a handsome plainsman from Texas when two gamblers, accompanied by two women, entered the coach. All of the newcomers were French. Soon a flirtation began between "Texas" and the younger woman. The next to enter the coach was a fat, foul-tempered German (Tucker had decided ethnic views), who complained of the crowding and insisted on smoking a strong pipe, despite the presence of ladies. Eventually he went to sleep leaning against the door and snored loudly. "Texas" reached around him and slipped the door latch; the door opened on the next bump and the German fell out. When his fellow passengers retrieved him, he furiously accused them of attempted murder and became so violent that they refused to let him reenter the coach, forcing him to ride on top.

The younger Frenchwoman so enjoyed this incident that her ardor for "Texas" increased. Her escort grew resentful, one thing led to another, and there was a challenge to a duel. The story has an air of improbable melodrama, but Tucker was a respected physician and he reported what followed as fact. As the stage reached a station in northern Texas, the recipient of the challenge, the Texan, chose revolvers as the dueling weapon. With Tucker and the older Frenchman acting as seconds, the duelists went to a corral behind the station. The two foes entered opposite gates, their pistols ready.

In Dr. Tucker's words: "Suddenly the Frenchman dropped his revolver and quickly fired two shots. At the second discharge, 'Texas' half-wheeled to the left and staggered. His exposed left arm was shattered near the wrist. He sprang forward several paces and fired." He missed, the Frenchman shot again, but neither was touched in this exchange. Blood was pouring from the Texan's arm as he approached his enemy; the Frenchman paused and then they fired together. This time, the Frenchman, still unhurt, knocked the Texan's hat off. Tucker continued: "Then 'Texas' dropped upon one knee and, resting his revolver across his wounded arm, fired with deliberate aim. His antagonist was at the moment also in the act of firing, but the Texan's bullet reached his heart before he could press the trigger. Throwing his arms in the air, the Frenchman fell dead!"

Leaving the dead man's friends to cope with his corpse, the rest of the passengers hastily took off. Tucker continued: "The driver had eaten his supper, fresh horses were in harness, and 'Texas' and myself could only seize some food and jump into the coach, as the six wild mustangs started off on a fierce gallop. I also carried off some shingles, to splint the broken arm."

Tucker learned from his driver that the French group were drifting gamblers. He was to hear no more of them, but years later he chanced upon the Texan, who had become a staid and wealthy cattle owner in his native state. Tucker went on to hold a variety of important positions in the California state government. But until the day that he died, in 1891, he considered his stagecoach ride the high point of his long life.

To keep the mail and passengers moving when winter blanketed the Sierra, some coach lines switched to sleighs that could skim over snow where it was packed hard enough to support the horses. In this 1871 sketch by W. H. Hilton two four-horse sled-coaches meet on the Placerville Road.

6 | Assembling a behemoth

In April of 1868, crowds turned out all across the country to gawk at a spectacle that provided a climax of sorts to the age of the expressmen. No fewer than 30 new stagecoaches were being shipped on flatcars from the Abbot-Downing factory in Concord, New Hampshire, to a railhead on the Missouri River. The record-breaking shipment had been ordered by Wells, Fargo & Company to expand the already superb service of its far-flung stage empire, which by then had absorbed or crushed every major competitor west of the Missouri.

Yet staging was just one of many activities of Wells, Fargo. Established in San Francisco in 1852 as a service for delivery of lightweight valuables, the company steadily overspread the West with branch offices manned by efficient, imaginative personnel; at the same time, it moved into all phases of transport. By ship, coach, freight wagon and mule train, its agents delivered practically everything—food, families, fire-fighting equipment and even fancy ladies—from any point in the world to new towns in the middle of nowhere.

When the 1860s drew toward a close, Wells, Fargo ranked as the biggest, richest and most versatile corporate entity in the West. Soon—sooner than the company's directors guessed—the completion of the transcontinental railroad would deal its staging fleet a heavy blow, but Wells, Fargo switched onto the rails and kept growing with the West that it had served so well.

A piggyback armada of stagecoaches rolls westward in 1868, bound for service under the Wells, Fargo banner.

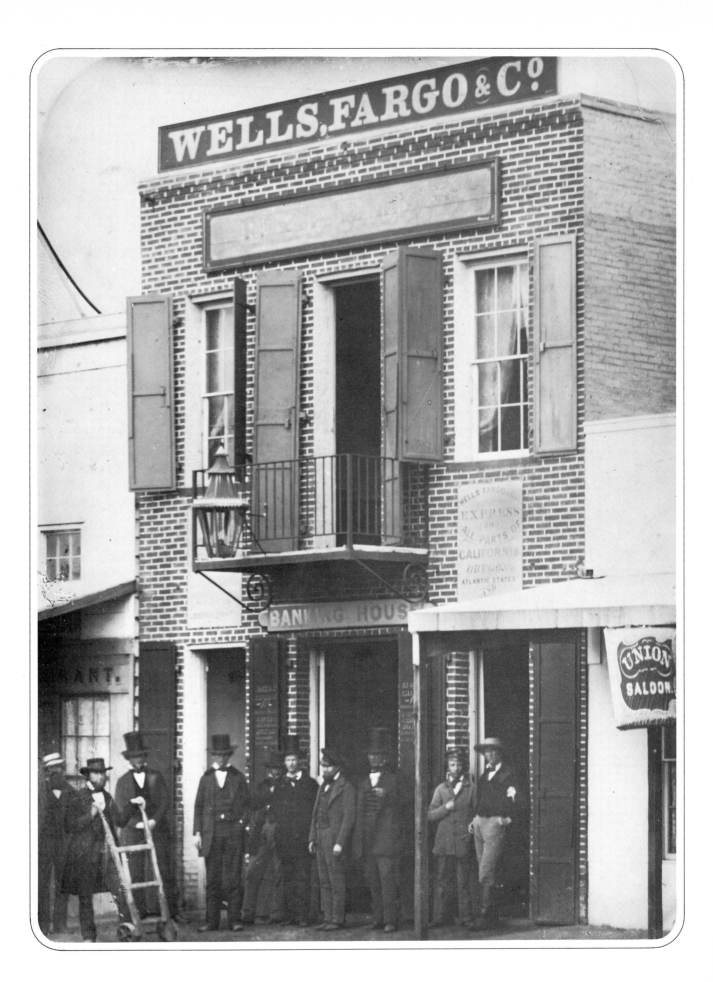

The Western express that "did almost anything for anybody"

Just about everywhere in the West in the late 1860s travelers were sure to see block-lettered signs that said "Wells, Fargo" and the distinctive green color that was a company trademark. Almost every stagecoach had "Wells, Fargo" blazoned on its elegant curved flank, and a green strongbox hidden inside. A Wells, Fargo office, with iron shutters — painted green — at the windows, was the focal point of commercial activity in more than 200 towns. Throughout California, Wells, Fargo mailboxes — green, of course — stood brazenly beside red boxes labeled U.S. Mail. Wells, Fargo green was, obviously, as good as gold.

If a curious visitor from the East chose to ask about Wells, Fargo, he was not likely to get a satisfactory answer. Just about every Westerner knew the company's name as well as his own; its success was legendary and its honesty and reliability so proverbial that miners swore "by God and by Wells, Fargo." But precisely because the company was so huge, so far-flung and so preeminent in so many different activities, no one could sum it up easily. Those who tried usually ended up with some grandiose platitude, like "ready companion of civilization." Possibly the best epitome was delivered by a long-time admirer of the company who wrote: "Wells, Fargo went everywhere, did almost anything for anybody, and was the nearest thing to a universal service company ever invented."

Specifically, this "universal service company" was, by the mid-1860s, the West's most important express agency, richest bank, farthest-ranging stage line and one of the largest freighting concerns. Taken as a whole, it was the most powerful institution of any kind in the

West — looming even larger than the U.S. government, whose departments had then only tenuously penetrated the trans-Mississippi frontier.

Wells, Fargo served as a sort of surrogate government. Its immense bureaucracy of agents, clerks and messengers handled more mail than the Post Office. Its shotgun guards, seated beside each driver on a careering stage, were often the only lawmen for miles around, and they chalked up a remarkable record of capturing highwaymen and recovering loot. The company tempered its exercise of power with enlightened responsibility. It collected relief funds and delivered food and clothing for victims of disasters, such as the great Sacramento fire in the fall of 1852. It helped keep the West informed by distributing out-of-town and Eastern newspapers, free of charge, to local editors for culling and excerpting. Naturally, editors repaid the favor with good publicity for Wells, Fargo, redounding in still more business for the company and still larger dividends (as high as 22 per cent a year) for its stockholders.

Steady profits over the long haul — that was Wells, Fargo's goal, and one that it richly realized. No other giant company in the field of East-West transportation and communication had managed this feat in an era when competition was cutthroat even for meager way-stop business in isolated frontier towns. Within 15 years of the founding of Wells, Fargo in San Francisco in 1852, every one of its major rivals — despite the fact that they had enjoyed hefty government mail subsidies — had been absorbed, bankrupted or forced to quit.

The two businessmen who gave their names to this California-based colossus were Easterners who, curiously enough, were content to stay in the East and direct the fortunes of their company from a distance of 3,000 miles. Henry Wells made only one brief inspection visit to the West Coast, and William G. Fargo seems never to have ventured beyond the Mississippi at

---

Wells, Fargo employees gather outside the firm's first office, built on San Francisco's Montgomery Street in 1852. The green iron shutters became a company trademark.

Wells, Fargo founders Henry Wells *(left)* and William Fargo *(right)* used acumen gained in the East to build a giant company that controlled virtually all stage lines between the Missouri River and California.

all. Apparently neither partner felt the need to know the West as intimately as their pioneer predecessors had known it. Alexander Todd, hauling miners' mail and gold dust, had learned about the Sierra foothills the hard way. James Birch, driving a ramshackle ranch wagon full of passengers, had come to recognize every rock along the rude trail on which his staging empire got its start. Wells and Fargo, though contemporaries of Todd and Birch, represented a new breed of entrepreneur, much more at home behind a desk than battling the rigors of the frontier. Theirs was a world of ledgers, directors' meetings and corporate maneuverings. Under the banner of Wells, Fargo, adventure was never lacking, but it was left to underlings.

Vermont-born Henry Wells was 35 and experienced as a steamboat operator on the New York waterfront when, in 1841, he went to work as an agent for William Harnden *(page 16)*, founder of the first express firm of them all. After a few months of learning the ropes, Wells left Harnden's employ and teamed up with another expressman, carrying mail and packages between Albany and Buffalo by means of the available stagecoach and rail services. Wells was husky and

broad-shouldered and entirely capable of the physical effort involved, but he also bubbled with shrewd ideas. He soon ensured the success of the new firm with a novel service that brought him customers by word-of-mouth publicity: to the delight of Buffalo's landlocked gourmets, he supplied a local restaurant with fresh Long Island oysters at three dollars a hundred.

By 1843, business was good enough for Wells to hire a messenger to take over his traveling chores — William Fargo, a frugal, hard-working New Yorker. Two profitable years later, Wells made him a partner, and they organized another firm that extended their express service to Cincinnati and Chicago.

Efficiency was the keynote of their expanding operations; they managed to get the job done faster and cheaper than their competitors. They turned a profit delivering letters at six cents each when the U.S. Post Office was charging 25 cents. The Post Office ordered Wells to stop undercutting its rates. He replied with a bold counterproposal: his company would contract to deliver all U.S. mail, anywhere in the nation, for six or even five cents a letter. The Assistant Postmaster General hastily declined the offer, reportedly exclaiming, "Zounds, sir, it would throw 16,000 postmasters out of office!" but Henry Wells had made his point. The Post Office soon dropped its rates in the East all the way down to three cents a letter.

By 1850, Wells and Fargo were big operators — and eager to get even bigger. The way to do it, they decided, was to merge their two firms with an express company controlled by John Butterfield. At the time, Butterfield's most celebrated venture — operating the first transcontinental stage line over the southern Oxbow Route — was still in the future. When Wells and Fargo approached Butterfield in New York, the proposed merger struck him as a fine idea. The deal was made and the resulting firm was named American Express.

It was an instant giant, and its very name reflected the founders' ambition to make it an all-encompassing, nationwide enterprise. But Wells and Fargo met stubborn resistance from some of their fellow directors on the board. Wells and Fargo wanted American Express to set up a base in California, in order to cash in on the gold riches that had been pouring out of the Mother Lode country since 1849. Customarily, the gold was brought by its finders to a California bank or express company — often one and the same firm — and shipped east to U.S. government mints in Philadelphia and New Orleans to be converted into gold coin, which was then shipped back to the West. For their services as expediters, express companies levied a charge of from 3 to 5 per cent of the value of the shipment. Just how neat a return this could bring them was evident from the fact that in 1851 alone the total gold shipped east was valued at $60 million.

Wells and Fargo were fully aware that an American Express operation in California would have to compete with companies already entrenched there, but they cheerfully felt that there would be profits enough to go round. Some of the other directors, Butterfield included, were less optimistic; they hung back, apparently in the belief that the gold bonanza would soon peter out.

Unable to budge them, Wells and Fargo decided to invade California on their own. They saw no reason to relinquish either their positions or their financial stake in American Express, since a connection east of the Mississippi was vital to the plan they had in mind. On March 18, 1852, the two men met at the Astor House Hotel in New York City with seven other financial backers and formed a new express company specif-

ically to serve California and the Western frontier. The new concern, capitalized at $300,000, was christened Wells, Fargo & Company.

Wells and Fargo acted with their characteristic swiftness. Less than four months later, early in July, two carefully selected agents — one to oversee banking services and one in charge of express services — opened the first Wells, Fargo office in a narrow red-brick building at 114 Montgomery Street in San Francisco. The red of the brick made a striking contrast to the green of the iron window shutters, which had been specially cast in Brooklyn and sent by ship to California. It may have been Wells, Fargo's founders themselves who thought up this added touch of decor. In any case, it caught the fancy of San Francisco's citizens, who also liked what they saw inside the building: a neat, well-planned office with an array of strongboxes standing ready to receive consignments of gold.

By the following February, when Wells paid his one and only visit to check on the operation and inspect the office and the books, business was off to a good start. Wells briefly surveyed the California scene, commented that "This is a great country and a greater people," and soon departed on his return sea voyage homeward. The lieutenants he left behind must have been pleasantly surprised; in an era of rampant individualism, most employers tended to be domineering and interfering, playing hunches that were sometimes brilliant but just as often disastrous. Wells had manifestly given his men in the West a resounding vote of confidence. Everyday operations were to be left entirely in the charge of capable and well-financed managers, while the directors of the company remained back in the East and planned their strategy for expansion.

Though the prospect of profits on gold shipments was the lure that had brought Wells, Fargo west, the company made clear from the start that it saw few limits to the services it could lucratively render. It ticked them off in an advertisement in San Francisco's leading daily, the *Alta California:*

"Wells, Fargo is now ready to undertake a general express forwarding agency and commission business; the purchase and sale of gold dust, bullion and bills of exchange; the payment and collection of notes, bills and accounts; the forwarding of gold dust, bullion and specie; also packages, parcels and freight of all descriptions,

By the late 1850s, as indicated by this poster, Wells, Fargo was operating on an international scale, but deliveries to California mining towns still ranked first among the many services the company provided.

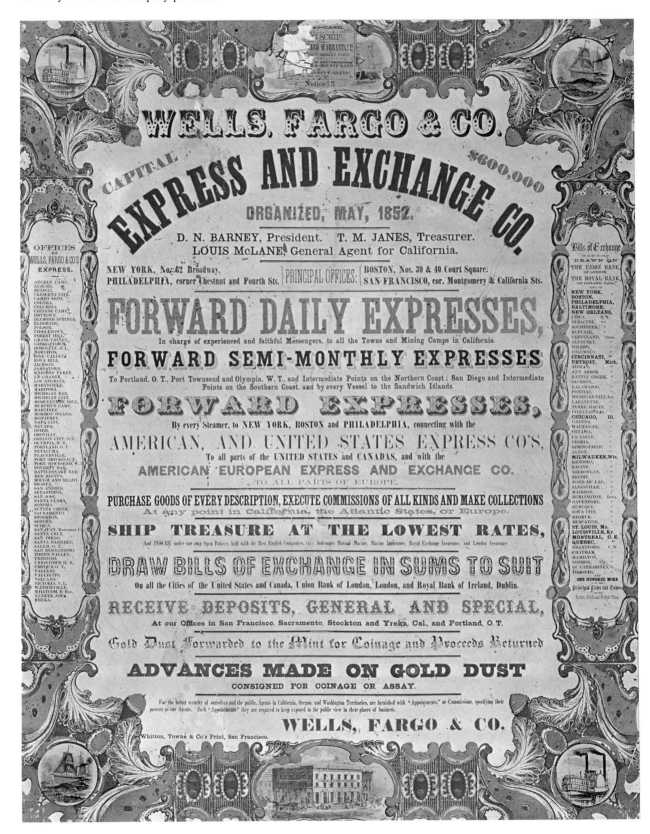

between the city of New York and the city of San Francisco, and the principal cities and towns in California."

Moreover, Wells, Fargo informed readers: "Energetic and faithful messengers furnished with iron chests for the security of treasure and other valuable packages" would accompany each shipment, inside California as well as beyond it—even in the Atlantic states.

This sweeping promise was made possible, so far as the East was concerned, through the connection Wells and Fargo retained in American Express. Shipments by sea from the Pacific Coast and across the Isthmus of Panama could be picked up at Eastern ports by American Express employees and transported to destinations anywhere in the network of cities covered by that company. The same arrangement could work in reverse for express shipments west. Within California itself, there were small, short-haul express lines whose facilities Wells, Fargo could hire—until it built up its own network or acquired other companies outright.

Before long, Californians and Easterners alike were ready to concede that this bold new enterprise was every bit as good as its word. Messengers assigned to guard gold and bullion on the long sea trips began to find that Wells, Fargo customers had trustingly committed other valuables to their charge—a piece of expensive jewelry or other prized personal possessions, sometimes even a wife and child traveling to join the family breadwinner. Customers in California found themselves relying more and more on Wells, Fargo's private mail service. No longer did they have to trek to a U.S. Post Office—then located in only a few of the larger towns—and wait interminably while clerks poked through mounds of backed-up letters. Instead, people could walk to the convenient Wells, Fargo branch office in their own town and pick up or send out their mail with no pain at all.

The establishment of branch offices was company policy from the outset. By the end of Wells, Fargo's first year it had opened them in Sacramento, Monterey, San Diego and other communities, a dozen in all, up and down the state. This move was one signal of its ambition to expand, but there was also another method of growth—buying out competitors.

Less than four years after the gold rush of 1849, ways of doing business in California were beginning to change drastically. The shrewdest businessmen now talked in terms of consolidation; the day of the lone entrepreneur, operating on a shoestring, was almost past. Mining offered a prime example of the changes afoot. A solitary gold seeker stood a decreasing chance of striking it rich because the surface veins he could probe with relative ease were beginning to play out. The mining country was still yielding up an immense treasure; some $81 million in raw gold passed through San Francisco during the peak year of 1852. But getting at the treasure now required the combined enterprise of men of substantial means, who could afford hydraulic rigs and other heavy machinery—yet who were prepared to pay miners no more than day wages.

Some of the ramifications of the change soon became evident in ordinary daily life. People seldom walked into stores any more and paid for small purchases with gold dust; instead they were using the gold coins, government-minted back East, that were being shipped west in increasing quantity. Now merchants no longer asked those applying for a clerk's job: "How much can you raise in a pinch?"—then hired the man with the biggest hands simply because in taking payment he was the one who could pick up more gold dust between his thumb and his forefinger.

Moves toward consolidation were taking place in businesses other than mining. The many small stagecoach companies that had sprung up in the first flush of gold fever were already debilitated by dog-eat-dog competition, and ready to throw in their lot with the most successful operator among them, James Birch; the California Stage Company, the giant monopoly that he fashioned in 1854, would absorb five sixths of the smaller stagecoaching firms.

Nor was the express business any exception to the trend. Lone messengers still rode from gold camp to gold camp, delivering letters as the original regular Western expressman, Alexander Todd, had done back in 1849. But the dozens of local one-man express outfits were fighting a rear-guard action against a few large, strong firms that were constantly extending their routes and expanding their power.

Thanks to their previous experience in the East, Wells and Fargo were old hands at the game of consolidation, and were more than willing to apply their knowhow in the West. In August 1852, only a month after Wells, Fargo & Company opened its doors in San Fran-

San Francisco's Montgomery Street, financial heart of the West, was the site of three successive Wells, Fargo headquarters. In 1854 the firm

occupied the arcaded edifice *(right foreground)* directly across from the Parrott Building —which was then home of the rival Adams & Company.

cisco, it bought out an express competitor with routes in Placer County — the heart of the Mother Lode country. In 1853 it acquired another competitor with routes in the southern mine region. In 1854 it bought out a third company — not only its express business but its offices and stage equipment. By the end of 1854, Wells, Fargo had 24 branch offices and only one major rival: Adams & Company.

The Adams company was, as Henry Wells conceded, "formidable opposition," considered by many Californians to be the state's leading corporation. The Western branch of a powerful Eastern express company of the same name, it had set up banking and express services in San Francisco in 1849, when its canny founder, Alvin Adams, whose rise from messenger paralleled that of Henry Wells, scented the prodigious sums to be reaped from the gold rush. Adams thus had a three-year jump on Wells, Fargo, and could claim the same advantage of an Eastern connection to help facilitate its services the country over.

In 1852, Adams signaled its success by moving into San Francisco's first stone structure, the new Parrott Building on Montgomery Street. The impressive façade was made of huge granite blocks shipped all the way from China. The city's Chinese population, by then numbering 20,000, took great pride in this fact. But as it turned out, the building was constructed in a way that they considered inauspicious, even accursed (*page 199*). They refused to enter it and proceeded to switch their banking and express patronage to Wells, Fargo. But the loss of these lucrative clients scarcely affected the high-riding Adams enterprise, or the banking firm of Page, Bacon and Company with which it shared the Parrott Building.

Though Henry Wells admitted that a declaration of war against Adams "demanded much courage and determination," Wells, Fargo decided to go on the offensive. One tactical thrust was symbolic; in 1854 it moved down Montgomery Street into new and larger headquarters directly opposite its competitor's granite temple of commerce. At the same time, the two firms engaged in a rate-slashing war, wooing each other's customers by reducing charges on gold and express shipments. In an ostensibly lighter vein, they also staged messenger races — supposedly sporting entertainment but actually contests intended to enhance the winner's

prestige and thus its business. One such race was run to see whose messenger would be the first to deliver in Portland, Oregon, the text of an important Presidential message that had arrived by ship in San Francisco. To speed the message north, each company stationed fresh horses and relief riders along the route.

William Lowden, who rode for Adams on a relay leg that started at Tehama, California, suggested some of the excitement of the race: "I sprang into the saddle with the bags, which weighed 54 pounds. I changed horses 19 times between Tehama and Shasta, touching the ground but once. This was at the Prairie House, where Tom Flynn, the man in charge of my horse, was actively engaged in a fight with the keeper of Wells, Fargo's horse and had let mine get loose. I rode my tired horse a little past where the fight was going on, sprang to the ground, caught the fresh horse by the tail as he was running away from me and went into the saddle over his rump at a single bound."

Lowden lost about one minute changing horses at Prairie House, but quickly made up the time and more: "All other changes I made while the horses were running, the keeper leading the horse I was to ride and riding his extra horse. When I reached him, the keeper would have my horse in a lively gallop, and I sprang from the one to the other. I reached Shasta, 60 miles, in two hours and 37 minutes."

Wells, Fargo not only lost that race but gained just a little financial ground on Adams, and that slowly. Records that were kept on shipments of gold to the East, dispatched every couple of weeks when a steamship left for the Isthmus of Panama, told the story plainly. On a random date in November 1854, Wells, Fargo shipped $177,000 in gold, Adams $350,000 and Page, Bacon $417,000.

But the two larger firms were growing careless and greedy. The high interest rates they charged for banking services — from 3 to 10 per cent per month — gave them the wherewithal to engage in a variety of business speculations. The general business climate was overheating dangerously. There were no banking controls in California; anyone with an office safe and plenty of nerve could declare himself a bank, accept deposits and make loans. And with so much gold being shipped to the East, even the big banks were often left with only a narrow margin of cash on hand. As long as the golden

A headquarters that had to be freed of Chinese demons

Wells, Fargo's third San Francisco headquarters building was as solid as the company itself—thanks, perhaps, to a rite of exorcism the company arranged before moving in.

It all began in 1851 when, after five fires swept through San Francisco in three years, millionaire Sam Parrott swore, "I'll put up a building this time that can't burn down." He ordered the granite for his building all the way from China, each stone to be marked at the quarry for its exact place in the structure. But when the granite blocks arrived, local Chinese masons absolutely refused to help with the construction. Baffled, Parrott brought the boss stonecutter over from China, and the mystery was solved —although, sadly not resolved. "You are placing your building on the wrong corner," the master mason said. "It should be on the opposite side. The stones are all marked for the other corner where no evil influences are to be encountered, as will be found here."

Work went on when Parrott's contractor promised to have the building exorcised. But, in the end, he reneged and, when Adams & Co., the big express rival of Wells, Fargo, moved in, Chinese customers took their business across the street to Wells, Fargo. Adams collapsed in a bank panic of 1855, and Wells, Fargo took over the building, first accepting the advice of its Chinese friends to have the accursed place purged. These solemn rites, involving the ceremonial burning of tea, rice and sacred papers, being duly completed, Wells, Fargo kept its Oriental clientele.

Whether the rites were effective or not, the fact is that the structure stood up well to ensuing evil influences. It came through unscathed when a box of nitroglycerin exploded in the building, killing 10. It survived the city's great earthquake and fire, and when it was razed 19 years later, wreckers had a terrible time tearing it down.

Completed in 1852, the Parrott Building became the head office of Wells, Fargo after its competitor, Adams & Co., went bankrupt there in 1855.

In a cartoon of the 1855 financial panic, a gloating gnome watches banks sink in San Francisco Bay. Below, a banker *(left)* indicates he is closed, while Wells, Fargo's rival, Adams & Co. *(right)*, crumbles.

stream continued to flow down from the mountains, no one seemed to care.

By early 1855, however, the stream was slackening. It was not only that the rich surface veins were petering out; just as ominous, an unusually dry season had lowered the mountain creeks that were essential to mining. Most miners found themselves out of work. In the East, too, there was financial unrest, partly because of overspeculation in stocks and commodities. As the crisis loomed, Wells, Fargo — smaller, better managed, and not as smug and complacent as its rivals — hunkered down to ride out the storm.

On February 18, 1855, the steamship *Oregon* arrived in San Francisco with the alarming news that

Page, Bacon's parent bank in the East had failed, a self-made victim of reckless speculation in railroad construction. Just before collapsing, the bank had stripped its San Francisco branch of $1 million in gold, leaving it woefully short of capital. Panicky depositors began withdrawing their funds. Anxiously, the manager called together the city's other bankers and, mustering considerable bravado, demanded their support. In turn, the bankers — among them William Tecumseh Sherman, soon to win fame as a Civil War general — demanded an audit of Page, Bacon's books. The manager refused and was abandoned to his fate. The run on the bank grew, and by February 22 its assets were exhausted. The run spread to other banks; on the same day Adams paid out more than $200,000. On February 23—afterward known as Black Friday—four of the leading banks in the city, including Wells, Fargo, did not open their doors for business.

At Wells, Fargo's request, an auditor immediately began to examine the books of its banking operations. At 10 p.m. on Saturday the firm issued a report that the *Alta California* printed the next morning: "Wells, Fargo & Co. have completed a balance of their accounts this day, and find to the credit of their house above every liability $389,106.23, and only ask of their friends a few days to convert some of their assets to resume payment." In fact, the firm reopened the following Tuesday morning and, after paying all its claims, had a surplus of more than $100,000 in cash. Page, Bacon went under. And not far behind it, embroiled in charges of embezzlement and other irregularities, was Adams' California branch. Adams filed a petition of insolvency and never reopened its doors. By the end of 1855 a total of 197 San Francisco business enterprises of every sort had failed, and another 140 toppled the following year.

In surviving the crash, Wells, Fargo achieved heroic stature in the eyes of frightened Californians. Henceforth they believed unquestioningly in the company and in its honesty, safety and integrity. In a flowery tribute, the *California Farmer* declared that, like gold "seven times purified," Wells, Fargo had emerged "from the fiery ordeal with increased lustre," and thus radiated "a name and fame that will endure."

To the victor went spoils as well as praise. Wells, Fargo moved across Montgomery Street into the great granite structure that had housed both Adams and Page, Bacon. Without any fanfare it brought in a Chinese priest, who performed a ceremony to rid the building at last of the evil emanations that made Chinese customers feel uncomfortable there. The company also inherited its defunct rivals' customers, and within a year or two it was firmly entrenched as the foremost business power in the West.

A new general manager of all California operations, appointed in 1856, symbolized Wells, Fargo's advance in status. Louis McLane, unlike previous company representatives in the West, was not content to remain anonymous. Member of a distinguished Baltimore family, he had first seen the West Coast as a naval officer attached to the U.S. expedition that seized the region from Mexico in 1846. Liking what he saw of the country, he resigned his commission and went into the shipping business. When Wells, Fargo sought a new Western manager after the panic of 1855, McLane's knowledge of transport and of California's affairs made him a natural choice.

His value to the company was soon proved in a wrangle with the U.S. government itself. The government's target was the private mail service that Wells, Fargo, along with other express companies, provided as a means of attracting customers. Heretofore the companies had charged only their own postage, but now Washington insisted that each of their letters also carry a government stamp. McLane and his counterparts in other firms fought the order and failed. But then McLane devised a way out of the dilemma. Figuring that by increasing Wells, Fargo's volume of mail he could absorb the additional cost per letter and still manage to come out ahead, he bought a supply of stamped government envelopes, printed the Wells, Fargo frank beside the U.S. postage, and sold the envelopes to customers. McLane's hunch proved correct; the envelopes turned out to be so popular with the public that by 1864 Wells, Fargo was selling more than two million of them a year and netting a neat profit.

Wells, Fargo further discomfited Washington by boldly installing its green mailboxes all over San Francisco and eventually throughout California. Patrons no longer had to come to Wells, Fargo offices to mail their letters, and the service in general was so much better that the green mailboxes attracted more business than the government's red ones.

Under McLane's stewardship, Wells, Fargo branch offices—a total of 55 in 1855—increased to 126 by 1859; and there were more to come as new mineral strikes created pockets of settlement in the frontier wilderness. To the Wells, Fargo agent who appeared to set up a new office, it made no difference if the raw new digs had primitive facilities, or none at all. When agent Dave Ward rode into Nevada's fabulous Comstock Lode country in 1860, the silver camp that was soon to become Virginia City was still nothing but a sprawl of tents and shacks. Across from the tent that housed the main mining headquarters, Ward pitched his own tent and hung a Wells, Fargo sign from its

A young agent's "days long to be remembered"

The Wells, Fargo representative was a big man in any community, in more ways than one. "You are aware that I am an Agent of the House of Wells, Fargo & Co., an express and banking house of a half-million dollars' capital and unbounded credit," 21-year-old John Q. Jackson wrote home from Auburn, California. "My position," he assured his father back in Virginia in 1852, "throws me in contact with the heaviest business men of the state —Bankers, Lawyers, Judges, Merchants & all do business through us. The office is my passport to any society in which I may choose to move and withal is one of good profit."

The proud letter writer was Wells, Fargo's first agent in Auburn, seat of gold-rich Placer County. Jackson had left home at 18 and sailed around the Horn to join the 1849 gold rush. When he found prospecting "Getting rather dull," he established general stores at Ophir and Bear Creek, California, served as an election official and was appointed a postmaster before joining Wells, Fargo in 1852.

It was a grueling seven-day-a-week job, busiest on Sundays. "What I have to do is quite confining," he wrote his brother, "staying in my office all day till 10 at night buying dust, forwarding & receiving packages of every kind, from and to everywhere —filling out drafts for the Eastern Mails in all sorts of sums and drawing checks on the Offices below, when men wish to take money to the cities." Gold dust had to be cleaned, weighed, sealed and packed for forwarding. Books had to be balanced. Incoming letters had to be sorted, out-

Agent Jackson at age 24

going letters had to be listed for the messenger who left at daybreak.

But the compensations were ample. "I might have stayed in Virginia," he told his brother, "and never had $1,000 entrusted to me or been worth anything myself." Now he had a "handsome" monthly income, of which part came from the 25-cent fee he collected for himself on every letter he picked up at the post office for forwarding by Wells, Fargo.

Social opportunities, by virtue of Jackson's position, were enticing. "I returned from a ball a few days ago after spending a very pleasant night in company with the *First* ladies of the County," he wrote to his father. And later he added: "There are some very fascinating married ladies here, one of whom might possible ilope [sic] with me should I [illegible] the matter."

Most satisfying of all, perhaps, Jackson had gained "the utmost con-

fidence of the 'Heads' of the Concern in San Francisco & Sacramento." His performance during the panic of 1855 proved their confidence was merited. "Yesterday & today," he wrote his father on February 24, 1855, "have been days long to be remembered by me. On the night of the 22nd I was present at a ball . . . where I remained until 4 a.m. At 8 o'clock I was awoke by a messenger handing me a telegraphic dispatch to the effect that Adams Co. had failed to prepare for a run. I instantly got up & at the moment I reached the door crowds were running towards the office. I knew that our funds would not meet all our outstanding draft certificates. Very soon Adams Co. here had paid out all their funds and still were short some $20,000. The crowd were now furious. I saw no other plan but to open [the office] and let it [cash on hand] go as far as it would—paying out commenced and the work got pretty warm. I made arrangements for funds to the amount of all the demands against us—the time ran smoothly till about 4 p.m. when it was telegraphed that *Wells, Fargo & Co. had suspended in San Francisco.* This felt like a death knell to me but as far as this office was concerned I could weather it. Soon the paying out was lively—but as there seemed to be no lack of funds and my giving assurance of their safety all was quieted for the day. This morning I received a dispatch from the San Francisco Office that their house would open on Monday next & I am in hopes that we will go through the storm safely. This is the proudest time of my life."

ridgepole. Just that simply, he was open for business.

Though the company sometimes adopted its rivals' practice of taking office space in a hotel, Wells, Fargo preferred to construct its own buildings in mining towns that seemed likely to last. If the building was made of wood, it was fairly certain to burn down sooner or later; fires were endemic in the new towns. In Grass Valley, California, only the office vault and its precious contents survived a fire in 1855; while the fire was still smoldering, the Wells, Fargo agent, an indomitable character named Alonzo Delano, picked up a flimsy shed and moved it by wagon to the ruin, positioned it in front of the safe and was back in business in a wink.

In places with proven diggings of gold, Wells, Fargo usually did its building or rebuilding with fireproof brick.

And when the inevitable green shutters arrived to provide the final touch, the miners knew that Wells, Fargo was there to stay, that their town was truly established and their links to the outside world indissoluble.

In brand-new digs the welcome accorded to Wells, Fargo was invariably jubilant. Charles Blake, who had gone to work for the company as a young Yale graduate in 1853, considered himself an unflappable veteran when, 10 years later, he journeyed to Idaho to open an office in a new mining camp near the Boise River. Yet Blake was dumfounded by the tumultuous greeting he received. He and his traveling companions reined their mules to a halt among a throng of miners who were busy cutting shingles for new buildings. Then, as Blake reported, "One of the crowd said to our guide,

203

Traveling in tandem for greater security, stagecoaches depart from the Wells, Fargo agency on the main street of Virginia City, Nevada, in 1866. The booming Comstock Lode town generated so much traffic that Wells, Fargo served it with a dozen coaches daily to and from California.

AMERICAN EXCHAN

205

This gold ingot, shown full size, was worth $325 when Wells, Fargo had it smelted in 1854. It was cast from about 16 ounces of gold dust that miners all over the West brought into Wells, Fargo express offices.

'Can you tell us anything about Wells, Fargo & Company? We understood that they were going to establish an agency here.' 'Yes,' says the guide, 'they are, and that man in spectacles is the agent.'

"The next instant," Blake went on, "I heard a shout taken up and repeated through the whole town, 'Wells, Fargo have come!' In less than three minutes I was surrounded by an excited crowd of two or three hundred men, who hardly allowed me time to get my saddle off my mule before they dragged me into a large unfinished building on the Plaza, as they called the square. The carpenters were at work, but were stopped at once, the shavings were cleaned out, one man ran for a whisky keg to make me a stool and another brought in scales and a yeast powder box to put gold dust in and installed himself to weigh for me."

The miners had further cause for joy when Blake produced about 400 letters he had brought and called them out to the rightful recipients. "The crowd increased," Blake reported, "and for eight mortal hours my tongue had to wag without cessation. I disposed of a great many letters at a dollar apiece, and about eight o'clock at night broke up business in spite of the crowd."

Blake's varied duties as agent were typical of Wells, Fargo routine in every branch. He stayed close to the office much of the time to assay gold dust as miners brought it in; he might buy the dust outright for coin, or accept it as a bank deposit against which the miner could draw checks for a service charge of one fifteenth of 1 per cent a day. Almost every day Blake and his assistants melted down the accumulated gold dust and cast it into bars for convenient transport to the mints. By now the federal government had opened a mint in San Francisco to reduce the time and cost involved in shipping the metal back East to be turned into currency, and at intervals Blake's fund of coins was replenished. He also received bags of letters to distribute and bundles of newspapers to sell.

Between waiting on miners, preparing his outbound mail, writing waybills for outgoing shipments of gold and parcels and doing the bookkeeping involved, Blake was kept busy until nine in the evening at least twice a week. And, as he reported, "One day when we had a big rush I did not finish my work until four o'clock next morning."

Blake had no chance in Idaho to perform any of those flamboyant feats of service that did so much to puff up Wells, Fargo's fame, but other agents filled the breach. One Wells, Fargo man escorted a fire-fighting wagon all the way from Baltimore by ship to San Francisco, then drove it inland and delivered it safely to its purchaser, the fire-prone city of Sacramento. Another agent arranged to keep the sporting houses in Virginia City supplied with fresh talent; as new girls began arriving, townsmen turned out eagerly to greet each incoming Wells, Fargo stage.

Thanks also to Wells, Fargo, silver- and gold-rich miners enjoyed an endless influx of culinary delicacies. Just as Henry Wells had once successfully delivered oysters to Buffalo, so his company continued to provide the Nevada and California treasure towns with firkins of reasonably fresh butter from Vermont and with wines and *pâté de foie gras* all the way from France. Wells, Fargo even shipped Californians cigars from Germany and cuttings of grapevines from Switzerland — the start of a local wine industry.

For these sensational feats, as well as in its more customary concerns, Wells, Fargo used every available mode and route of transport: steamers to San Francisco around the Horn or by way of the Panama portage; Sacramento River boats; local California railroad cars on the Sacramento-to-Folsom line; heavy freight wagons and light express wagons to haul supplies; mule trains to carry freight and mail where wagons could not go; even men on snowshoes to get mail through mountain blizzards. But the major means of transport the company employed was the stagecoach, whose speed best served the needs of overland express.

Yet, until 1860, Wells, Fargo's position in staging was anomalous. Logically, a company of such varied and sprawling enterprises should by now have owned a great fleet of coaches and operated its own far-flung stage lines. Wells, Fargo did own some feeder lines; but for the most part it sent its express shipments via the coaches of other carriers, notably the California Stage Company, the mammoth concern consolidated by James Birch. California Stage controlled all but a relatively small fraction of the state's staging business, and Wells, Fargo scrupulously avoided any semblance of competing with Birch's firm.

In 1860, however, two events occurred which were to plunge Wells, Fargo willy-nilly into staging, and transform it almost overnight into a giant in the field. One of these unexpected developments stemmed directly from Louis McLane's fascination with horses. An expert rider himself, he had inevitably acquired a parallel interest in staging. He did nothing concrete about it until, in 1860, he learned of the impending

sale of the Pioneer Stage Company, whose coaches plied the Sierra between Placerville, California, and Carson Valley, Nevada. Acquiring Pioneer was not only a potential dream come true for McLane, but an irresistible investment. The Comstock Lode, near Pioneer's Nevada terminus, had been discovered only the year before and was pouring forth untold riches in silver — all of which had to be transported to banks and mints, at a substantial fee for the carrier.

With his brother as partner, McLane bought Pioneer. He did not feel it necessary to give up his position at Wells, Fargo, nor did the company feel the need to deprive itself of his talents. A mutually beneficial arrangement was made whereby Wells, Fargo shipments rode Pioneer stages to and from Nevada and the two firms shared offices. In a few years Wells, Fargo was to buy Pioneer from the McLanes, though still discreetly keeping the fact a secret lest it annoy

A stagecoach strongbox, measuring about two feet by one by one, was painted Wells, Fargo's inevitable green—and filled up with gold.

In this *Police Gazette* re-creation of a
Wells, Fargo stage holdup in Nevada in
1866, highwaymen plunder a pair of
coaches while one gallant bandit offers a
female passenger a seat off to the side.

competing stage lines whose services it might occasionally require.

The other momentous event of 1860 was to take
Wells, Fargo much further afield in staging. It involved
an old friend and onetime financial cohort of Henry
Wells and William Fargo—John Butterfield. By now
Butterfield's celebrated stage line on the long Oxbow
Route across the southern part of the country was in
deep trouble. Despite his zeal and efficiency, and despite a $600,000-a-year government mail contract, the
expense of upkeep and repairs along the meandering,

perilous route was impossibly high; to deliver each letter he carried, Butterfield once morosely figured, cost
his company more than $60 apiece. Wells, Fargo had
made a number of loans to help keep Butterfield going,
but his inability to repay strained and finally snapped
the friendship. In March 1860, Wells, Fargo took control of the Butterfield Overland Mail and summarily de-
posed its founder.

A year later, on the eve of the outbreak of civil war,
history played into Wells, Fargo's hands. When Confederate irregulars cut the Oxbow Route and Wash-

ington ordered the stage line moved northward to the safer central route, Wells, Fargo suddenly found itself the prime stage operator on the western end of the only remaining transcontinental link, tying in with the C.O.C. & P.P. at Salt Lake City. Once committed to staging, Wells, Fargo spent lavishly—but the expenditures were amply justified: the western part of the central overland route was bullion-rich territory, offering great profit to the line that transported the treasure.

Still, this latest undertaking by Wells, Fargo was not without its troubles. Most of them stemmed from the operators of the eastern part of the central overland route —the 1,200-mile stretch linking Salt Lake City and Missouri River towns. The first operator with whom Wells, Fargo had to contend was the perennial promoter, William Russell, then dreaming the last of his dreams of glory and nearing the end of his rope. When Russell's operation foundered, the man who took over was even less palatable to Wells, Fargo's hard-working officials. Russell at least had personal charm; Ben Holladay was all gall.

Without full cooperation between the operators of the eastern and western parts of the central overland route, any claim of providing travelers with an uninterrupted journey clear across the continent was at least arguable. Wells, Fargo was willing to cooperate. It took over management of the western end of the Pony Express—Russell's prized scheme for proving the utility of the central overland route—before the Pony itself was nosed out by the East-West telegraph. Wells, Fargo collaborated with Holladay as well; the passengers and packages and mail his stage line delivered to its terminus at Salt Lake City were carried further westward in Wells, Fargo's charge.

To Holladay, however, cooperation was a distasteful concept. The fact that Wells, Fargo stages commanded one part of the overland route did not prevent him from charging stiff rates for Wells, Fargo express matter that traveled over his part of the route. Louis McLane, still ensconced as Wells, Fargo's Western manager, could not abide Holladay. In turn, McLane's arrogance—he was capable of calling anyone who disagreed with him an "egregious ass"—infuriated Holladay. The hard feelings were reinforced by invidious newspaper editorials that lauded Wells, Fargo's service and condemned Holladay's, complaining that he charged

too much for passenger fares, took poor care of his equipment and animals and generally was running his stage line into the ground.

In this climate of acrimony, Wells, Fargo's directors were understandably stunned when, in 1866, Holladay abruptly allowed them to buy him out. What made him do so was his own secret; he had simply read the handwriting on the wall and decided that staging would not long survive the completion of the oncoming transcontinental rail link. But Wells, Fargo leaped at the chance Holladay offered and paid $1,800,000 in cash and stock for his stage line. Only after a few years' experience would the directors discover that because of growing rail competition along Holladay's part of the overland route, their net profits showed a reduction of about $80,000 a year. But for the moment the directors had valid reasons to congratulate themselves. They had realized the dream of William Russell and the other great expressmen: they now possessed a monopoly on long-distance staging and mail service west of the Missouri River.

In 1866 the West was Wells, Fargo's oyster. The company had 196 branch offices, and business was bigger and better than ever. Wells, Fargo's other stage line, Pioneer, had grown explosively with the silver boom around Virginia City: it now ran four stages daily in both directions between there and Placerville. (McLane saw to it that the mountainous route was scraped of snow in the winter to keep it passable, and watered in the summer to keep it smooth and dust-free.) As far as Wells, Fargo's directors could see, the only cloud on their corporate horizon was a minor one, though a vexing problem for staging entrepreneurs—the growing trouble with robbers.

Back in the early gold rush days of 1849, expressman Alexander Todd had carried an old butter keg filled with $150,000 in gold dust some 70 miles to San Francisco without benefit of gun or guard, certain that everyone was so busy trying to survive and strike it rich that no one had the time or inclination to attempt to rob a traveler. But that atmosphere had changed as California grew more populous, wealthier and more—or less—civilized.

The first robberies had been small affairs, presumably because the new mining towns were just starting

An express wagon carrying a quarter million dollars' worth of gold to the railroad for cross-country delivery rolls out of the Homestake Mine in South Dakota in 1890. Valuable shipments such as this rated four Wells, Fargo guards.

As Wells, Fargo's chief detective for 32 years, James B. Hume hunted down hundreds of stage and train robbers by combining new methods such as ballistics analysis with dogged pursuit of his quarry.

Five of Hume's colleagues gather to mark the capture of the celebrated bandit Black Bart. The sheriff of Calaveras County, California, poses *(center)* with an ax like the one Bart used to smash money chests.

to produce treasure. At this point, thieves seemed to provoke more amusement than indignation. In 1859 the Wells, Fargo agent in Sonora, California, was about to retire for the night on his bunk at the back of the office when he heard a suspicious noise. The agent, Canfield by name, searched the area and finally looked under his bed. There he spied a man who was armed with an ax. Unarmed himself, Canfield dashed outside to look for help, and the would-be bandit escaped. The Stockton *Argus* reported the nonevent with a strained pun: "We apprehend that that fellow intended to *ax* Canfield for his money."

Soon, however, robbery ceased to be a joke. Stage holdups increased, and sometimes were pulled off by entire gangs. Often the bandits waited in hiding at the top of a steep grade, where the tired stage horses had slowed to a walk. One bandit, with his confederates covering him from the brush, would step or ride his horse into the path of the oncoming stagecoach brandishing a double-barreled shotgun. Then he would call out an order that before long became all too familiar: "Throw down the box!"—the green Wells, Fargo treasure chest.

Bullion coming down from the mines in the mountains was the main prize; at first robbers rarely molested passengers or stage men. When one brigand with an innovative turn of mind ordered everyone aboard a stage to empty his pockets, the driver roared angrily, "You are the meanest man I ever saw in the business. There never was a driver before who was asked to give up a cent." The bandit, thoroughly abashed by the scolding, returned the driver's money.

Wells, Fargo suffered its first road robbery near Shasta in 1855—a holdup of a mule train. A gang led by the notorious bandit Rattlesnake Dick, so-called because he had launched his career of crime in the California mining camp of Rattlesnake Bar, made off with $80,000 in gold dust. Rattlesnake Dick was eventually killed in a shoot-out near Auburn in 1859, about the same time that real rattlesnakes came into use as an improvised method of bandit control. The idea was to stash a live rattler inside the treasure box: the robbers might get the gold, but with it they would also get a nasty surprise.

Holdups became so commonplace that Wells, Fargo printed up a standard form for use as a "stage robbery report," with blanks for the agent to fill in with the details. The epidemic of holdups had Californians enraged and ready for vigilante action. After three local stagecoach robberies within one week, the *Yreka Union* printed a thinly veiled threat: "This is getting somewhat monotonous for the people of Shasta County and we expect to hear, about the next thing, that some highwaymen have been seriously hurt."

Wells, Fargo went to work on the bandit problem in every conceivable way. Treasure chests consigned to transport by stage were bolted down to the floor boards of the coach or built into passenger seats. But even a bolted strongbox could be opened, and so the company took pains to conceal its plans when particularly big shipments were due to go out. A gold shipment from Sonora worth $190,000 remained a perfect secret—until the stage hit a rut. The weight of the gold broke the coach frame in half, and a stream of gold dust spewed out onto the roadway.

To protect stages carrying bullion from Comstock country—popular targets of robbers—Wells, Fargo put not only a shotgun guard on the box beside the driver,

Tom Cunningham,   B. K. Thorn,   H. N. Morse,
        Capt. A. W. Stone,   J. N. Thacker

A Wells, Fargo reward poster for the robber Black Bart presents facsimiles of the handwritten doggerel he tauntingly left in the treasure boxes he plundered. Bart signed his verses as "the Po8," meaning poet.

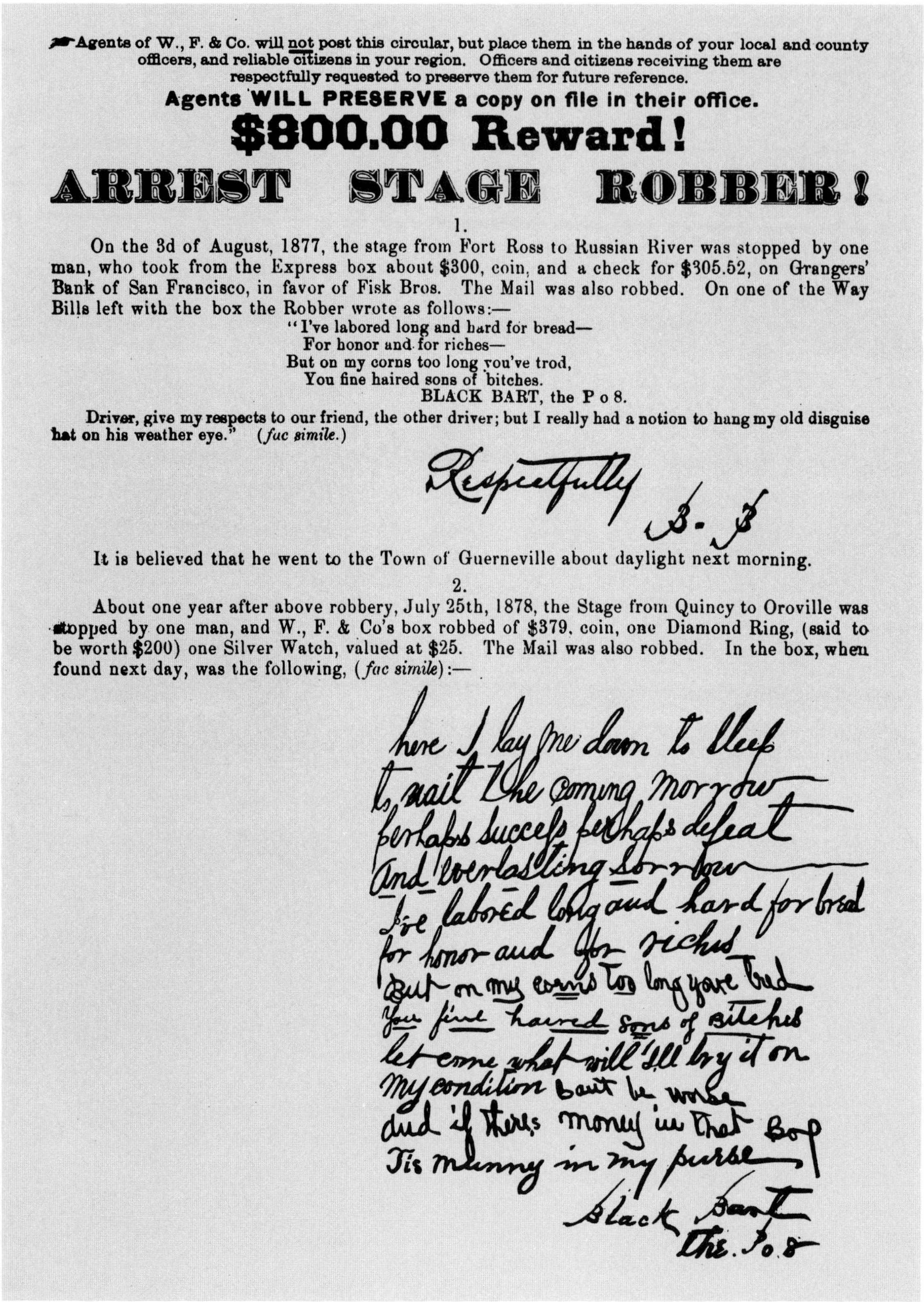

Agents of W., F. & Co. will not post this circular, but place them in the hands of your local and county officers, and reliable citizens in your region. Officers and citizens receiving them are respectfully requested to preserve them for future reference.

Agents WILL PRESERVE a copy on file in their office.

$800.00 Reward!

ARREST STAGE ROBBER!

1.

On the 3d of August, 1877, the stage from Fort Ross to Russian River was stopped by one man, who took from the Express box about $300, coin, and a check for $305.52, on Grangers' Bank of San Francisco, in favor of Fisk Bros. The Mail was also robbed. On one of the Way Bills left with the box the Robber wrote as follows:—

"I've labored long and hard for bread—
For honor and for riches—
But on my corns too long you've trod,
You fine haired sons of bitches.
BLACK BART, the P o 8.

Driver, give my respects to our friend, the other driver; but I really had a notion to hang my old disguise hat on his weather eye." (*fac simile.*)

Respectfully
B. B.

It is believed that he went to the Town of Guerneville about daylight next morning.

2.

About one year after above robbery, July 25th, 1878, the Stage from Quincy to Oroville was stopped by one man, and W., F. & Co's box robbed of $379, coin, one Diamond Ring, (said to be worth $200) one Silver Watch, valued at $25. The Mail was also robbed. In the box, when found next day, was the following, (*fac simile*):—

here I lay me down to sleep
to wait the coming morrow
perhaps success perhaps defeat
And everlasting sorrow
I've labored long and hard for bread
for honor and for riches
But on my corns too long you've trod
You fine haired sons of bitches
let come what will I'll try it on
My condition can't be worse
and if there's money in that Box
Tis munny in my purse
Black Bart
The Po8

but another on top of the coach and two more riding on horseback 50 yards to the rear. That maneuver helped, and so did an idea that originated with some California shippers who had their silver smelted and cast into forms too heavy for robbers to carry off. One smelter turned out silver cannonballs that weighed 700 pounds each. Another poured almost a ton of silver and gold into an immense ingot which he inscribed, appropriately enough, "Champion."

As holdups continued virtually unchecked into the 1860s, Wells, Fargo built up a large force of private detectives and police. Company pride demanded the expenditure: it was a matter of living up to its unofficial watchword, "Wells, Fargo never forgets." (It first appeared — so the story goes — on the tombstone of a bandit hanged in Virginia City.) The force proved to be a sound — if heavy — investment. It was company policy to reimburse shippers for any gold stolen while in Wells, Fargo's care; and in 14 years, the losses from 313 robberies totaled $415,000. In the same period, the company paid out roughly an equal amount in salaries and operating expenses for its police and detectives. Still, it reaped the satisfaction of knowing that they had not only recovered large amounts of loot, but had thwarted 34 stage holdups and captured and secured the conviction of 240 bandits.

Wells, Fargo's plague of robbers was finally brought under control by James B. Hume, a cigar-loving native of New York's Catskill Mountains who had racked up an impressive record of arrests as a peace officer in California and Nevada. In 1873, Hume, then 46 years old, went to work for the company as chief of detectives. Patient and diligent, as orderly as Wells, Fargo itself in his approach to his business, Hume believed in law-book law rather than Western gun law. To make sure that the bandits he apprehended were convicted on solid evidence when they reached court, he pioneered in the science of ballistics and other new methods of crime detection.

Hume was a big man who tried to make himself inconspicuous under a black felt hat. Out of personal reticence and professional discretion, he shunned publicity, declined interviews and avoided the limelight. On one occasion when Hume found himself — to his annoyance — in a discussion of his own successes, he merely made

Mug shots and criminal records fill the pages of chief detective Hume's "black book" of bandits who were arrested for crimes against Wells, Fargo. The roster typifies Hume's systematic sleuthwork.

14.

N.384

Ramón Ruiz
Robbed Stage in Butte &
Calaveras Co. in 1875 & 76
with Old Joaquin & others

Antone Savage
Robbed Stages in Calaveras Co
in 1875 & 76 with Ruiz and
"Big & Little Mitch"

15.

J.W. Ratovich
Robbed Stages in Calaveras
in 1875 & 76 with Joaquin,
Ruiz, and others

Harry Norton
Robbed Stage from La Porte
to Oroville July 20 - 1876
with John Doe

the laconic rejoinder, "My salary has been increased from time to time."

Hume's most famous case involved Black Bart, a masked bandit who punningly called himself the "Po8" (poet), for the doggerel he composed. Bart's intelligence and style made him a worthy adversary for Hume. To make the contest even more fascinating to the public at large, Bart never stole much gold (a total of only $18,000 in 28 or 29 holdups) and not once did anyone physical harm.

Apart from breaking the law, the real offense that Bart committed was to wound Wells, Fargo's pride. And he kept rubbing salt in the wound. The spectacle of a lone man outwitting a business colossus endeared him to everyone who worked hard for low wages and watched others grow rich. As events proved, it was this very sentiment that inspired Bart to torment Wells, Fargo exclusively.

The man who became renowned as Black Bart made his criminal debut on July 26, 1875, at the crest of a hill near Copperopolis, California, in the High Sierra. As a stage driven by John Shine labored up to the top of the rise, a weird-looking figure armed with a double-barreled shotgun stepped into its path. The bandit was wearing a flour-sack mask with two eyeholes, a long, soiled white-linen duster that concealed his clothing and build, and cloth wrapping around his boots—obviously to blur his footprints.

The shrouded apparition spoke. "Please throw down the box," he said politely in a voice of surprising depth and timbre. Luckily for him, this particular box was not bolted down. As Shine fumbled with the Wells, Fargo box, the bandit called over his shoulder, "If he dares to shoot, give him a solid volley, boys." Shine looked around him and saw several barrels leveled at him from the surrounding cover. Hurriedly he dropped the treasure box onto the ground.

The bandit chopped it open with a small ax and began stuffing the bags of gold coins it contained into the pockets of his linen duster. At that point a hysterical woman passenger voluntarily threw down her purse. The bandit paused, picked up the purse, handed it back to its owner and said grandly, "Madam, I do not wish your money. In that respect, I honor only the good office of Wells, Fargo." He then finished emptying the strongbox and waved the stage on. When Shine, looking back, saw him run off the road into the brush, he decided to return to pick up the box. He was horrified to see that the rifles of the bandit's confederates were still aimed at him—until he realized that the weapons were only sticks, carefully aligned and tied in place. The robber had been alone.

Thus began the legend of the solitary bandit of the trackless wilderness. In later robberies his method of operation remained the same. Always he appeared out of the brush at the top of a hill on a lonely road. His costume never varied and his manner was consistently calm, even pleasant.

Black Bart added the touch that was to make him famous when he held up his third stagecoach on the road to Duncan Mills on the Russian River. In departing with his loot, he left behind a scrap of paper on which he had written a one-stanza poem, with each line in a different style of handwriting. The verse expressed the feelings of all men who considered themselves exploited and oppressed by the wealthy:

I've labored long and hard for bread
for honor and for riches
But on my corns too long youve tred
You fine haired Sons of Bitches.

It was signed, "Black Bart, the Po8." In a stroke, the bandit had created a character and had given him both a name and a personality. Thereafter, newspapers wrote about him extensively and romantically; and from time to time Bart rewarded them with other bits of doggerel to quote—taunting messages for Wells, Fargo detectives. His string of holdups grew longer, but they occurred at unpredictable intervals. Sometimes months would pass between his robberies; once he struck two stages within 24 hours, at two places 30 miles apart.

Through interviews with ranchers and farmers in the vicinity of Bart's crimes, Hume learned that many had seen one particular stranger. From their descriptions Wells, Fargo's ace detective gradually pieced together a good picture of his suspect. He was an erect, spare, gray-haired man of about 40 or 50, standing five feet eight inches tall. His clothes were rough, his boots were badly worn (and slit open to ease the pressure on the corns referred to in Bart's poem), and he usually wore a derby hat. Slung over a shoulder he carried a blanket roll in which, Hume surmised, he toted his highwayman's tools: a small ax, a small sledge hammer, a pry bar and, of course, a shotgun. He moved quietly about the country posing as an itinerant laborer, presumably observing stage routes and schedules. Many an unsuspecting family had taken him in for a meal, which he repaid with good conversation and interesting, well-told stories. People invariably liked him.

As Hume had deduced, Bart was able to elude capture easily because he was a superb walker, capable of covering great distances quickly. He never used a horse because hoofprints were easy to track, and he never paused or stopped overnight within 12 miles of the scene of a robbery. Once, trackers followed him through 60 miles of wilderness before they lost his trail.

Bart's downfall commenced on the same hill near Copperopolis where he had perpetrated his first robbery. Stage driver Reason McConnell was making his regular run. Alongside of him on the box was a young friend, Jimmy Rolleri, who was going hunting. As the stage started up the hill the boy dropped off to scout the woods for game, planning to meet the coach on the far side. Near the top of the hill Black Bart stepped into the road with his shotgun leveled. McConnell stopped. As it happened, the Wells, Fargo treasure box was bolted to the floor of the carriage. The bandit ordered McConnell to unhitch the horses and take them over the hill so he could do his plundering at leisure. He then climbed into the coach to chop open the box.

By the time he finished, Jimmy Rolleri had rejoined McConnell. The driver, having surrendered his rifle to Bart, grabbed the boy's rifle and fired twice at the man as he backed out of the stage. McConnell missed both times, whereupon Rolleri snatched his rifle back, saying, "I'll get him and I won't kill him either." He fired and hit the fleeing bandit. Bart stumbled, dropping something but keeping a grip on the gold, then scrambled up again and disappeared into the brush.

When detective Hume arrived on the scene he found the ground littered with belongings he recognized as Black Bart's. They included field glasses, a derby hat, a razor and a knotted handkerchief full of buckshot. Not one of the items seemed to offer an identifying clue —until a closer look at the handkerchief revealed a faint laundry mark: F.X.O.7.

Hume checked laundries in a dozen towns before he found one in San Francisco that recognized the mark. It belonged to a certain Charles E. Bolton, apparently a prosperous mining man who made regular trips to San Francisco and while there stayed at the Webb House hotel. A Wells, Fargo detective, Harry Morse, persuaded the laundry owner to accompany him to the hotel to see if Bolton was there. As they approached, Bolton stepped out of a doorway and spoke to the laundryman, who introduced him to Morse.

Quietly scrutinizing the stranger, Morse saw that he neatly fit the physical description Hume had constructed, though hardly the scruffy sartorial image. Morse described him as "elegantly dressed, carrying a little cane. He wore a natty little derby hat, a diamond pin, a large diamond ring on his little finger and a heavy gold watch and chain. He was about five feet eight inches in height, straight as an arrow, broad-shouldered with deep sunk-

Railroad caps on three Wells, Fargo messengers in a Reno, Nevada, office proclaim a new era for the express business, but shotguns, sacks of silver and a strongbox indicate that the risks have not diminished.

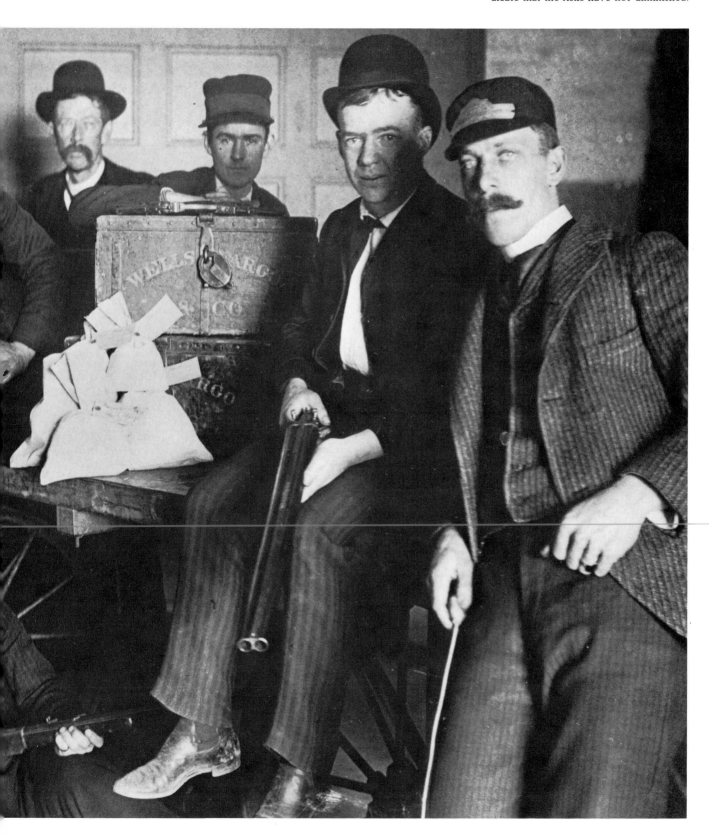

Grateful Wells, Fargo executives presented this ornate gold watch to A. Y. Ross, a company guard who stood off a band of train robbers in a three-and-a-half-hour siege of his express car at Montello, Nevada.

en bright blue eyes, high cheekbones and a large handsome gray mustache." Morse added: "One would have taken him for a gentleman who had made a fortune and was enjoying it. He looked anything but a robber."

Nonetheless, Black Bart he was; the folk hero had been caught. It turned out that "Bolton" was actually Charles E. Boles, a restless ne'er-do-well who had abandoned a wife and four children in the Middle West. In consideration of his abjuring of violence and his return of most of the gold he had stolen, Boles was permitted to plead guilty to only one count of armed robbery. He was sentenced to six years in the state penitentiary at San Quentin. The outcome was such an anticlimax that diehard romantics chose to believe that the "real" Black Bart still roamed the forests, and that every robbery pulled off by a lone bandit was his handiwork.

Probably the greatest loss suffered by Wells, Fargo as the result of a road robbery was the $80,000 taken by Rattlesnake Dick in 1855. But the greatest single holdup of Wells, Fargo took place not on an open road but in a locked conference room in Omaha. And it cost the directors millions of dollars—in fact, the loss of their hold on the company.

The scene was set for this inside hijacking in 1867, and the leading player—the villain or hero who became president of Wells, Fargo—had already made his presence felt. He was Lloyd Tevis, a lawyer from Kentucky, who had shown considerable business acumen before gold fever drew him West in 1849. He soon learned that the key to great wealth lay less surely in the gold diggings than in the business opportunities that abounded in the fast-growing Western cities. In California, Tevis moved in and out of many profitable ventures, among them a water-supply company, telegraph companies, mines, a stage line and real estate.

Tevis once claimed that he could think five times faster than any other man in San Francisco, and his thoughts about the railroad business demonstrated that his boast was not an idle one. He was well acquainted with the group of ambitious railroad men that would soon become known as the Big Four—Charles Crocker, Leland Stanford, Mark Hopkins and Collis P. Huntington. And he took them at their word when they told him that their Central Pacific Railroad, working eastward from California, would meet the Union Pacific Railroad, advancing steadily westward from Omaha, in Utah in 1869.

To most people—including Wells, Fargo's directors—this projected date for a transcontinental linkup of rails seemed decidedly overoptimistic. But Tevis invested heavily in the Central Pacific, and he did so at a time when it was making its slowest and costliest progress into and over the snowy Sierra. The venture was taking more capital than the railroad men could scrape together in New York and San Francisco to buy all the machinery and equipment they needed, send it by ship to San Francisco, and keep the tracks inching forward despite the obstacles posed by the mountains. And completing the job would require millions of dollars more.

Tevis did not wait for the union of the rails to make his investment pay off. He realized that the rights to carry mail and bullion on the completed railroad would be worth a fortune, and he persuaded Charles Crocker, the dominant member of the Big Four, to form an express firm and award it the contract for those rights. The papers creating the Pacific Union Express Company were drawn up in May 1867.

At the time, the directors of Wells, Fargo were keeping half an eye on the railroads' progress; as overlords of Western transport they could hardly do less. But they did not regard the transcontinental linkage of the rails as a serious threat to stagecoaching. Wells, Fargo was already shipping some express matter westward on the Union Pacific as far as its track had been laid, and the company casually assumed that it would eventually do the same over the entire line.

Both the directors of Wells, Fargo and its horse-fancying general manager, Louis McLane, were old-line conservatives with set ways and attitudes, and they really did not like the idea of railroading. They not only declined to invest in the rails but encouraged their associates not to participate. The future rail magnates would remember all this with anger.

As the Central Pacific Railroad broke through the Sierra and passed Reno, Nevada, the new express company operated by Lloyd Tevis began competing with Wells, Fargo stages for express business between the Reno railhead and Virginia City, 20 miles to the south. The competition included a rate-slashing war and the sort of messenger races that Wells, Fargo used to lose to its rival, Adams & Company. Each side hired skillful riders for the races and stationed four fresh horses about four miles apart. In one contest in July 1868, the famous Pony Express veteran, Bob Haslam, rode for Wells, Fargo and Frank Henderson for Tevis' outfit, with results that made news in the *Sacramento Union:* "The Pacific Express rider got about 10 yards start (Bob delayed until his bag was firmly fastened on his back) but Bob soon overhauled and passed him (in one

mile) and kept ahead of him the rest of the distance."

But the races that Wells, Fargo won were hollow victories. As the Central Pacific drove its rails through the Nevada desert and the Union Pacific advanced well into Wyoming, their crews working harder and faster, it finally occurred to Wells, Fargo's directors that the linking of the rails was not a decade away, but imminent.

Too late, they concluded that the future was riding in on rails, not coach wheels. They turned against the stagecoach suddenly, almost vindictively, as if it had betrayed them. In May 1868, McLane was thunderstruck by an order he received from the Wells, Fargo board in New York. He was to sell all of the company's stage lines, retaining only the rights to transport express matter over the routes operated by the new buyers. To McLane, the order was incomprehensible and heartbreaking, but he dutifully began the mournful task of dismembering the magnificent staging empire, coaches, animals and all. It was his last real service to Wells, Fargo. He soon left its employ, perhaps involuntarily.

By the spring of 1869, the two railroad crews were fairly flying toward each other, the Union Pacific crossing the great desert west of Salt Lake City and the Central Pacific crossing the Bonneville salt flats. Charles Crocker's crew, which had grown to 10,000 men, set a one-day record, laying a full 10 miles of track. And still the directors of Wells, Fargo, who now knew their express shipments would have to ride those tracks, made no known overture to the railroad.

Exactly why remains obscure. Perhaps the directors already knew the horrible truth—that Lloyd Tevis' Pacific Union Express had an exclusive contract. Perhaps they thought that their early refusals to invest in the railroad had made it futile to ask for an accommodation now. In any case, the rails finally came together in Utah on May 10, 1869, and Tevis' exclusive contract soon went into effect. Wells, Fargo was out in the cold, and its empire was threatened.

It was not until October 4 that its fate became clear. On that momentous day, Wells, Fargo's directors met with Lloyd Tevis in Omaha. Present among the directors was William Fargo, now 51 years old; Henry Wells absented himself. Behind closed doors the conferees reached a settlement.

Wells, Fargo was obliged to pay Tevis five million dollars for the piece of paper that had granted Tevis'

One of the most elusive bandits who preyed on Wells, Fargo rail shipments, John Sontag lies mortally wounded in a haystack near Visalia, California, as his captors gather triumphantly around him. When the posse cornered him, Sontag was sheltered by local farmers hostile to the railway.

company exclusive express rights on the railroad. That arrangement terminated the short life of Pacific Express and guaranteed that Wells, Fargo would survive.

Tevis had more news for the directors. Wells, Fargo's unhorsed and railless plight—together with the losses it had suffered in its rate war with Tevis' express—had sent the company's stock plummeting from $100 a share to as low as $13, and Tevis had quietly been buying it up at the depressed prices. In the room in Omaha, the directors were forced to concede that Lloyd Tevis now controlled Wells, Fargo.

In time, Wells, Fargo customers—the people of the West—concluded with relief that the new regime was determined to preserve the virtues of the old. The company they had trusted, relied on and believed in, was still intact, with its sound brick buildings and strong vaults, its honest scales and efficient agents. Now, of course, the company rode the rails. But Wells, Fargo itself still delivered the goods, attracted the treasure and continued to grow.

Yet in some ways Wells, Fargo had changed, for the West itself was changing rapidly. Wells, Fargo became a California firm in 1870, when Lloyd Tevis transferred its headquarters from New York to San Francisco. That was a move of symbolic importance, reflecting the maturity that the West had acquired in a period of just two decades.

Many other things had changed in that time. Alexander Todd had plodded the Sierra foothills alone, hauling letters up to miners and bringing gold down. Alexander Majors had ridden the overland trail with his freight-wagon trains, supping with his bullwhackers by a buffalo-chip fire and sleeping on the ground. In those years the West was only a scattering of settlements in the wilderness, isolated from everything but hope. But Todd and Majors and men like them—the stage drivers and shotgun messengers and the Pony Express riders—had traveled weary, dangerous, lonely miles bringing Westerners all they needed to survive. Thanks to the expressmen, the West was now united and linked indissolubly to the East. When the railroad came, the expressmen knew that their strenuous era was near an end, and they were a little sad to see it go. In the saloons of San Francisco, trail-hardened veterans sang in whiskey-hoarse voices, "Farewell to romance. The old days are gone, we shall not see their like again."

The many facades of Wells, Fargo

The rapid conveyance of people, documents and precious metals underwent a startling metamorphosis as the West matured. In just over two decades, the deeds of larger-than-life expressmen like Alexander Todd, Hank Monk and Ben Holladay gave way to the sobersided responsibility of a sprawling corporation. Pursuing the business of minding other people's property, the Wells, Fargo express company shaped a new kind of West in its own image. As quickly as restless and adventurous men moved on and found ways to extract new wealth from mine, farm, forest or river, Wells, Fargo joined them to take reliable charge of the proceeds. In hundreds of towns this one company's arrival to do business was taken as proof of stability and permanence.

In the years that followed the opening of its first office in San Francisco in 1852, the company extended its aegis into every corner of the West. By 1893, Wells, Fargo was making deliveries over a total of 37,766 miles of express routes, and the corporation operated 2,829 branch offices—each of which was the center of commercial life in its area. Through prosperity and panic, boom and bust, Wells, Fargo was there—everywhere—to serve the new West it had helped so much to create.

A knot of natty customers congregate in front of the Wells, Fargo office in Portland in 1852.

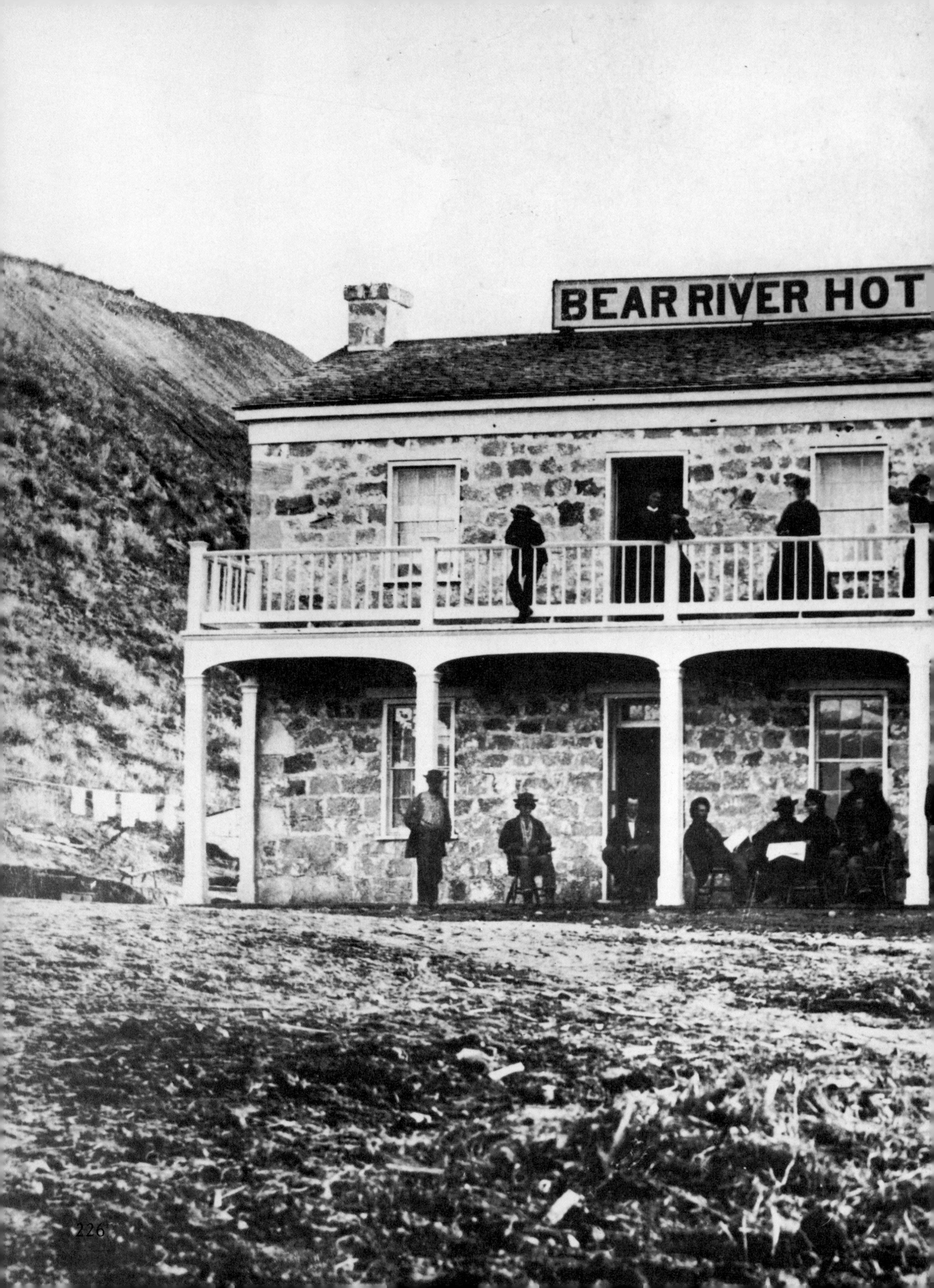
BEAR RIVER HOT

At the California gold town of Applegate—named for the owner of this hotel—a celerity stagecoach pulls up to the Wells, Fargo agency.

At the adobe-block village of Phoenix, Arizona, about 1880, Wells, Fargo occupies quarters in a general store.

ELLS, FARGO & CO.,
VERLAND MAIL
XPRE OFFICE.
WESTERN UN
Telegrap
OFFICE
ELLS FARGO

Passengers wait at the Wells, Fargo office as a stagecoach halts on the snowy main street of Virginia City, Montana.

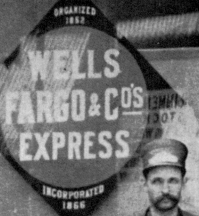

By 1892, Wells, Fargo was solidly housed on Arapahoe Street in the city of Denver, where the proud staff stood for a portrait outside the iron-and-glass building.

233

PICTURE CREDITS

The sources for the illustrations in this book are shown below. Credits from left to right are separated by semicolons, from top to bottom by dashes.

Cover— *The Old Stagecoach of the Plains,* Frederic Remington, courtesy Amon Carter Museum, Fort Worth, Texas. 2—From the Arizona Collection of John and Lillian Theobald. 6 through 11—Oliver Willcox, courtesy Thomas Gilcrease Institute of American History and Art, Tulsa, Oklahoma. 6,7—*Wagon Boss,* Charles Russell. 8,9—*Thru Hostile Country,* O. E. Berninghaus. 10,11—*The Coming and Going of the Pony Express,* Frederic Remington. 12—Courtesy The Bancroft Library. 14, 15—Courtesy Library of Congress. 16—Courtesy General Research and Humanities Division, The New York Public Library, Astor, Lenox and Tilden Foundations. 18,19—Courtesy Library of Congress. 20—Map by Rafael Palacios. 22—Courtesy American History Division, The New York Public Library, Astor, Lenox and Tilden Foundations. 25,26,27—Courtesy The National Archives. 28, 29—Courtesy Library of Congress. 30—Courtesy Wells Fargo Bank History Room, San Francisco, California. 32—Courtesy The Bancroft Library—Courtesy General Research and Humanities Division, The New York Public Library, Astor, Lenox and Tilden Foundations. 33—Courtesy The Huntington Library, San Marino, California. 34—Frank Lerner, courtesy David Jarrett. 35—Frank Lerner, courtesy Frank S. Stevens Home for Boys Inc., Swansea, Massachusetts. 36,37—On indefinite loan to the California Historical Society (San Francisco) from the M. H. de Young Memorial Museum. 38—Courtesy The National Archives. 39—Courtesy Minnesota Historical Society, St. Paul—Courtesy The New-York Historical Society. 40 through 43—Courtesy The National Archives. 44,45—Courtesy Nebraska State Historical Society, Lincoln. 46 through 49—Courtesy Library of Congress. 50,51—Courtesy The Haynes Foundation. 52—Courtesy General Research and Humanities Division, The New York Public Library, Astor, Lenox and Tilden Foundations. 53—Courtesy Nebraska State Historical Society. 54,55—Courtesy Denver Public Library, Western History Department. 56,57—Photographed in 1885 by R. L. Kelly, submitted by his son Daniel S. W. Kelly. 58,59—Drawings by Nicholas Fasciano. 61—Courtesy Denver Public Library, Western History Department. 62—Courtesy Private Collection of Dorothy J. Russell (Mrs. John W. Russell, Jr.); J. R. Eyerman, courtesy Mrs. Waddell F. Smith, Pony Express Retreat, San Rafael, California. 63—J. R. Eyerman, courtesy Mrs. Waddell F. Smith, Pony Express Retreat, San Rafael. 64—Courtesy Miss Louisa P. Johnston. 65—Courtesy The Huntington Library, San Marino. 66,67—Courtesy Denver Public Library, Western History Department. 69—Courtesy Library, The State Historical Society of Colorado, Denver. 70,71—Courtesy John A. Anderson Collection, Nebraska State Historical Society. 72,74—Courtesy Library of Congress. 76—Courtesy Denver Public Library, Western History Department. 77—Courtesy The Huntington Library, San Marino. 79—Courtesy The Oakland Museum, Andrew J. Russell Collection. 80,81—Courtesy The Huntington Library, San Marino. 82,84,85—Courtesy Montana Historical Society, Helena. 86,87—Benschneider, courtesy National Park Service (2) —Courtesy Nebraska State Historical Society; courtesy Denver Public Library, Western History Department. 88,89,90—Courtesy Pony Express Stables Museum, St. Joseph, Missouri. 93—Benschneider, courtesy Pony Express Stables Museum, St. Joseph. 94—J. R. Eyerman, courtesy Mrs. Waddell F. Smith, Pony Express Retreat, San Rafael. 95—Courtesy California Historical Society, San Francisco/San Marino. 96,97—Courtesy Wells Fargo Bank History Room, San Francisco. 98,99—Courtesy General Research and Humanities Division, The New York Public Library, Astor, Lenox and Tilden Foundations. 100—Courtesy The Huntington Library, San Marino. 101—Courtesy Library, The State Historical Society of Colorado. 104—Benschneider, courtesy Pony Express Stables Museum, St. Joseph. 106, 107—Courtesy The Oakland Museum, Andrew J. Russell Collection. 108—Courtesy General Research and Humanities Division, The New York Public Library, Astor, Lenox and Tilden Foundations. 109—Courtesy Nevada State Historical Society, Reno. 111—J. R. Eyerman, courtesy Wiltsee Collection, Wells Fargo Bank History Room, San Francisco. 112—Courtesy Rare Book Division, The New York Public Library, Astor, Lenox and Tilden Foundations. 113—Courtesy General Research and Humanities Division, The New York Public Library, Astor, Lenox and Tilden Foundations. 114, 115—Courtesy Western Electric Company. 116 through 121—Courtesy Pony Express Stables Museum, St. Joseph. 122,123—Courtesy Library of Congress. 124—Courtesy *The Oregonian.* 126,127 —Courtesy Kansas State Historical Society, Topeka. 128,129—Courtesy Wells Fargo Bank History Room, San Francisco. 130,131—Courtesy Library of Congress. 132—Courtesy Denver Public Library, Western History Department. 134,135—Courtesy The New Hampshire Historical Society, Concord. 136,137—Gjon Mili, courtesy Wells Fargo Bank History Room, San Francisco. 139—Courtesy Montana Historical Society, Helena. 140—Reproduced by permission of the director, The Bancroft Library. 143—Courtesy Library, State Historical Society of Colorado. 144,145—Courtesy General Research and Humanities Division, The New York Public Library, Astor, Lenox and Tilden Foundations. 146—Courtesy Oregon Historical Society, Portland. 147—Courtesy Southern Pacific. 148,149—Courtesy Oregon Historical Society. 150,151—Photo by Frederick Monsen, courtesy The Huntington Library, San Marino. 152,153—Courtesy Denver Public Library, Western History Department. 154,155—Courtesy Library of Congress. 156,157—Courtesy Pioneers' Museum, Colorado Springs, Colorado. 158—Courtesy The Bancroft Library. 160,161—Courtesy Minnesota Historical Society. 162—Courtesy Wells Fargo Bank History Room, San Francisco. 163—Courtesy Omaha Public Library. 164, 165—Courtesy The Huntington Library, San Marino. 166,167—Courtesy Denver Public Library, Western History Department. 168,170 —Courtesy Wells Fargo Bank History Room, San Francisco. 171, 172,173—Courtesy The Bancroft Library. 175—Courtesy General Research and Humanities Division, The New York Public Library, Astor, Lenox and Tilden Foundations. 176,177—Courtesy Joslyn Art Museum, Omaha. 178,179—Courtesy Denver Public Library, Western History Department. 182,183—Courtesy The Bancroft Library. 185 —Courtesy Montana Historical Society, Helena. 186, 187—Courtesy California Historical Society. 188, 189—Courtesy New Hampshire Historical Society. 190,192—Courtesy Wells Fargo Bank History Room, San Francisco. 194—J. R. Eyerman, courtesy Southern Oregon Historical Society Collections. 196, 197—Courtesy Wells Fargo Bank History Room, San Francisco. 199—Al Freni, *The Illustrated News,* Feb. 19, 1853. 200 through 205—Courtesy Wells Fargo Bank History Room. 206—©Ted Mahieu, courtesy The Bank of California, "Museum of Money of the American West." 207—Benschneider, courtesy Wells Fargo Bank History Room. 208—Courtesy Library of Congress. 210 through 219—Courtesy Wells Fargo Bank History Room. 220—Benschneider, courtesy David L. Ross. 222,223—Courtesy Brown Brothers. 224 through 229—Courtesy Wells Fargo Bank History Room. 230,231—Courtesy Montana Historical Society, Helena. 232,233 —Courtesy Wells Fargo Bank History Room.

TEXT CREDITS

For full reference on specific page credits see bibliography.

Chapter 1: Particularly useful sources for information and quotes: "The Birch-Stevens Crypt," *The Harvester*, Sept. 9, 1972; "The Fabulous and Mysterious James E. Birch," *The Harvester*, Sept. 25, 1954; LeRoy E. Hafen, *The Overland Mail 1849-1869*, AMS Press, 1969; Ralph Moody, *Stagecoach West*, Thomas Y. Crowell Co., 1967; Alexander L. Stimson, *History of the Express Business*, Baker & Godwin, 1881, *History of the Express Companies, Including the Origin of American Railroads*, 1858, Finch Press Reprints; Ernest A. Wiltsee, *The Pioneer Miner and the Pack Mule Express*, California Historical Society, 1931; Oscar O. Winther, *Express and Stagecoach Days in California*, Stanford Univ. Press, 1936, *Via Western Express & Stagecoach*, Univ. of Nebraska Press, 1969; 23 — Livingstone and Kincaid paraphrase, Walker, pp. 158-160; 24-25 — Chorpenning-Woodward incident, paraphrased Huntington Rare Book #89198; 25-27 — Weller quote and paraphrase, California quote, W. T. Jackson, *Wagon Roads*, pp. 161-162. Chapter 2: Particularly useful sources for information and quotes: Josiah Gregg, *Commerce of the Prairies*, J. W. Moore, 1851; William E. Lass, *From the Missouri to the Great Salt Lake*, Nebraska State Historical Society, 1972; Alexander Majors, *Seventy Years on the Frontier*, Ross & Haines, Inc., 1965; Merrill J. Mattes, *The Great Platte River Road*, Nebraska State Historical Society, 1969; Frank A. Root & Wm. E. Connelley, *The Overland Stage to California*, courtesy The Rio Grande Press, Inc., enlarged and indexed 1970 edition; Raymond W. and Mary Lund Settle, *Empire on Wheels*, Stanford Univ. Press, 1949, *War Drums and Wagon Wheels*, Univ. of Nebraska Press, 1966; Henry P. Walker, *The Wagonmasters: High Plains Freighting from the Earliest Days of the Santa Fe Trail to 1880*, copyright 1966 by the Univ. of Oklahoma Press; Walker Wyman, "Bullwhacking: A Prosaic Profession Peculiar to the Great Plains," *New Mexico Historical Review*, Vol. VII, Oct. 1932 (quotes reprinted by permission of the *New Mexico Historical Review*); 53 — freight yard quote, Greeley, p. 38; 68 — water tank quote, Holt, pp. 277-278; 75 — coffee pot quote, whiskey barrel quote, Taylor, pp. 13-14; 77 — engine quote, Robinson & Warner, p. 37; 79 — Indian attack quote, Garrett, p. 90; trip's end quote, Russell, p. 30; 83 — trip's end quote, Brown, p. 113; 86 — Jackson quotes, L. R. and A. W. Hafen, pp. 43, 50, 54, 82. Chapter 3: Particularly useful sources for information and quotes: Roy S. Bloss, *Pony Express — The Great Gamble*, Howell-North Books, 1959; Raymond W. and Mary Lund Settle, *Saddles and Spurs*, Stackpole Co., 1955, *War Drums and Wagon Wheels*, Univ. of Nebraska Press, 1966; 92 — Richardson quote, G. Root, p. 53; 94 — Sacramento pony quote, Hafen, p. 173; 97 — acclaim for pony quote, Hafen, p. 166; 98 — Morehead quote, G. Root, p. 40; 100 — mare ad, G. Root, p. 40; 102 — Twain quote, Twain, p. 64; Keetley quote, Hafen, p. 180; 103 — Wilson quote, Winther, *Via Western Express*, p. 132; 113 — pony eulogy quote, Chapman, p. 302. Chapter 4: Particularly useful sources for information and quotes: J. V. Frederick, *Ben Holladay: The Stagecoach King*, The Arthur H. Clark Co., 1940; Ellis Lucia, *The Saga of Ben Holladay*, Hastings House Publishers, Inc., 1959; Ralph Moody, *Stagecoach West*, Thomas Y. Crowell Co., 1967; Frank A. Root & Wm. E. Connelley, *The Overland Stage to California*, courtesy The Rio Grande Press, Inc., enlarged and indexed 1970 edition; (Abbot-Downing essay, pp. 134-137) Elmer M. Hunt, "Abbot-Downing and the Concord Coach," *Historical New Hampshire*, Vol. 1, Nov. 1945; Harry N. Scheiber, "Coach, Wagon and Motor-Truck Manufacture, 1813-1928 . . ." *Historical New Hampshire*, Vol. XX, No. 3, Autumn 1965; (Slade box p. 139) Lew L. Callaway, "Joseph Alfred Slade: Killer or Victim?" *The Montana Magazine of History*, Vol. III, No. 1, Jan. 1953; Thomas J. Dimsdale, *The Vigilantes of Montana*, copyright 1953 by the Univ. of Oklahoma Press; 139 — change quote, Twain, p. 71. Chapter 5: Particularly useful sources for information and quotes: Wm. and George H. Banning, *Six Horses*, Century Co., 1930; Horace Greeley, *An Overland Journey*, Alfred A. Knopf, 1964; Albert D. Richardson, *Beyond the Mississippi: From the Great River to the Great Ocean*, Bliss & Co., 1867, Johnson Reprint Corp., 1968; Frank A. Root & Wm. E. Connelley, *The Overland Stage to California*, courtesy The Rio Grande Press, enlarged and indexed 1970 edition; Mark Twain, *Roughing It*, New American Library, 1962; Oscar O. Winther, *Transportation Frontier: Trans-Mississippi West 1865-1890*, Holt, Rinehart & Winston, 1964; 163 — travel agonies quote, Tallack, p. 13; 184 — Barnes quote, Barnes, p. 71; 186 — Tucker excerpts, Tucker, pp. 183-185. Chapter 6: Particularly useful sources for information and quotes: Richard Dillon, *Wells Fargo Detective*, Coward-McCann, Inc., 1969; Edward Hungerford, *Wells Fargo: Advancing the American Frontier*, Random House, 1949; W. Turrentine Jackson, "A New Look at Wells Fargo, Stagecoaches and the Pony Express," reprinted from *California Historical Society Quarterly*, Dec. 1966; "Wells Fargo, Staging over the Sierra," reprinted from *California Historical Society Quarterly*, June 1970; "Wells Fargo: Symbol of the Wild West," reprinted from the *Western Historical Quarterly*, April 1972; "Wells Fargo's Pony Expresses," reprinted from *California Historical Society Quarterly*, June 1970; Noel M. Loomis, *Wells Fargo, An Illustrated History*, Clarkson N. Potter, Inc., 1968; Oscar O. Winther, *Via Western Express and Stagecoach*, Univ. of Nebraska Press, 1969; 202 — John Q. Jackson letter excerpts, courtesy Wells Fargo Bank History Room; 217 — bandit quote, Moody, p. 310.

ACKNOWLEDGMENTS

The editors give special thanks to the following persons: Tony Chiu and Keith Wheeler, who wrote portions of the book; Dr. W. Turrentine Jackson, Professor of History, University of California, Davis, and Dr. William E. Lass, History Department, Mankato State College, Mankato, Minn., who commented on portions of the text.

The editors also acknowledge: Andrew Anderson, Ass't Gen'l Public Relations Mgr., Southern Pacific Transportation Co., San Francisco; Carolyn Baldwin, Manuscripts Librarian, Rita Camp, New Hampshire Historical Society, Concord; Susan Burns, Assoc. Researcher, The Oakland Museum, Oakland, Calif.; Eugene Decker, Archivist, Kansas State Historical Society, Topeka; Merrilee Dowty, Director, Elaine Gilleran, Ass't. Director, Wells Fargo Bank History Room, San Francisco; Richard Engeman, Photographs & Maps Librarian, Oregon Historical Society, Portland; Suzanne Gallup, Reference Librarian, The Bancroft Library, University of California, Berkeley; Ronald E. Grim, Cartographic Archives Div., Charlotte Palmer, Archivist, Michael Stanche, Cartographic Archives Div., National Archives, Washington, D.C.; Oliver Willcox, Thomas Gilcrease Institute of American History and Art, Tulsa; Frances M. Gupton, Registrar, Marjorie Morey, Curator of Photographic Collections, Amon Carter Museum of Western Art, Fort Worth; Allen Haeker, Exec. Secretary, Oregon Trail Museum, Gering, Neb.; Isabel M. Haynes, President, The Haynes Foundation, Bozeman, Mont.; L. James Higgins Jr., Curator of Manuscripts, Nevada State Historical Society, Reno; Parsons Holladay, Huntington Beach, Calif.; David Jarrett, New York; Jerry Kearns, Prints & Photographs Div., Library of Congress, Washington, D.C.; Gary Kurutz, Mary Wright, Henry E. Huntington Library, San Marino, Calif.; Hazel Lundberg, Agostino Mastrogiuseppe, Western History Div., Denver Public Library, Denver; Terry W. Mangan, Colorado State Historical Society, Denver; Hal F. Marks, Curator, Museum of Money of the American West, Bank of California, San Francisco; Harriet Meloy, Librarian, Lory Morrow, Photo-Archivist, Montana Historical Society, Helena; Harry Owens, Frank S. Stevens Home for Boys, Swansea, Mass.; Basil C. Pearce, Vice President, Wells Fargo Bank, San Francisco; Robert C. Pettit, Curator of Collections, Opal Jacobsen, Photo Librarian, Nebraska State Historical Society, Lincoln; Don L. Reynolds, Ass't. Director, St. Joseph Museum-Pony Express Museum, St. Joseph, Mo.; David L. Ross, Sandy, Utah; C. C. Roumage, Auburn, Calif.; Mrs. Mariana B. Smith, Pony Express History & Art Gallery, San Rafael, Calif.; Bonnie Wilson, Minnesota Historical Society, St. Paul; James Woodson, Curator of Exhibits, Catherine Hoover, Ass't. Curator of Exhibits, California Historical Society, San Francisco.

BIBLIOGRAPHY

The American Philatelist. The American Philatelic Society, November, 1930.

Angel, Myron, ed., *History of Nevada.* Thompson and West, 1881. Reprinted 1973 by Arno Press, Inc.

Banning, William and George H., *Six Horses.* Century Co., 1930.

Barnes, Demas, *From the Atlantic to the Pacific Overland.* D. Van Nostrand, 1866, reprinted by Arno Press, 1973.

Berthold, Victor, *Wells, Fargo and Company's Hand-Stamps and Franks.* Scott Stamp and Coin Co., 1926.

Billington, Ray A., *Far Western Frontier 1830-60.* Harper & Row, 1956.

"The Birch-Stevens Crypt," *The Harvester* (Swansea, Mass.), Sept. 9, 1972, p. 7.

Bloss, Roy S., *Pony Express: The Great Gamble.* Howell-North Books, 1959.

Bott, Emily Ann O'Neil, "Joseph Murphy's Contribution to the Development of the West," *Missouri Historical Review,* XLVII, No. 1, Oct., 1952.

A Brief History of the Mail Service, Settlement of the Country, and the Indian Depredations Committed upon the Mail Trains of George Chorpenning on the Several Routes between Salt Lake and California from May 1st, 1850, to July 1860. Washington, 1870. Huntington Rare Book # 89198, Henry E. Huntington Library, San Marino, Calif.

Brown, Jesse, "The Freighter in Early Days," *Annals of Wyoming,* Vol. 19, 1947.

Callaway, Lew L., "Joseph Alfred Slade: Killer or Victim?" *The Montana Magazine of History,* Vol. III, No. 1, Jan., 1953.

Carter, Kate B., *Utah and the Pony Express.* Utah Printing Co., 1960.

Chapman, Arthur, *The Pony Express.* Cooper Square Pubs., Inc., 1971.

Corle, Edwin, *John Studebaker: An American Dream.* E. P. Dutton and Co., Inc., 1948.

Dillon, Richard, *Wells Fargo Detective.* Coward-McCann, Inc., 1969.

Dimsdale, Thomas J., *The Vigilantes of Montana.* University of Oklahoma Press, 1953.

Dines, Glen, *Overland Stage: The Story of the Famous Overland Stagecoaches of the 1860's.* Macmillan Publishing Co., Inc., 1961.

Dunbar, Seymour, *A History of Travel in America.* Bobbs-Merrill Co., 1915. Reprinted in 4 vols., Greenwood Press, Inc., 1968.

Egan, W. M., "Recollections of the Pony Express." Original manuscript courtesy of the Yale University Library.

"The Fabulous and Mysterious James E. Birch," *The Harvester,* Sept. 25, 1954.

Frederick, J. V., *Ben Holladay: The Stagecoach King.* The Arthur H. Clark Co., 1940.

Garrett, T. S., *Annals of Wyoming,* Vol. 3, July, 1925.

Glasscock, C. B., *Bandits and the Southern Pacific.* Frederick A. Stokes Co., 1929.

Goetzmann, William H.:
Army Exploration in the American West 1803-1863. Yale University Press, 1959.
Exploration and Empire. Alfred A. Knopf, 1971.

Gray, A. A., "Camels in California," *Quarterly of the California Historical Society,* Vol. IX, No. 4, Dec., 1930.

Greeley, Horace, *An Overland Journey.* Alfred A. Knopf, 1964.

Gregg, Josiah, *Commerce of the Prairies.* J. W. Moore, 1851. (Various reprints available.)

Hafen, LeRoy R., *The Overland Mail.* AMS Press, Inc., 1969.

Hafen, LeRoy R., and Ann W. Hafen, eds., *The Diaries of William Henry Jackson.* The Arthur H. Clark Company, 1959.

Hagen, Olaf, "The Pony Express Starts from St. Joseph." *Missouri His-*

torical Review, Vol. XLIII.

Harlow, Alvin F., Old Waybills. D. Appleton-Century Co., 1934.

Holt, R. D., "Old Texas Wagon Trains," Frontier Times, Vol. 25, Sept., 1948.

Hungerford, Edward, Wells Fargo: Advancing the American Frontier. Random House, 1949.

Hunt, Elmer Munson, "Abbot-Downing and the Concord Coach," Historical New Hampshire, Vol. 1, Nov., 1945.

Jackson, William Henry, Time Exposure: The Autobiography of William Henry Jackson. G. P. Putnam's Sons, 1940. Reprinted by Cooper Square Publishers, Inc., 1971.

Jackson, W. Turrentine:
"A New Look at Wells Fargo, Stagecoaches and the Pony Express." Reprinted from the California Historical Society Quarterly, Dec., 1966.
Wagon Roads West. Yale University Press, 1965.
"Wells Fargo, Staging over the Sierra." Reprinted from the California Historical Quarterly, June, 1970.
"Wells Fargo: Symbol of the Wild West." Reprinted from the Western Historical Quarterly, April, 1972.
"Wells Fargo's Pony Expresses." Reprinted from the California Historical Quarterly, June, 1970.

Jensen, Lee, The Pony Express. Grosset & Dunlap, Inc., 1955.

Kelly, Clyde, United States Postal Policy. D. Appleton and Co., 1931.

Lass, William E., From the Missouri to the Great Salt Lake: An Account of Overland Freighting. Nebraska State Historical Society, 1972.

Lewis, William S., "The Camel Pack Trains in the Mining Camps of the West," Washington Historical Quarterly, Vol. XIX, No. 4, Oct., 1928.

Lillard, Richard G., and Mary Hood, Hank and Horace: An Enduring Episode in Western History. Wilmac Press, 1973.

Loomis, Noel M., Wells Fargo: An Illustrated History. Clarkson N. Potter, Inc., 1968.

Lucia, Ellis, The Saga of Ben Holladay. Hastings House Publishers, Inc., 1959.

Majors, Alexander, Seventy Years on the Frontier. Ross & Haines, Inc., 1965.

Mattes, Merrill J., The Great Platte River Road. Nebraska State Historical Society, 1969.

McClure, Alexander K., Three Thousand Miles Through the Rocky Mountains. J. B. Lippincott and Co., 1869.

Monaghan, Jay, ed., The Private Journal of Louis McLane U.S.N. Dawson's Book Shop, 1971.

Moody, Ralph, Stagecoach West. Thomas Y. Crowell Co., 1967.

Mullan, John, "Report on the Construction of a Military Road from Fort Walla Walla to Fort Benton," Senate Executive Document 43, 37th Congress, 3rd Session, 1862-1863.

Nathan, M. C., Franks of Western Expresses. Collectors Club of Chicago, 1973.

Richardson, Albert D., Beyond the Mississippi: From the Great River to the Great Ocean. Bliss and Co., 1867. Johnson Reprint Corp., 1968.

Robinson, A. P., and Edward Warner, Overland Traction Engine Company. Wright and Potter, Printers, 1865.

Root, Frank A., and William E. Connelley, The Overland Stage to California. The Rio Grande Press, Inc., 1970.

Root, George A., and Russell K. Hickman, "Pike's Peak Express Companies," Kansas Historical Quarterly, Vol. 24, 1944.

Russell, Marian, Land of Enchantment. Branding Iron Press, 1954.

Scheele, Carl H., A Short History of the Mail Service. Smithsonian Institution Press, 1970.

Scheiber, Harry N., "Coach, Wagon and Motor-Truck Manufacture, 1813-1928: The Abbot-Downing Company of Concord," Historical New Hampshire, Vol. XX, No. 3, Autumn, 1965.

Scott, Edward B., The Saga of Lake Tahoe. Sierra-Tahoe Publishing Co., 1957.

Settle, Raymond W. and Mary Lund:
Empire on Wheels. Stanford University Press, 1949.
Saddles and Spurs. Stackpole Co., Pa., 1955.
War Drums and Wagon Wheels. Univ. of Nebraska Press, 1966.

Simpson, James H., "Report of Explorations Across the Great Basin of the Territory of Utah . . ." Government Printing Office, 1876.

Smith, Waddell F., The Story of the Pony Express. Hesperian House, 1960.

Stansbury, Howard, "Exploration and Survey of the Valley of the Great Salt Lake of Utah . . ." Senate Executive Document 3, 32nd Congress, Special Session, March 1851.

Stimson, Alexander L.:
History of the Express Business. Baker & Godwin, 1881.
History of the Express Companies, Including the Origin of American Railroads. 1858. Finch Press Reprints.

Tallack, William, "The California Overland Express: The Longest Ride in the World." Leisure Hour, Vol. 14, London, 1865.

Taylor, T. V., "In the Days of Frontier Freighting," Frontier Times, Jan., 1925.

Thompson, Robert Luther, Wiring a Continent. Princeton University Press, 1947.

Truman, Major Ben C., "Knights of the Lash," Overland Magazine, March-April 1898, courtesy Wells Fargo Bank History Room, San Francisco.

Tucker, Joseph C., To the Golden Goal and Other Sketches. William Doxey, 1895.

Twain, Mark, Roughing It. The New American Library, 1962.

Walker, Henry P., The Wagonmasters: High Plains Freighting from the Earliest Days of the Santa Fe Trail to 1880. University of Oklahoma Press, 1966.

Warren, Sidney, Farthest Frontier: The Pacific Northwest. Macmillan Publishing Co., Inc., 1949.

Wiltsee, Ernest A., The Pioneer Miner and the Pack Mule Express. California Historical Society, 1931.

Winther, Oscar Osburn:
Express and Stagecoach Days in California. Stanford University Press, 1936.
Transportation Frontier, Trans-Mississippi West 1865-1890. Holt, Rinehart and Winston, 1964.
Via Western Express and Stagecoach. University of Nebraska Press, 1969.

Wyman, Walker:
"Bullwhacking: A Prosaic Profession Peculiar to the Great Plains," New Mexico Historical Review, Vol. VII, Oct., 1932.
"Freighting: A Big Business on the Santa Fe Trail," Kansas Historical Quarterly, Vol. 1, 1931.